THE NEW HISTORICISM: STUDIES IN CULTURAL POETICS
Stephen Greenblatt, General Editor

Another Kind of Love

Another Kind of Love

Male Homosexual Desire in English Discourse,
1850–1920

CHRISTOPHER CRAFT

University of California Press

BERKELEY   LOS ANGELES   LONDON

Chapters 2, 3, and 4 were previously published in slightly different forms.
Chapter 2 appeared under the same title in *Genders* 1 (Spring 1988): 33–101.
Chapter 3 was published as "Kiss Me with Those Red Lips" in *Representations*
8 (Fall 1984): 107–33. Chapter 4 appeared under the same title in
Representations 31 (Spring 1990): 19–46. Reprinted with permission.

University of California Press
Berkeley and Los Angeles, California

University of California Press, Ltd.
London, England

Library of Congress Cataloging-in-Publication Data

Craft, Christopher, 1952–
    Another kind of love : male homosexual desire in English discourse,
  1850–1920 / Christopher Craft.
        p. cm. — (The new historicism : studies in cultural poetics ; 30)
    Includes bibliographical references and index.
    ISBN 0-520-08492-6 (alk. paper)
    1. English literature—19th century—History and criticism.
  2. Homosexuality and literature—Great Britain—History.
  3. Lawrence, D. H. (David Herbert), 1885–1930. Women in love.
  4. Gay men in literature. 5. Desire in literature. 6. Love in
  literature. I. Title. II. Series: New historicism ; 30.
  PR468.H65C73   1994
  820.9'353—dc20

                                        93-25759
                                          CIP

Printed in the United States of America

9 8 7 6 5 4 3 2 1

The paper used in this publication meets the minimum requirements of
American National Standard for Information Sciences—Permanence of
Paper for Printed Library Materials, ANSI Z39.48-1984.

Contents

Kiss and Tell
A Preface

The first thing we love is *a scene*.
—Roland Barthes, *A Lover's Discourse*

I began with the desire to kiss the dead.

Or rather, more accurately, with the desire *to be kissed by them*.

This desire, marked as it is by an insistent cathexis between passivity and morbidity, points "no doubt" to a pathological subject, the kind whose "specification" and "implantation," in Michel Foucault's famous argument, have occupied the formidable taxonomic energies of the modern regime of sexuality. But this is hardly a pathology that can be remanded to the precincts of a particular subjectivity (say, for instance, my own), quarantined on the one side by the anecdotes of personality (*One day, as a small boy, I saw* . . .) and on the other by the definitive vocables of a proper name. Quite the contrary. A persistently heterosexist culture has found the dissemination of this "perversion," as of many others, to be extremely useful in the propagation and regulation of individuals, genders, and sexualities. No dearth of standardized deviations; exempla everywhere. As a consequence, my strange desire had no difficulty finding multiple textual incitements. A perverse late-Victorian kiss, for instance, was enough to send my mind wandering:

In the moonlight opposite me were three young women, ladies by their dress and manner. I thought at the time that I must be dreaming when I saw them, for, though the moonlight was behind them, they threw no shadow on the floor. They came close to me and looked at me for some time and then whispered together. . . . All three had brilliant white teeth, that shone like pearls against the ruby of their voluptuous lips. There was something about them that made me uneasy, some longing and at

the same time some deadly fear. I felt in my heart a wicked, burning desire that they would kiss me with those red lips . . .

I was afraid to raise my eyelids, but looked out and saw perfectly under the lashes. The fair girl went on her knees and bent over me, fairly
gloating. . . . Lower and lower went her head as the lips went below the
range of my mouth and chin and seemed to fasten on my throat. . . . I
could feel the soft, shivering touch of the lips on the supersensitive skin
of my throat, and the hard dents of two sharp teeth, just touching and
pausing there. I closed my eyes in a languorous ecstasy and waited—
waited with a beating heart.[1]

If *Another Kind of Love* may be said to possess, or to be possessed by,
a primal scene to which all of its overdetermined elaborations subsequently refer, then this scene of impending vampirism from *Dracula*—
and the adjacent scene of a particular reader reading it, reading "with a
beating heart"—would constitute that "originary" moment. I mean this,
first, in the pedestrian and literal sense that the earliest of the words
printed here were written in excited response to my first reading of Stoker's tremendous potboiler,[2] an encounter that occurred in the highly motivated context of a graduate seminar in Victorian literature offered by
Carol Christ at the University of California, Berkeley. Out of that reading, according to the conventional seminar itinerary, a paper sprang; from
that paper a research project was generated, Alex Zwerdling by this time
having pointed me in the direction of a book by Havelock Ellis called *Sexual Inversion* (1897); from that research project a dissertation ensued
(speed of cold molasses), thereafter to be elaborated (same speed) into the
book you now hold in your hands. As I say, a conventional enough academic itinerary.

But I also mean to invoke the primal scene in all the genealogical duplicity that Freud's genius conferred upon it. As a scene, first of all, that
may or may not have occurred "in fact" and, if so, may or may not have
been experienced as such by the unblinking witness whose erotic life
would thereafter be inflected, not to say dominated, by the baffling visual
information he receives but cannot yet incorporate; as a scene, moreover,
whose traumatizing effects (most famously: the male subject's introduction to promissory castration) are not experienced "primally" or "originally" in the here and now of immediate sensory perception, but are conveyed instead according to a strange temporal syncopation, a time delay
that activates the trauma secondarily and belatedly, in a recursive fantasmatic movement spurred on by the superaddition, many years later, of a
specifically sexual knowledge that would not have been available to—or,

if available, could not have been assimilated by—the spectator-subject at the time the scene was being seen, if indeed, as I say, it ever was; and, finally, as a scene whose now thoroughly invaginated "reality" could never be definitively corroborated by direct access, say, to an irrefutably authentic memory, since (in the first place) memory presents its artifacts via a temporal palimpsest in which the fantasmatic has already laminated the real and since (in the second) all access to the scene occurs only through the aperture opened (contour of the keyhole) by still another highly mediated recursive action: the uneven interlocution, I mean, of the analyst and the analysand, the former reconstructing the scene's truth from the dissociated fragments embedded in the enforced speech of the latter. Freud: "scenes, like this one in my present patient's case [the Wolf Man], which date from such an early period and exhibit similar content, and which further lay claim to such extraordinary significance for the history of the case, are as a rule not reproduced as recollections, but have to be divined—constructed—gradually and laboriously from an aggregate of indications." Thus understood as an analytic assemblage, a montagelike "product of construction,"[3] the primal scene can only dispense an odd prime truth: the recognition that its own action necessarily evacuates the primacy—the claim to a first, unmediated origin—to which it nonetheless continues to make its bald-faced appeal. What the primal scene locates, then, is not exactly the (of late) heavily advertised death of the origin; it imposes, instead, the melancholy illumination that any account of beginnings must proceed from the unnatural animation of an origin that has, as origin, already given up the ghost. The morning, therefore, in which the origin first reveals its primeval freshness turns out to be none other than the night of the living dead.

So also with my appeal above to the manifestly "heterosexual" kissing scene from *Dracula*. It was, "in truth," in response to this scene that the writing of *Another Kind of Love* began, but the origin thus honestly specified is so riddled with lacunae, distorted with displacements, and congested with blockages that it would be disingenuous, not to say downright fatuous, to present this as an origin innocent of antecedents all its own: antecedents in the primal sense of something dispersed and occluded, something deferred and recursive, accessible only through an interpretive action destined to read the aftermath of the genesis it had hoped to find, and finding, lay bare. As regards *Dracula* in its entirety, just what I understand these lacunae, displacements, and blockages to be will be made clear in the extended discussion of the novel I offer in Chapter 3. But as regards the kissing scene adduced above, some preliminary remarks may be offered here, if only to help situate the writing that follows. Undoubtedly what first arrested, and subsequently detained, this writer's reading eye was the enthralling spectacle of a supine masculine subject (here a very proper Jonathan Harker, whose journal entry we are considering) suffering the enchantment of an inescapable passivity, *a passivity that has chosen him.* As the burdens of individual agency, not to mention of motor control, are magically suspended by vampiric compulsion, a preternaturally heightened consciousness entertains the "wicked, burning desire that they would kiss me with those red lips." What does this scene present if not a congested erotic tableau posed and poised on the cusp of an "unnatural" penetration, the luxurious incipience of which is imagined from the (more usually foreclosed) position of what forensic discourses were once pleased to call a "male pathic"? As the lips "seemed to fasten on my throat . . . I could feel [their] soft, shivering touch . . . on the supersensitive skin of my throat, and the hard dents of two sharp teeth, just touching and pausing there." *As the lips fastened, I could feel*: the imminence of the vampiric kiss ignites a knowledge hitherto dampened within the benumbed precincts of the normative male subject—the knowledge, specifically, that his upright being has been slipped into a "supersensitive" epidermal envelope that can't wait to be opened. "Touching," "pausing," "beating": how exquisitely the slo-mo advance of the lover's tooth corresponds to the furor of the patient's heart, to the blind languor of his wideeyed "waiting," to the ambivalent affect ("some longing and at the same time some deadly fear") that now enriches his mandatory passivity.

Our primal scene offers, then, a transfixing display of transfixed masculinity. So compelling—and so anxiogenic—is this tableau that one cannot but hear the rustle of the defensive adjectives ("feminine"/"homosexual") that have descended categorically (that is, as historically determinative categories) in order to monitor such displays and marshall their considerable truth effects. Stoker's narrative, too, keeps itself busy defending against the same "wicked" imputations that it also profitably solicits. The manifest (and manifestly duplicitous) heterosexuality of the scene at hand is only the most immediate example of this deeply ambivalent narrative activity; Stoker is careful, after all, to deploy *three* women to unman Harker here, as if so overdetermined a ratification of the boy-girl linkage would be enough to keep everything straight. But it is worth remembering in this regard that the erotic thrill, or threat, that charges the novel's opening movement (the portion exactly coextensive with Harker's journal) derives from the much-anticipated, and endlessly deferred, *Blutbrüderschaft* between Dracula and Harker; given this emphasis, the "weird sisters" (who will ultimately end up "doing" Harker for the Count) are disclosed as supernumerary and belated simulacra—cross-gender replicants who diffuse unmediated homosexual connection. The scene that "tells" in this regard is the famous one in which the profusion consequent upon Harker's having nicked himself while shaving instantly excites Dracula's hunger. Yet just as surely as *Dracula* will sustain its flirtation with an originary homosexual desire—the desire, anyway, with which the novel first lures its readers—so will it prophylactically refuse to gratify that desire directly. As if to explain the absence of the male-to-male vampiric kiss, the Count himself obligingly explicates the novel's "triangular" or "homosocial" articulation of homosexual desire; late in the novel, after having successfully vamped Lucy and while in the process of repeating himself upon Mina, Dracula admonishes Van Helsing and his ithyphallic phalanx thus: "my revenge has just begun! I spread it over centuries, and time is on my side. Your girls that you all love are mine already; and through them you and others shall yet be mine" (365). *Through them you shall yet be mine*: this patently substitutive logic everywhere governs *Dracula's* perverse heterosexual distribution of homosexual desire; given such an erotics of substitution, Harker's submission to the weird sisters bespeaks a deflection or transposition of homosexual desire across gender, the weirdness of the sisters lying therefore in the wayward course that leads homosexual desire to monstrous heterosexual enactment.

The pages to follow will explore some of the literary and historical ramifications of this figural strategy. Anything but isolate or idiosyncratic, Stoker's transposition of the homo into and through the hetero partakes of a broadly diffused explanatory paradigm, specifically, an erotics of inversion. As classically articulated in the sexological discourses of the late nineteenth century, "sexual inversion" defines and explains (away) a problematic homosexuality by dismissing it as a kind of displaced heterosexuality—the heterosexual impulse having, as it were, taken up residence at the wrong anatomical address, as in the case of the male "invert" (*anima muliebris virili corpore inclusa*) who cuts the formulaic and decisive figure in these discourses. As the Latin formula (usual English rendition: "a female soul trapped in a male body") so schematically indicates, the inversion paradigm deploys a metaphorics of gender crossing—rhetorically speaking, a metathesis of gender—in order to explicate what John Addington Symonds called "this persistent feature of human psychology";[4] it is, after all, the suppositional woman-in-the-man whose presence alone "explains" why a man might want another man. Feminization of the male is thus an intrinsic aspect of the inversion figure, the very ground of its taxonomic coherence: any and all desire for a male is encoded, from the first, as a specifically feminine desire, despite its incongruent placement in a male body. As, therefore, part criss-cross and part double bind, inversion offers no conceptual space for even the possibility of a virile or masculine male homosexuality, a literally homophobic denial that, among other things, perpetuates the regime of a compulsory heterosexuality whose axiomatic normalcy may thus reign without question. Very much the same conceptual duplicity informs the articulation of male homosexual desire in *Dracula*. This is notable not only in the novel's general economy of homosocial distribution ("through them you and others shall yet be mine"), but also in its continuing incitement of the embrace whose liminal presence it cannot do without, but whose direct representation it cannot bear to countenance: a man in another man's arms. Consider in this regard just how our primal scene ends. The progress of the scene has been arrested, as in a freeze-frame, on the lip of the kiss, the spellbound male subject immobilized by "the hard dents of two sharp teeth, just touching and pausing there." But Harker's pulsing and panting at the end of the paragraph ("waited—waited with a beating heart") only seem to be the last notations of a consciousness about to be submerged in a fathomless kiss; for what actually succeeds this phrase is not the kiss itself but rather its spectacular interruption: penetration denied or deferred. Dracula himself breaks into the room, drives the women away from Harker, and admonishes them harshly: "How dare you touch him, any of you? How dare you cast eyes on him when I had forbidden it? Back, I tell you all! This man belongs to me" (53). Dracula's intercession here imposes two noteworthy effects: on the one hand, it suspends and diffuses throughout the text a "passive" desire maximized on the brink of an involuntary penetration, a desire that the novel will hereafter attribute only to women, as if belatedly to repress (the cat after all being well out of the bag) the novel's insistence on an originary, passive homosexual desire; and on the other, it repeats and intensifies the threat of a more direct libidinal embrace between Dracula and Harker ("This man belongs to me"), as if compulsively to reassert the origin it is also busy repressing. If I stress this antinomical distribution of male homosexual desire (intensification and dispersal, tumescence and subsidence), this is because the doubleness thus emphasized will figure crucially in the chapters to follow. And not merely, as will become clear, in the texts being read, but also in the writing that struggles so to read them.

To whom, then, does *this* man belong? Shall he be granted kisses? and if so by whom? What are his allegiances, filiations, proclivities, orientations? And to what degree do such determinations, however opaque or uncertain or shifting, in turn determine the writing subject's relation to the subject of which he presumes to write? Or does he intend seriously to maintain the imposture of anonymity and neutrality assumed by yesterday's "expert in the field?" Less circumspectly: Are you gay? and if not, what particular perversities ("Do you like to watch?") inflect and motivate your cool engagement with, if not quite your hot enjoyment of, the gay male body and the historical discourses that have surrounded, bound, and inscribed that body? Writer, specify your commitment to your subject: Does your body have the courage of your prose? Dare you put your penis where your pencil is, or your asshole where your eye has been? Or again: Does not the hypertrophic masculinity (not to mention the buoyant good health) with which you affront the public eye simply rehearse the overfamiliar mendacity of the (only) seeming heterosexual who, having failed either to come out or act up, prefers instead to enjoy the show (always the scholar: pencil in hand) from the protected wings of a spectacle he continues to disown? Worse than a "closet case" then. How else to explain how deep and well-appointed (down to the Armani black label!) your armoire appears to be?

Before dutifully submitting to these demands for explanation (each of which has been addressed to me—with what shades of aggressivity and contempt I need not here recall—since I began writing this book), it may be useful to resist them, if only for a while—"*long enough, at any rate, to draw attention to what is most compelling in the demand for them.*"[5] Demand indeed: the inquisitorial verve propelling such questions may itself provide the strongest motivation for withholding answers to them; surely the requirement that one put one's papers and one's life in parallel, synchronic order partakes of the same disciplinary (not to mention voyeuristic) impulse that infuses virtually every interstice of the conceptual grid we have learned to call modern sexuality. (Gender cops of both sexes, and of various sexualities, keep extending the dragnet: "Just the facts, ma'am.") Far more than merely a violation of the confidence that should obtain between lovers, to kiss and tell has become one of the performative obligations exacted from anyone whose writing or thinking approaches the highly unstable (and therefore heavily defended) borders of identity politics; and, to make matters worse, such obligations are only too reflexively introjected by the writing subject, in whose murky consciousness they are likely to resurface in the guise of desires for self-justification or even self-exposure. The writerly anxieties associated with this imperative to disclose by naming (one's desires, one's practices, one's compatriots in desire and practice) have resulted in some remarkable permutations of style: most notably, perhaps in the work of Roland Barthes, whose recourse to the ablation of the signified (strategies of fragmentation, obliquity, severe parataxis, semantic drifting, etc., etc.) demonstrates the supple rigor of the practiced contortionist who repeatedly escapes the locks and chains with which his bespangled assistant (her name: the image repertoire) has bound him hand and foot. Barthes's intolerable: to be put in his place by the language of others. Correspondingly, his defensive strategies of the atopic: to repudiate the efficacy of all names, proper and improper, however doomed he is to their use (luckily: "the tyranny of language is not absolute");[6] to deform wherever possible the stratifications of what it pleases him to call the *Doxa*; above all, to outmaneuver (by feint, by fall, never by "manly" confrontation) the fatal capture with which the strong arm of every adjective threatens him. Hence: for all the transparent gayness of his writing (transparent in a double sense: as clear to the eye as air, but "aerated to the point of invisibility"), the preponderance of what Barthes calls *le travail du mot* consists in undermining the prestige and appeal of categorical denotation—the very signifying practice, we might note, that posits the homosexual/heterosexual binarism as one of the fundamental determinants of our being.[7] Better the dispersion of affect than its congelation into "sexuality": "the very task of love and language is to give to one and the same phrase inflections which will be forever new, thereby creating an unheard-of speech in which the sign's form is repeated but is never signified; in which the speaker and the lover finally triumph over the dreadful *reduction* which language (and psychoanalytic science) transmits to all our affects."[8] However naïve may be the aspirations embedded within the sophistication of this prose ("inflections . . . forever new," "finally triumph," etc.), one implication at least is clear: no parading (Barthesian term) of a homosexual thematics.

Another Kind of Love pursues a different tack entirely: homosexual thematics and very little but. There are surely many (more fashionably, *too* many) reasons for this, both personal and historical, some of which even the writer himself may be thought to understand. Most obvious among these is the simple fact that anyone writing about gender and sexuality in the 1980s and 1990s cannot help but register (however impossible it is to assimilate) the "discursive explosion" whose deafening reverberations alternately trigger and overwhelm cognition. To mention, in passing, only a recent few: divergent feminisms of first, second, and subsequent waves, the tidal effects of which have left even the Great Unwashed rocking on their heels; the post-Stonewall efflorescence of multiple gay voices, male and female, the diversity and subtlety of which should be enough to obliterate forever the perduring fantasy of disclosing a Definitive Truth about a Singular Homosexuality; in contrapuntal response to this multiplicity, the brutal monotone of homophobic oppression, repellent always, but especially so at a time when the fatal predations of a mindless virus are being heartlessly accelerated by a government that refuses to care for its *entire* citizenry; the round-the-clock transmissions of a popular culture (video, radio, records, film) whose frenetic play in the fields of sex and gender ensures, first, that no spectatorial desire shall go unsatiated, and second, that every satiety shall then be immediately converted back into a "fresh" desire for more of the same; finally, and most preposterously, the excruciating acoustics of the so-called men's movement (heady jamborees at The Tom-Tom Club, itself something of a traveling circus), the major impetus behind which seems to be to dispel a circumambient sissy-boy anxiety by forging fashionably dysfunctional males into iron men and warrior dads. Despite the semantic overkill inherent in such a discursive environment, there are still good reasons, again both personal and historical, for a straight man—in any event, this straight man—to pursue an explicit homosexual thematics. Not the least of these is his need to generate an instrumental genealogy of his "own" sexual desire, in both its heterosexual and homosexual manifestations, and also of his own sexual practice, especially since the insistently heterosexual modalities to which he has submitted his body so obviously fail to correspond to the rhythms of desire. I take it as axiomatic (proofs to follow nonetheless) that this disjunctive relation between desire and practice itself constitutes one of the crucial pivots around which normative male heterosexuality has historically been taught to dance its ugly sidestep.[9] It is here that homosexual desire intersects explosively with a virtually mandatory homophobia: the kind, anyway, that in the Los Angeles of my youth propelled a group of pseudotoughs down Hollywood Boulevard where, from the protective confines of an orange Dodge, we could with impunity heckle the queers we were afraid to talk to, more afraid still to become.

Not many years after thus discharging my meanness into the hot Hollywood night, I would in turn be required, again in Los Angeles, to enlist myself, if only momentarily, under the regime of the same rude epithet

("Faggot!") with which I had previously attempted to bolster an evidently faltering sense of masculinity. This event marked the first time ever I understood that someone else (someone, that is, other than my most secret self) might have sufficient reason to refer the gay possibility to my person—that reason being, apparently, my own momentary leap into sartorial extravagance. The extravagance in question seems modest enough fifteen years later: nothing more than a pair of navy-surplus trousers, very baggy, of blue-almost-black wool, held up by extremely bright carmine suspenders, which in turn were matched by an equally bright and equally carmine shoulder bag. It was, presumably, the shameless conjunction of bag and suspensory device that triggered the emission of the epithet (from which man in the crowd, obviously seeing red, I could never quite tell) as I made my way across the stereotypically sun-drenched main quad at UCLA. What must have been the flagrant effeminacy of the bag may in part be explained by the fact that I had borrowed it from a woman (the strap upon my own more conventionally masculine appendage having recently given way under the gravitational pull of *The Norton Anthology of Literature* and companion volumes); but the apparently equally legible gayness connoted by the bag confounded me some, not least (but also not only) because I had just become, as we say, "involved" with the same petite *danseuse* whose not very innocent wardrobe had provided the offending item. Could not a resolutely heterosexual genital practice guarantee a corresponding heterosexual identity, discernible from afar? Was I not as manifestly straight as the concrete path along which I was making my way, no longer to class but to her? Some time later, after much anxious polishing of the masculine body armor so effortlessly pierced by the point of the epithet, I began to think the experience through, with the productive result that I was able to translate the microtrauma of the event into a minirevelation I could then put to use; always the quick undergraduate, I realized that I had been submitting all along to a vestimentary code whose efficient operation in no way required a vocal pledge of allegiance from me and whose inadvertent violation would just as efficiently stimulate public abuse from another male. Another male, whomever he may have been, just like myself.

More than a simple exercise in the operation of tacit social codes, this anecdote is meant to suggest the complex interaction between linguistic exchange, identity formation, and sexual desire in a culture whose ardent promotion of heterosexual normalcy requires nothing less than its continual incitement of a categorical homosexuality; the anecdote also indicates one of the prevampiric origins (I wouldn't read *Dracula* for another five years) of the present study. Distilled to its rudiments, my narrative offers a neat parable about the boomerang trajectory of the brutal little noun *faggot*: sometime in 1971 or 1972 I hurled the epithet maliciously into the night air, sometime in 1976 or 1977 it returned from behind to catch me unaware. I became in that moment the unwitting object of my own previous denunciation. This story also exemplifies just how assiduously the male heterosexual subject must work to sustain the serenity of his presumably natural sexual identity; it exemplifies, that is, the open violence of homosocial exchange in contemporary American culture. For just as surely as the epithet's first emission marked an act of homophobic disidentification on my part, so did the second indicate a symmetrically homophobic act of identity attribution. And if, as should be obvious, the overcharged circulation of the language of faggotry continually teased one with the possiblity of erotic engagement between men, so conversely did the tenor of the particular exchanges guarantee that this possibility would go unexplored, here and now, between *these* men. In just this way—perhaps only in this way—could the gay possibility be maintained as both perpetually open and immediately foreclosed, a temptation ever ready to be transformed into a threat. Finally, my anecdote invites skeptical appreciation of anything that purports to mark an advance in critical thought. Certainly my undergraduate insight into the oppressive operation of vestimentary codes must count as one of the first steps I took on the road to gay-affirmative thinking and feeling: if only for a moment, and if only on the protected ontological ground of an *as if*, I was required to experience just one of the social exactions that others were daily compelled to suffer as the very condition of their being. But just as surely did the very nimbleness of my recognition allow me to elude the indelible application of the epithet whose cruelty I had just begun, a little piously, to explicate. After all, could I not drop that perilous identity attribution as readily as I could my pants?

Not so readily escaped or eluded, however, are the pervasive entanglements that bind together normative heterosexuality, homophobia, and certain decisive formulations of homosexual desire. Nor does the writing to follow claim exemption from these entanglements. Quite the contrary, in fact, since this book implicitly argues that the homophobia fundamental to (at least) post-Renaissance figurations of homosexual desire is not simply something earnestly to be renounced, like yesterday's adultery or the petty theft of the day before; it is, rather, a genuinely perverse imperative whose violence must be measured as it traverses not merely in-dividual psychology and personal history but also those cultural forms (even the outmoded ones) that continue to fashion our desires and aver-sions. From among the many forms that together constitute a geneaology of our present, I have here emphasized certain British literary texts of the nineteenth and twentieth centuries in which homosexual desire and ho-mophobia are to be found locked in passionate embrace: a high-Victorian elegy in which the death of the beloved object instigates a specifically erotic yearning in the male poet whose grief exceeds the bounds of all dis-cretion; a blood-crazed piece of late-Victorian "trash" in which a vampiric "father or furtherer of a new order of beings" possesses his sons by inter-posing a demonically virilized female whose business it is to kiss them into bliss; an earnestly closeted homosexual farce in which a preposterous gay signifier—a name, literally, without a character—must be formally ex-pelled in order to facilitate, before the curtain drops, the requisite het-erosexual coupling; and, finally, a great modern novel whose notorious intractability derives at least in part from the deep interfusion of its ho-mosexual and homicidal impulses. Beyond these specifically literary ex-amples, I also read some neglected texts from a now-superannuated sex-ology, and certain of Freud's decisive studies. Throughout it all, even as I tried to maintain something of the scholar's sobriety and decorum, I struggled to insinuate into the writing what professional criticism more usually struggles to leave out: a not entirely unembarrassed recognition of the erotic and political bias that no reading can hope to escape. In the pres-ent case, this has meant a continuing acknowledgment of my own am-bivalence ("some longing and at the same time some deadly fear") when faced with the temptation that lay at the vampiric origins of *Another Kind of Love*: the galvanic promise of something more than just another kiss.

No matter how solitary the practices of reading and writing ultimately prove to be, they are nonetheless almost always fostered by the generosity of friends and the kindness of strangers; even a dismissive antagonist may haplessly end up advancing the cause of a writing he has come to detest. Accordingly, I want to acknowledge the many debts whose simple reck-oning exceeds whatever power I might summon to discharge them. Thanks are due, therefore, to the following persons for the assistance they so readily provided along the way: Janet Adelman, Carol T. Christ, Ed Co-hen, William A. Cohen, Stephen Greenblatt, Catherine Gallagher, Wayne Koestenbaum, Thomas Laqueur, Eve Kosofsky Sedgwick, and

Alan Sinfield; I am saddened to think that the cruelties of the flesh preclude me from thanking Joel Fineman in anything but spirit. Beyond these, however, there are a special few who deserve (at any rate, are going to receive) what award committees like to call special mention. The first to be thus sentenced to gratitude must be Laura Richards Craft, whose love and support (intellectual, emotional, financial) made it possible for me to work at all; I think she will remember, as affectionately as I do, the friction generated by a nearly prehistoric argument (its topic: a "cowboy belt") that had for me the value of an annunciation: in that undergraduate contest gender was reborn before my eyes as a political activity, even as it passed away as one of Nature's gratuities. In subsequent years, three splendid individuals—Jessica Ashley Craft, Ariel Samantha Craft, and Deirdre Ann Force—each helped to make the author's life worth living, most especially when certain brute evidence seemed to suggest that it was otherwise. During the protracted composition of this book, Alex Zwerdling provided unstinting paternal (but never paternalistic) care to a writer whose youth never quite matched his age; Alex's sufferance during this time has been almost enough to give fathers a good name, though I suspect that we will never resolve our dispute about the ethics of punning. Finally, the pride of last place (rhetorically, of course, the first) goes to a dear friend who has instructed me variously in the intensities of writing and the complexities of human relationship, not to say love; the name on his office door, itself more distant than I would like it to be, reads D. A. Miller, but in my sometimes "Michelangelesque" imaginary he is simply David.

I

Alias Sodomy

It was my primary object when I began these autobiographical notes to describe as accurately and candidly as I was able a type of character, which I do not at all believe to be exceptional, but which for various intelligible reasons has never yet been properly analyzed. I wanted to supply material for the ethical psychologist and the student of mental pathology, by portraying a man of no mean talents, of no abnormal depravity, whose life has been perplexed from first to last by passion—natural, instinctive, healthy in his own particular case—but morbid and abominable from the point of view of the society in which he lives—persistent passion for the male sex.

— *The Memoirs of John Addington Symonds*

Read *The Memoirs of John Addington Symonds* (written between 1889 and 1891 in a fever of self-disclosure, consigned immediately thereafter to the closet, not to see public light until the Grosskurth edition of 1984)[1] and before long you will find yourself entertaining a fantasy of metalepsis, a dream of historical reversal: *it is obvious, Symonds has been reading Foucault*. Impossible, of course. Yet Symond's autobiography unfolds like the efflorescence of a Foucaldian paradigm: "I am not talking about the obligation to admit to violations of the laws of sex, as required by traditional penance; but of the nearly infinite task of telling—telling oneself and another, as often as possible, everything that might concern the interplay of innumerable pleasures, sensations, and thoughts which, through the body and the soul, had some affinity with sex."[2] In just this way, on page after page of the *Memoirs*, a hyperconscious modern subject anxiously interrogates the minutae of his sexual desire in order to disclose, at once and forever, the fundamental truth of his being; Symonds *knows*, and sets out in writing to prove to an unknowing world, that his entire identity pivots upon the "persistent passion for the male sex" that (he has good reason

stridently to claim) is "natural, instinctive, [and] healthy in his own case."
To dissect that passion and "properly [to] analyze" the "type of charac-
ter" that descends from it: such is the "primary object" of the Symonds
Memoirs. *La volonté de savoir*, and with a vengeance.

Such exigent appeals to the sexual as the very ground or foundation of
the subject's truth are anything but natural or inevitable; they are among
the instruments of a cultural formation whose genealogy is still being
written. Foucault has read the epistemological appeal to sex as part of the
symptomatology of the modern, one of the key indicators pointing to a
crucial transformation in which the modern experience of sexuality
emerges from the antecedent experience of the flesh. Yet the distinction
between these divergent "experiences" is hardly self-extolling, nor by any
means is it clear just what emerges in the eighteenth and nineteenth centuries as sexuality. What, then, are the differences implied by Foucault's
counterposing of these two concepts, terms, experiences? What would a
comparative typology of the flesh and sexuality actually show? "The term
itself ["sexuality"] did not appear until the beginning of the nineteenth
century, a fact that should be neither underestimated nor overinterpreted.
It does point to something other than a simple recasting of vocabulary,
but obviously it does not mark the sudden emergence of that to which
'sexuality' refers."[3] By "sexuality," then, Foucault certainly does not mean
the coming to light of a heretofore undisclosed reality or truth, a transindividual substratum ontologically prior to its own disciplinary containment or "subversive" incitement; nor conversely does he indicate the uni-
lateral advance of a microdiscipline whose powers of diffusion and
insinuation, like those of the vampire, leave no corpuscle uncolored, no
capillary untapped. In resisting the symmetrical totalizations of both "nature" and "culture," Foucault, like Wilde before him, locates sexuality
at—indeed, as—a crossroads or terminus.[4] As the switchpoint for dis-
parate vectors, sexuality marks the experience of a convergence, a collision, a coming together: "the modern experience of sexuality" must be
"understood as the correlation between fields of knowledge, types of nor-
mativity, and forms of subjectivity in a particular culture."[5]

This "correlation" or "ensemble" is never fixed or unitary. There exists
no transhistorical zero point from which to graph its movement; and its
component "axes" or vectors—knowledge, power, subjectivity—imply
discursive forms and social practices that themselves are subject to historical, institutional, and individual torsions. At times the historical pressures exerted upon these axes may intensify and ramify until they take on

the force of a paradigm shift, an irrecuperable modification in the relations of knowledge, power, and subjectivity within the sexual field. Foucault's distinction between flesh and sexuality points to such a shift—points, that is, to different ways of articulating desires, of generating sexualities, of inciting and controlling bodies. But a caution is in order: nowhere does Foucault press the distinction between flesh and sexuality into a rigid opposition; these two terms do not map an epochal scission on either side of which lie incommensurable experiences, discourses, institutions, practices. Between flesh and sexuality, then, our reading must disclose not a simple, binary division, but rather a complex passage subject to "overlappings, interactions, and echoes."[6]

And yet there are differences to be marked, and a historical process to be engaged. The "perversions" provide the historically crucial example. In the Christian discourse of the flesh, sexual acts were carefully codified but distinct sexualities were not. A proscribed sexual act implicated the actor as a juridical subject, someone whose activity did or did not conform to civil or canonical law; the commission of a particular sexual act might signal the perpetrator's "inequity" or even threaten his life, but it did not disclose a singular or definitive sexuality, a "perversion" in the modern sense of the term. And this for good reason: the discourse of the flesh presupposed a postlapsarian body exquisitely and dangerously attuned to the insistent impulsions, "natural" or otherwise, of a general concupiscence; this was a fallen body always ready to fall again, a body ever liable to seduction by its own desire for pleasure. And pleasure itself was understood as a mobile tropism, a power of perverse turning implicating all bodies and consuming (potentially) any object. Given these polytropic dynamics, reason was obliged to channel and subdue the flesh according to divine injunctions and interdictions, as these were mediated first by ecclesiastical and later by secular institutions. Reason worked, in other words, to patrol the erotic errancies to which fallen flesh was inescapably heir. The corresponding logic of articulation and control here is juridical: codes are promulgated and imposed, individual behaviors are filtered through those codes, confessions are solicited, penance and punishment are administered accordingly.

Even so cursory an account of the experience of the flesh will help us discern the emergence of sexuality and, more specifically, of homosexuality. Symonds's *Memoirs* are instructive here, for they engage this historical process at exactly the juncture whose importance Foucault has taught us to appreciate: the juncture, precisely, of discourse and desire, where

strands of language and strands of sexuality are woven inextricably together. Symonds is as earnest in his writing as in his desire: "It was my
primary object . . . to describe as accurately and candidly as I was able a
type of character . . . and to supply material for . . . the student of mental
pathology." The embarrassment (not to mention the thrill) of publicly
unpacking one's richly imbricated subjectivity finds abundant recompense only in the promise of dispensing a historically unprecedented, and
specifically homosexual, knowledge—"the disclosure of a type of man
who has not yet been classified."[7] This gesture manifests a radical contradiction that should not be sublated or reconciled: the very freedom to disclose or uncloset one's (here gay) desire erupts as the pursuit of a new taxonomic encasement, an emergent type, a fresh classification. Symonds
consequently centers his autobiography on his "lifelong struggle [with]
this tyrannous desire," a desire he later calls "an incurable malady," "that
more deeply rooted perversion of the sexual instincts (uncontrollable, ineradicable, amounting to monomania) to expose which in its relation to
my whole nature has been the principal object of my memoirs."[8] Submitting to the conjoint duties of exposure and analysis, Symonds offers
himself as the subject/object of an insistent will to knowledge that both
is and is not "his own"; in so doing, he enacts a discursive cathexis in
which the subject's impulse to self-representation fuses with a circumambient cultural imperative to produce a "proper understanding of the *vita
sexualis*."[9] In this autobiographical and autodiagnostic text, therefore, self
and homosexual desire *must* explicate each other.

"This being the case," Symonds continues, "I shall not shrink from
continuing the analysis which I have undertaken, painful as it is to do so,
and extraordinary as the needful confession will have to be."[10] The convergence in this sentence, as in the *Memoirs* generally, of "painful analysis" and "needful confession" bespeaks the infusion of Symonds's personal courage with a transindividual urgency that is itself symptomatic of
modern sexuality, one of whose chief operations is to repress the his-
toricity of the "truths" it thereby generates; only recently have we acknowledged that "our experience of sexuality is a product of systems of
knowledge and modalities of power that bear no claim to ineluctability."[11]
Symonds's "sterile self-delineation" (unfortunate but telling phrase) necessarily occurred within particular political, economic, and institutional
contexts, just as his verbal and ideational vocabulary derived from a contradictory discursive reservoir whose tributaries included a virulent anti-
sodomy tradition, contemporaneous thinking on evolutionary biology,

the advancing influence of psychiatric medicine, and the emerging language of prepsychoanalytic sexology. And however pressing his subjective exigency, Symonds's drive to enlist himself under the master sign of sexual inversion was itself cognate with a more pervasive cultural effort at sexual redefinition, "a new taxonomic and labelling zeal," as Jeffrey Weeks has called it, "which attempted to classify 'scientifically' the characteristics and increasingly the aetiologies of the forms of sexual variety, and in doing so helped construct them as objects of study and as sexual categories."[12] Aligned from the beginning with a eugenic concern for the social body, this classificatory impulse would yield what Foucault calls "the perverse implantation," the development of essentializing typologies that would establish the perversions or paraphilias on a new ontological basis. What had once been a mere capacity of undifferentiated lust would in the late nineteenth century be hypostasized as pivotal sexual differences defining new types of individuals: the masochist, the transvestite, the fetishist, etc.

Yet it would be naive to think that all perversions are created equal. In the case of modern Euro-American discourse, homosexuality (or its late-Victorian counterpart, sexual inversion) indisputably constitutes the paradigmatic or exemplary deviation, the perversion with a future—no doubt, in part, because it could be strategically aligned in a pseudo-opposition with that other emergent category, normative heterosexuality. What for centuries had been thought of as a multivalent sexual flux, a polytropic wandering inherent in *all* flesh, in *every* body, would be effectively arrested by a kind of taxonomic freeze-framing; the fluid vagrancies of the flesh would be crystallized into discrete and hermetic categories, especially into sexualities whose disjunctiveness would be determined along the axis of object choice: either the homo *or* the hetero. Simultaneously the convenient figure of "bisexuality" would be promulgated to bridge the gap between sexualities that remained fundamentally distinct. Nor did the homo/hetero dyad advene as a diagnostic or "cartographic" advance; certainly it did not arrive as an improved mapping of an ontological substrate that had for centuries eluded correct analysis or description. On the contrary, the binarism operated as an instrument whose formidable incisiveness would help shape modern being and culture; it worked to fashion the reality it would then go on to describe. But how does such an instrument come to hand? and how are its edges sharpened? How else than by a subtle modification of an instrumentation already at work, already in the process of articulating bodies and fashioning selves? In the case of the paraphilias, the precedent but conceptually distinct classification out of which homosexuality arose was sodomy—"that utterly confused category," as Foucault had good reason to call it.[13] Not accidentally, both the sexologists and the gay polemicists of the turn of the century labored intensively to differentiate the deep truth of inversion or homosexuality from the merely epidermal play of sodomy. From the periphery of the epidermis to the center of being: a trajectory worth considering.

This is the monstruosity of love, lady, that the will is infinite
and the execution confin'd, that the desire is boundless and the
act a slave to limit.
                                        —*Troilus and Cressida* (3.2.87–90)

Sodomy is a spacious word. In contemporary English and American usage, it usually refers to anal intercourse, whether heterosexually or homosexually enacted. But in its most general historical signification, sodomy denotes a more inclusive class or set of reprobated, nonreproductive sex acts whose correct name—the name for which "sodomy" itself stands in as but an expedient and allusive alias—is, precisely, no name. For of course the major Western discursive traditions—religious, legal, medical, literary—have reflexively identified sodomy as *the* unmentionable act: *peccatum illude horibile non nominandum inter Christianos*; or, in Lord Alfred Douglas's famous and very loose translation, "the love that dare not speak its name."[14] As the *non plus ultra* of copulatory deviation, sodomy has been historically constructed as one of the bournes of representation, a verge or limit beyond which no action, thought, or discourse may go. "It is wrong [even] to speak of it."[15] In a very duplicitous and anxiogenic way, therefore, proper language takes up the subject of sodomy only to spit it out again, very conventionally, as "a subject the very nature of which is a disgrace to human nature," and of which, therefore, "the least mention is the best."[16]

But of course, by way of the paradox of preterition, a deed without a name has always already been named as such—has been named, that is, as *non nominandum*. The very convention of namelessness thus belies itself, thereby revealing the strategically foreclosed gap whose very unspeakability is articulated within and by discourse. The unspeakable, in other words, is always spoken by a historically contingent structure of beliefs, institutions, and practices to which the unspeakable must thereafter refer, even in its reverse or revisionary forms. Sade's loquacity is exemplary here; for it is precisely the imbrication of politics, ideology, and perversion that gives Sadian sodomy its destructive, or deconstructive, force—its power of apostasy and outrage. "The sodomist act," writes Pierre Klossowski, "has no significative value save as a conscious transgression of the norms represented by conscience."[17] And as Jane Gallop's intertextual readings of Sade and Klossowski have demonstrated, sodomy can operate as the "key sign" or master trope in Sade's texts because it "seems to imply a simple substitution, as a result of which the couple male/female is replaced by the opposition active/passive."[18] Yet, Gallop stresses, this act of substitution is anything but simple or stabilizing. What might at first seem an act of parodic or inverted simulation (i.e., of resemblance or metaphor) instead entails a decentering metonymic slide in which barely perceptible transitions link a whole series of contiguous pleasures. Precisely because the overlay of substitutions is asymmetrical, because there is no necessary correlation between the anatomical (male/female) and the conceptual (active/passive) orderings, sodomy initiates a proliferation of simulacra whose destructuring effect is as "corrosive of individual identities" as it is productive of diverse and mobile pleasures.[19] What had seemed merely a parodic repetition—the "natural" conjugal act gone preposterously awry—instigates what Gallop calls a "vertiginous spin" in which an insistent ideology of penile/vaginal centerings is opened to lubricious exchange. Gallop explains:

> Once any exchange is possible, once the telos (the vagina) is equated or equitable, then the substitutions can proliferate. The absolute value of a telos means its value is not a function of anything, not subordinate to any function. The possibility of an equivalent relativizes the value. The very positing of a substitute for the vagina assumes a grammar explaining that equivalency. That grammar opens the door for a potentially unending series of paradigmatic equivalents.[20]

Sodomy in this sense both initiates and represents a radical slippage for which the dilation of the anus is no longer an adequate figure. Once "the substitutions can proliferate," the possibility of *any* equivalent "opens the door," not merely on a predictable set of sphinctered orifices, but upon the entire cutaneous envelope of the body itself. Sodomy everywhere.

Sade, it might be objected, is an extreme and unrepresentative case— nothing less than the apotheosis of perversion. Nonetheless, as I now want to show, the disseminal vertigo of Sadian sodomy in fact realizes, however, hyperbolically, the conceptual and taxonomic instability that had always lain implicit in the category "sodomy," even in its most severe and repressive formulations. In order to give this claim the historical and textual specificity it requires, we return to the English context in order to ask the questions that I have suspended until now: Just what does sodomy signify? and what are the historical circumstances of these significations? Perhaps the authoritative English definition (and a voluble one, given the passion for reticence that governs English discourse on the subject) is provided by the Renaissance jurist Sir Edward Coke in *Third Part of the Institutes of the Laws of England* (1644), where he interprets 25 Henry 8, 6, the English statute of 1533 that transposed sodomy or buggery (the two terms are semantically interchangeable) from ecclesiastical to civil jurisdiction. Of course this transposition was itself politically motivated and must be "seen as part of a large-scale renegotiation in the boundaries between the Catholic Church and the British state."[21] Indeed, as the first in a series of civil statutes that recodified canon law and appropriated ecclesiastical privilege, 25 Henry 8, 6 marks the subsumption of the individual body by the affined powers of the king and the state. As the tenth item in an extensive list of crimes against the state, Coke's chapter "Of Buggery, or Sodomy" defines the "shamefull sin," now a felony, as follows:

> Buggery is a detestable, and abominable sin, amongst christians not to be named, committed by carnall knowledge against the ordinance of the Creator, and order of nature, by mankind with mankind, or with brute beast, or by womankind with brute beast.[22]

To a modern eye, this passage seems dense with obscurities, periphrases, elisions, even downright confusions. What, for instance, does the phrase "committed by carnall knowledge" actually indicate? What are the anatomical and behavioral implications of such a phrase? In subsequent paragraphs Coke acknowledges the need to gloss "the words of the said description of buggery" and almost provides the definitive details: "there must be *penetratio*, that is *res* in *re*, either with mankind, or with beast, but the least penetration maketh it carnall knowledge." "Least penetration" and "*res* in *re*," the thing in the thing, suggest some specificity— they would seem to designate an act of "unnatural" penetration conjoining distinct bodies—but the generality of "things" here simultaneously points away from exact indication, an ambivalence very typical of this discourse. Yet the operations of a practical jurisprudence would require more specific detail: If "the least penetration maketh it carnall knowledge," how, if at all, does ejaculation signify? Coke's answer: *"Emissio seminis maketh it not buggery, but is evidence in case of buggery of penetration."* Orgasm for Coke corroborates, but is insufficient to establish, the "detestable, and abominable sin."

If Coke's circumspection leaves much occulted, this much at least is clear: as a jurist defining proscribed behavior (not abnormal desires), Coke's disciplinary emphasis falls upon the conjunction of bodies and the acts that conjoin them. But what constitutes an "unnatural" conjunction? Answer: any act of "carnall knowledge [committed] against the ordinance of the Creator, and order of nature," an elliptical enough locution by which Coke gestures toward acts of copulation that, of their very nature, preclude reproduction. "Against nature," then, signifies traduction or circumvention of God's procreative imperative.

Thus defined, sodomy entails a deviant wandering, a heretical turning from the right to a wrong vessel, a movement that, theoretically at least, could include oral and manual as well as anal permutations; its transgressivity is determined not by aberrant desire but by the superimposition of an interpretive grid across the devious topography of a postlapsarian body. What sodomy emphatically does *not* indicate is a sexuality characterized by homosexual alignment of subject and object; it marks instead both the disjunction of the penis and the vagina and the lubricious sliding that may attend such disjunction. This mobile and labile quality, which Sade exploits and organizes so ruthlessly, also underwrites the chain of prepositional phrases in which Coke defines who can commit sodomy and with whom: "by mankind with mankind, or with brute beast, or by womankind with brute beast." Coke here wants to suggest, without precisely delineating, the postural combinations subsumable under the category of "Buggery, or Sodomy," and his phrasing indicates that the taxonomic principle governing this category—the principle that decides which variations are and are not admissible here—clearly derives from the notion of the unnatural adduced above. That is, bestiality (mankind or womankind with beast) may be categorically identified with what we recognize as male homosexuality ("mankind with mankind") because both contravene the "natural" (divine and supernatural) requirement that sex be deployed only for reproduction; this is the interpretive assumption that fuses or confuses persons and beasts here. But Coke's prepositional chain also performs some remarkable elisions and exclusions. Note for instance that this definition, strictly construed, does not entail heterosexual sodomy, although, as we shall see, subsequent juridical practice would subsume this variation under 25 Henry 8, 6. And furthermore, if Coke's subject includes genital relations between members of the same gender, why don't we find one more prepositional phrase, womankind with womankind, added to this disciplinary chain? Why is lesbianism so blithely elided here and elsewhere in English sexual discourse?[23] Both in its articulations and elisions, then, Coke's definition points to the taxonomic pliability of sodomy, to its counterposed powers of subsumption and exclusion. In doing so, Coke's definition witnesses the truth about sodomy that Jonathan Goldberg has put so succinctly: "the term remains incapable of exact definition."[24]

Let us then ask the obvious question. Is sodomy, for Coke, and for subsequent English discourse, primarily a question of anal intercourse? The general answer here is a qualified yes, the more exact answer is yes and no according to the historical conditions. The vagaries of this answer will seem less perverse if we examine briefly the vexed relation within English juridical practice between penetration and emission as proofs of sodomy. Recall that in Coke's definition penetration is primary ("there must be *penetratio*") and emission secondary ("*Emissio seminis* [alone] maketh it not buggery"). Yet in 1631, some ten years before the first edition of Coke's *Institutes*, the soon to be beheaded Mervin Touchet, ninth Lord Audley, second Earl of Castlehaven in the peerage of Ireland, had been convicted of sodomy although anal penetration was never proved. An extensive analysis of this complicated case, which also involved indictments for the earl's abetting the rape of his wife and stepdaughter, and which further entailed questions of treason, is beyond us here; we are concerned only with the sodomy indictments, of which there were two, for relations with male servants, one named Fitz-Patrick and another named Brodway, although we should note in passing that the sodomy indictment is framed within a larger context of extravagant lust, not of "homosexual" deviance. In their examinations before the court, Fitz-Patrick and Brodway agreed as to the earl's sexual practice. Fitz-Patrick testified "that the Lord *Audley* made him lie with him, at *Founthill*, and at *Salisbury*, and once in the Bed, and emitted between his thighs, but did not penetrate his Body; and that he heard he did so with others."[25] Brodway similarly deposed "that the Earl us'd his Body as the Body of a Woman, but never pierc'd it, only emitted between his thighs." Given the consistency of this testimony, the question of guilt was indistinguishable from a question of definition: "Whether it were to be accounted *Buggery* within the statute [25 Henry 8, 6], without Penetration?" The court's response was emphatic: "The Judges resolve that it was: and that the Use of the Body, so far as to emit thereupon, makes it so." Thus the question of "whether it be *Crimen Sodomiticum sine Penetratione*" admits of two opposed answers: in 1631, according to this court's decision, the answer is yes; in 1644, according to Coke's *Institutes*, it is no. What this interpretive dispute reveals is less the flatness of a contradiction than an example of how a labile disciplinary instrument may yield multiple, equivocal, or even contradictory articulations.

During the eighteenth and nineteenth centuries, English juridical practice did not so much resolve this equivocation as distribute its uncertainty across two separate kinds of indictment. First, a felony indictment for committing "the unnatural and detestable sin of sodomy," conviction for which required proof of penetration and (until 1828) of emission *in ano*;[26] such a conviction yielded the death sentence until 1861, when the Offences Against The Person Act removed the death penalty and replaced it by sentences of ten years to life. Second, a misdemeanor indictment of easier proof for "assault with the Intent to commit the unnatural and detestable sin of sodomy," conviction for which was punished by a fine and a stand in the pillory (itself sometimes fatal) and up to two years' imprisonment. Of this misdemeanor indictment we should further note two things: that it represents a common-law or nonstatutory attempt to suppress certain "sodomitical practices" that stopped short of indictable sodomy, and that despite the violent implications of the word "assault," the indictment was employed during the eighteenth and nineteenth centuries to prosecute consensual as well as nonconsensual sexual acts between males.

A representative case illustrating the two kinds of indictments is that of George Duffus, unsuccessfully prosecuted for sodomy in December 1721 and then successfully prosecuted in March 1722 for the misdemeanor charge of assault with intent to commit same; both prosecutions referred to the same sexual episodes. The evidence provided by the prosecution's two primary witnesses recalls the testimony in the Castlehaven case above. Nicholas Leader stated that Duffus "suddenly seized me by the throat so that he had almost strangled me, turned me upon my Face, and forcibly entered my Body about an Inch as near as I can guess; but in struggling, I threw him off once more, before he made an Emission, and having thus forced him to withdraw, he emitted in his own Hand, and clapping it on the tail of my shirt, said, *Now you have it!*" In a corroborating statement, one Mr. Powell testified that Duffus "endeavor'd to convey my Hand to his Privities. I turned from him and lay upon my Back; he got upon me, kept me down, and thrust his Yard betwixt my thighs, and emitted." If the narrative details here stand in striking parallel to the Castlehaven case, then the divergence of the decisions is equally striking. Similar evidence produces opposite results, for in this case the judges "agreed in their Opinion that the Prisoner had not completed the Felony of which he stood indicted," largely because the "Spermatic Injection" (emission *in ano*) had not been proved. Hence the misdemeanor indictment and conviction.[27]

This misdemeanor indictment bears tellingly upon the historical argument being made here, for it once again indicates the definitional pliability of the "utterly confused category" of unnatural copulation. The range of "sodomitical practices" clearly outreaches the anus, and may include acts that do not involve penetration at all. Thus sodomy's propensity to slide metonymically into other paraphilias could be put to both revisionary and normativizing uses, depending upon institutional and textual pressures. In Sade's discourse, as we have seen, sodomy's mobility initiates a proliferation of substitutions whose effect is to corrode identities even as it mobilizes or enflames contiguous pleasures. But the same mobility or pliability also enabled a disciplinary advance, as in the English misdemeanor indictment, which made it possible not only to punish acts that were not sodomy in the strict sense but also to identify and police what research in gay history has shown to be the emergent urban male sodomitical subcultures of the eighteenth century. In the late nineteenth century, with the passage of the Criminal Law Amendment Act of 1885, this nonstatutory attempt to regulate male homosexual practice was codified. Under the provisions of section eleven of this law, all "acts of gross indecency" between males, whether public or private, became misdemeanors punishable by up to two years' hard labor. In referring only to sexual activity between males, this statute in effect legally ratified the emergent category of male homosexuality; as Weeks has noted, it "brought within the scope of the law all forms of male homosexual activity."[28]

But this last paragraph only too readily elides the historical difference that the rest of this chapter will work to elaborate: the difference between sodomy and homosexuality as models of same-gender sexual relations. Weeks, among others, has been careful to stress that "the construction of homosexuality" was no unitary achievement; surely it did not occur by discursive fiat, and just as surely it fluctuated according to the differential pressures of class, gender, and race. "Older notions of the immorality or sinfulness of homosexual behavior did not of course die in the nineteenth century. But from the nineteenth century they were inextricably entangled with would-be scientific theory which formed the boundaries against and within which homosexuals had to define themselves."[29] Weeks is astute in his double emphasis here: although the older model of sodomitical deviance would persist in an inextricable entanglement with newer theorizations of homosexuality, the definitional and conceptual boundaries had indeed changed. That change had the force of a paradigm shift—a shift entailing major transformations in notions of desire, gender, and the desiring subject. Hence in 1897 Havelock Ellis defined "congenital sexual inversion" as "sexual instinct turned by inborn constitutional abnormality toward persons of the same sex";[30] under this definition, it is the desire and not the act that proves taxonomically decisive. But in order to secure a better understanding of this paradigm shift, we must consider sodomy in relation to the broader economy of desire within which it is defined. We turn first to Thomas Aquinas for a representative account of unnatural lust, and then, jumping five centuries, to Jeremy Bentham for a rather more anomalous account.

Of Thomas Aquinas's *Summa Theologicae*, John Boswell has written that it "became the standard of orthodox opinion on every point of Catholic dogma for nearly a millennium and permanently and irrevocably established the 'natural' as the touchstone of Roman Catholic sexual ethics."[31] Such a touchstone entrains as its inescapable corollary a codification of "unnatural" acts, a taxonomy of perversions whose postulates would be transmitted intact to the Protestant English sodomy discourse, where, as we have seen, they would be redeployed and transformed in an increasingly secular and civil context. In the *Summa* Aquinas subsumes sodomy [*vitium sodomiticum*] as a specific subset within the more inclusive genus of unnatural vice or lust [*vitium* or *luxuria contra naturam*], for which he provides the following synopsis:

> It may happen variously. First, outside intercourse when an orgasm is procured for the sake of venereal pleasure; this belongs to the sin of self-abuse, which some call unchaste softness. Second, by intercourse with a thing of another species, and this is called bestiality. Third, with a person of the same sex, male with male and female with female, to which the

Apostle refers, and this is called sodomy. Fourth, if the natural style of intercourse is not observed, as regards the proper organ or according to other rather beastly and monstrous techniques.[32]

Quite clearly, the generic principle that affines the species of perversity enumerated above ("It may happen variously") is decidedly not a disorder or confusion in the relation between desire and gender; the vices numbered one, two and four are unaccountable according to the principle of the heterosexual alignment of an already gendered desire. Rather, as Aquinas's analysis makes clear, the generic postulate governing the category *vitium contra naturam* is a failure to constrain the pursuit of pleasure, itself inspecific as to gender, according to what Aquinas calls "the natural pattern of sexuality for the benefit of the species"—that is, according to God's procreative imperative. Obviously enough, this definition restricts the spectrum of the natural to the monochromatism of heterosexual vaginal intercourse while simultaneously determining a polychromatic range of the unnatural. In each of Aquinas's enumerated perversities—masturbation, bestiality, sodomy, nongenerative "heterosexual" variations—it is the failure of the given sex act to conform to the procreative imperative, and not any malformation in desire itself, that defines transgressivity. Furthermore, as a continuing reminder of the definitional vicissitudes of sodomy, we should note that Aquinas restricts *vitium sodomiticum* to unspecified genital relations between members of the same gender (he includes what Coke will omit: womankind with womankind) and in doing so diverts what we would call heterosexual sodomy to that other category of "rather beastly and monstrous techniques."

Two aspects of Aquinas's thought deserve emphasis: his rigorously delimited notion of "the natural pattern of sexuality" and his understanding of the play of pleasure in relation to that pattern. What precisely is the "patterning" that makes generative sex the only natural sex? What disciplinary machinery insures that pleasure's extravagance will accommodate itself—or, rather, be accommodated—to the shrunken parameters of Aquinas's well-ordered sex act? Given the ease of perversity, how are the rigors of the natural achieved? The brief answer is that in Aquinas's account the coordination of pleasure and nature is the function, at once hermeneutical and disciplinary, of the "higher powers" of "right reason." Reason's agency may be called hermeneutical because reason alone is dispassionate enough to read aright God's procreative intention, and disciplinary because reason alone is potent enough to chasten the excursivity of pleasure. A cool power submits the heat of pleasure to the standard of divine intentions:

> In the realm of human activity a sin implies a breach of the reasonable plan of life, which requires that things be fittingly ordered to their ends. If the end be good and if what is done is well-adapted to that, then no sin is present. Now as the preservation of the bodily nature of the individual is truly a good, so that of the nature of the race is an even greater good. And as food is for the first so sex is for the second. Augustine draws the parallel, *What food is for the health of a man, that intercourse is for the health of the race*. So then, as the use of food is without sin, if taken in due manner and order and for the body's welfare, so also is the use of sex in keeping with its purpose that people should be fruitful.[33]

Prior to the Fall this alignment between the "due manner and order" of the sexual act and God's "purpose that people should be fruitful" was, theoretically at least, an Edenic automatism, an achievement so spontaneous that Augustine could theorize a perfectly "passionless generation" implicating bodies but not pleasures. Of course, this "ideal of Edenic placidity," as Stephen Greenblatt calls it, was expelled from secular history, which is the history of the continuing dysfunction of flesh and reason.[34] Aquinas writes: "That sexual desire and pleasure are not subject to the sway and moderation of reason is part of the penalty of original sin, for as appears from Augustine, by rebelling against God we deserved to have our flesh in rebellion against our reason." As Adam stood against God, so flesh stands against reason; and with the specifically sexual implication that now "there is an excess of pleasure in any sexual act," an excess "so absorbing" that "reason cannot function." If once reason had been concomitantly the motive and the mode of human sexuality, it now arrives belatedly in the form of regulatory agency whose work is to chasten and correct the violence of desire: "Here is a matter where the order of reason is urgently required."[35]

Yet if the urgency of reason works to subdue the excursivity of desire, it must labor ceaselessly because postlapsarian sexuality—which is to say, sans Christ, all sexuality—is everywhere installed with a principle of unnatural extravagance; it always already tends to wander, turn, go the wrong road. Slightly transvaluing Aquinas, we may say that desire *naturally* tends toward the unnatural: a reflexive pleasure tropism. At the level of subjective affect, this entails an indiscriminate *delectatio venereorum* or "sex pleasure." Aquinas: "The goal of lechery is sex pleasure, the greatest there is to sensory appetite, and therefore highly desirable, both because of the vehemence of the pleasure and because it is so bound up with our nature."[36] As the naturally unnatural "vehemence of pleasure" overmasters the "sway of reason," a civil war among the members ensues:

> One consequence of the lower powers being powerfully affected by their own interests is the blocking or derangement of the activities of higher powers. Now in lechery the lower appetites, namely those of the desirous emotions, are vehemently intent on an object because of the strength of the pleasure. A result is that the higher powers of mind and will are put out of gear.[37]

Here, in the idea of an undifferentiated and self-delighting pleasure principle, is Aquinas's conceptual pivot. As pleasure's intrinsic vehemence neutralizes the higher powers of reason and self-control, the lower powers, motivated only by "their own interest" in polymorphic gratification, are free to solicit satisfaction anywhere. With reason thus disengaged, nothing remains to steer the sensual trajectories of *delectatio venereorum*, whose native modes are excess and excursus; and the very contours of gender, whose recognition is required by the higher powers and ignored by the lower, are simply erased by "the strength of pleasure."

For Aquinas, then, sexual desire is not a dyadically structured energy motivating the concussion of genital opposites; heterosexuality is not desire's intrinsic configuration. God's scriptural imperative to generativity and his interdictions against nonprocreative variations are necessary precisely because excursivity is native or natural to postlapsarian desire. Without the directional guide of reason (tab A invariably inserted *according to instructions* into slot B), desire itself is *polytropos*, of many turnings and various contrivances. Sodomy is thus one of the various unnatural turns that polytropic desire so naturally takes; and as such it belongs as a subset to the broader taxonomic category of unnatural vice, which represents a disorder in the relation between reason and pleasure and not, as in sexual inversion, a disorder in the alignment between psychical desire and anatomical sex.

Something like this conceptual schema—which holds transgressivity to be specific as to act and inspecific as to desire, and which holds desire itself to be a polytropic pursuit of pleasure—would govern the West's sodomy discourse from Aquinas's time through the end of the eighteenth century, when the controlling paradigm began to shift toward the inversion or homosexuality model that would dominate late nineteenth and twentieth century discourses, both sexological and psychoanalytic, on same-sex eroticism. If the historical, institutional, and social specifics of this paradigm shift still remain opaque, it is nonetheless clear, in broad terms anyway, that the sodomy paradigm remains dominant until the later decades of the nineteenth century. An instance from the English discourse will clarify this assertion. Circa 1785 Jeremy Bentham wrote, but did not publish, an extended essay (over sixty manuscript pages) on the moral and legal aspects of sexual relations between men. Louis Crompton, who edited Bentham's essay and published it for the first time in 1978, calls it "the earliest scholarly essay on homosexuality known to exist in the English language."[38] We may concur with Crompton's claim of temporal priority while pausing to demur at the word "homosexuality," for Bentham, writing in the last decades of the eighteenth century, had no access to the conceptual category of homosexuality and instead entitled his essay "Offences Against One's Self: Paederasty." It is a title worth lingering over.

The phrase "Offences Against One's Self" alludes generally to a tradition of political and juridical representation and specifically to a contemporaneous legal text, and when thus contextualized the phrase registers as well a certain conceptual plasticity regarding the self's relation to authority and desire's relation to community. The specific textual allusion is to William Blackstone's *Commentaries on the Laws of England*, volume 4, *Of Public Wrongs*, chapter 15, "Of Offences Against the Persons of Individuals," in which Blackstone, "having in the preceeding chapter considered the principal crime, or public wrong, that can be committed against a private subject, namely, by destroying his life," then proceeds "to inquire into such other crimes and misdemeanors, as more particularly affect the security of his person, while living."[39] Blackstone's ascending catalog of "such other crimes" begins in mayhem (by which he means dismemberment), moves to the forcible abduction of heiresses, escalates to rape, and then climaxes with that offense "of a still deeper malignity; the infamous *crime against nature*, committed either with man or beast." As one of the "crimes of a public nature," sodomy (a word Blackstone refuses to write because, as we have seen, "the very mention of [it] is a disgrace to human nature") breaches both the "King's peace" and the individual's "security" or "person"—that is, his or her bodily integrity. Yet Blackstone's catalog of security violations contains a noteworthy anomaly. Except for the infamous crime against nature, all the transgressions enumerated therein involve traductions of consent: an individual's body or person is *forcibly* violated or overwhelmed, but in the case of sodomy the issue of consent is simply elided. Hence consensual sodomy, for reasons Blackstone disdains to explain, constitutes a violation of the communal body itself and therefore counts as a "public wrong."

Bentham, whose reasoning on this subject is everywhere more explicit and composed than Blackstone's, presses Blackstone on exactly this point:

> Neither does this lawyer or any English lawyer in his comments make any distinction between this kind of filthiness when committed with the consent of the patient and the same kind of filthiness when committed against his consent and by violence. It is just as if a man were to make no distinction between concubinage or rape.[40]

And again:

> If either of them be unwilling, the act is not that we have here in view; it is an offense totally different in its nature of effects; it is a personal injury; it is a kind of rape.[41]

Bentham's specification of consent as a pivotal issue in the contradistinction of "paederasty" and "a kind of rape" registers two large differences in the way Blackstone and Bentham regard their subject. First and most obvious is the startling ease with which Bentham analogizes same-sex and other-sex relations; his unembarrassed parallelism between consensual sodomy and concubinage quite simply overturns a whole tradition of phobic masculine representation. Secondly, by simply discounting God's scriptural interdictions and His spectacular correction of Sodom and Gomorrah (a precedent for punishment that Blackstone still regards as "an universal, not merely a provisional precept"), Bentham seeks to refer consensual sodomy—and implicitly all voluntary sexual practice—neither to God nor to king, nor even to the social body at large, but rather to something he simply calls the "self." Unless consensual sodomy tends to "diminish the public force" (and Bentham argues that it does not), then it deserves inclusion "within the list of offences against one's self, of offences of imprudence."[42] Thus the provinces of the body and the trajectories of sexual behavior are for Bentham, as they emphatically are not for Blackstone and his predecessor Coke, matters of personal jurisdiction, and this is so because the individual, quite simply, owns the body and the self. In Bentham's argument, the public is not wronged because the communal/national/divine body is not invoked. For the purposes of abrupt contrast, consider Coke's discourse, where the chapter "Of Buggery, or Sodomy" is situated within *The Third Part of the Institutes*, the subtitle of which is "Concerning High Treason and Other Pleas of the Crown." Coke can account sodomy a species of treason because, according to the dominant Renaissance metaphysic conveniently known as "the great chain of being," all human bodies, especially male ones, repeat, reflect, and represent the king's (male) body, itself both personal and communal, which in turn represents God's (also presumptively male) body. Hence Coke, quoting Fleta, can write "*Sodomie est crime de majestie, vers le roy celestre.*"[43]

Yet if the first half of Bentham's title—"Offences Against One's Self"—signals this large difference in the conceptualization of the subject and the subject's relation to divine and secular communities, then his title's second half—"Paederasty"—should remind us that historical change is simultaneously a process of cultural continuity, that sameness and difference must accommodate each other in fluctuant interplay. Bentham's mistaken employment of the word *paederasty* (derived from the Greek root *paido*: *boy* or, more generally, *child*) to represent all same-sex erotic relations is doubly instructive here: first because it may stand metonymically for the insistent and enduring androcentric bias of English discourse on sexuality (Bentham's sixty manuscript pages contain exactly three perfunctory sentences on erotic relations between females; like Coke, indeed like the whole English legal tradition, he prefers to ignore womankind with womankind), and second because his large allusion to the Greek example forecasts the nineteenth century's fantasmatic quest (Symonds, Pater, Wilde) for a noneffeminated intermasculine sexuality.[44] What, then, is "paederasty" as Bentham defines it? Answer: It is one variety of the "offences of impurity," one of the "irregularities of the venereal appetite which are stiled unnatural."

Stiled unnatural: Bentham's past participle concretizes his revisionary impulse by referring both nature and unnature to the arbitrary cultural process of semantic codification. Bentham implicitly revalues sexual deviance as a kind of lexical or syntactical oddity, and sodomy becomes a merely culturally anomalous or "irregular" way of "procuring sensations." And yet if a revolutionary change is (only) potentiated here,[45] there is also indication of a telling continuity. If, to be sure, Aquinas and Coke would pale at Bentham's stylization of the natural, they would nonetheless recognize as familiar certain foundational assumptions informing the generic phrase "irregularities of the venereal appetite." Consider, for instance, Bentham's enumeration of the "varieties" of "these irregularities," which, he says, "consist either in making use of an object":

1. Of the proper species but at an improper time: for instance, after death.
2. Of an object of the proper species and sex, and at a proper time, but in an improper part.
3. Of an object of the proper species but the wrong sex. This is distinguished from the rest by the name of paederasty.
4. Of a wrong species.
5. In procuring this sensation by one's self without the help of any other sensitive object.

The affinity between this catalog of sexual irregularity and those of Aquinas and Coke is manifest. Despite hierarchical variations within this taxonomic structure (example: contra Aquinas and Coke, Bentham, in a phobic gesture typical of the eighteenth century, will rank masturbation as "the most incontestably pernicious" of the variations), these three writers agree that the genus of the "unnatural" (Aquinas, Coke) or the "irregular" (Bentham) subsumes a special series of transgressive or impure acts whose essential relatedness derives from a shared principle or, better, from a common property. "The abominations that come under this head," Bentham writes, "have this property in common, in this respect, that they consist in procuring certain sensations by means of an improper object." Thus the generic affinity of, say, heterosexual fellation, homosexual sodomy, and individual masturbation derives from a libidinal economy of sensations and their loci, of pleasure and mobile gratifications; it is precisely the indifference of sensation to the sites of its gratification that motivates the strict organization of members and orifices. Once again desire is *polytropos*, a wanderer. And most importantly, this is not an economy of desire in gender and gender in desire. Indeed, for Bentham the difference in sexual object (whether a difference in gender or species or person) does not constitute a critical or explanatory difference, because each object is a merely circumstantial or accidental telos of pleasure's polytropic inclinations. This notion of desire grounds Bentham's use of "paederasty" as a representative deviation. He writes that "in settling the nature and tendency of this offence we shall for the most part have settled the nature and tendency of all the other offences, that come under this disgusting catalog." The comprehensiveness of this exegetical claim may be astonishing, but it is coherent given the double postulate that grounds Bentham's account of eros: that, first, desire is an indifferent wanderer and, second, that transgression is act-specific—a matter of doing, not of feeling or of erotic orientation. If, as is the case, this taxonomic logic did not survive the nineteenth century intact, it was because those two postulates, for reasons that remain partly occulted, would be overturned. Or, perhaps better, inverted.

Before turning to the "discursive explosion" of nineteenth century sexuality and to the paradigm shift implicit in it, I want briefly to consider three eighteenth-century texts that bear directly upon the historical argument being made here. The first text, which presents a rather extensive analysis of the legal implications of a particular heterosexual sodomy case (*Rex* v. *Wiseman*, 1716), provides compelling confirmation of our assertion that sodomy derives from a gender-inspecific conceptualization of desire; the second and third texts, both phobic satires upon the burgeoning homosexual subculture of early eighteenth-century London, complicate our argument by indicating the ways in which social practices may outspeed discursive norms; by definition, the "preposterous" sidesteps the normative.[46] Indeed, the very appearance in the eighteenth century of an institutionalized gay male subculture, which has been definitively established by, among others, Alan Bray and Randolph Trumbach, itself suggests a cultural turn toward the articulation of a specifically homosexual identity.[47] Bray writes: "Alongside the old forms of society in which homosexuality had appeared new meanings were now being attached to homosexuality: it was more than a mere sexual act."[48] Yet we must stress, if only in passing, that such individual and cultural recomposition, never an instant accomplishment, is rather the result of a variable revisionary process, a conflictual interchange among discourses, institutions, subcultures, and identities, an interchange in which the presumptively opposed functions of complicity and resistance are not always so easily distinguished. As Weeks, following Foucault, has correctly noted, methods of domination (moral, legal, medical) produced an "inevitable contradictory effect," an enhanced awareness of the homosexual possibility, "and this in turn created the elements of resistance and self-definition that led to the growth of distinctive homosexual identities."[49]

To return to the sodomy paradigm: on 16 March 1716 Richard Wiseman, "the master of a workhouse at Maidstone in Kent," was tried and convicted at the assizes at Rochester under "an indictment for committing of sodomy, in ano, with a girl of eleven years of age," one Jane Mills.[50] For our purposes, the interest of this case does not center, as it would today, on the girl's age—the statutory age of sexual consent at the time was ten—but rather on her gender and its relation to the crime of sodomy. The importance of this case lies in its adjudication of the status of heterosexual sodomy; in the words of Justice Fortescue Aland, whose compilation of trial *Reports* provides the text I am using here, the question before the court was "whether it [i.e., anal intercourse between male and female] was buggery within the statute [25 Henry 8, 6] or not." Despite Wiseman's conviction, this question was sufficiently vexing to prompt a Mr. Justice Probyn temporarily to reprieve the prisoner "in order to have the opinion of all the Judges, on this offence"; the case was then referred to the King's Bench Division at Westminster for further consideration. Fortescue Aland's report describes these appellate deliberations:

> The Judges met once or twice on this occasion, and the case was argued by them, and a few were of opinion that this was not express buggery within our law; though as Justice Fortescue A. remembered there was a great majority, that were of opinion it was plain buggery by our law; but yet, because two or three Judges held out there was no further meeting and consequently no unanimous opinion given.
>
> But Justice Fortescue A. was exceeding sorry, that such a gross offence should escape without any punishment in England; when it is a crime punishable with death and burning at a stake, all over the world besides.
>
> It being so horrid and great a crime, that no colour should be given to such an offence, Justice Fortescue A. wrote to the Earl of Macclesfield, then Chancellor of Great Britain, concerning this matter; and his answer was by way of letter, that he wondered at a variety of opinions; that he had not the least hesitation in agreeing it to be plain sodomy, that he could not think of one objection, to which he should be able to give the appearance of an argument; that it is a crime exactly of the same nature, as well as it is the same action, as if committed upon a male, the difference of the subject only makes it more inexcusable, and it is within the letter of the Act of Parliament, as well as within the meaning, that it seems little to the purpose to say, that possibly the law-makers might not think of this crime; whether they did or not, appears not; the words reach it, and the reason of the law reaches it; and when crime is forbid in

general, it is not necessary that every species of it should be under consideration, unless such species should be less criminal.

From this remarkable passage we may deduce the following assertions. First, sodomy or buggery was a category of sufficient conceptual dubiety to produce a significant rift in legal interpretation, a dispute as to whether heterosexual anal intercourse counted as "express buggery within our law," 25 Henry 8, 6, which did not specify "mankind with womankind" but did specify "womankind with brute beast." Second, this interpretive dispute issued in a very anxious textual production (e.g., Fortescue Aland's letters of inquiry to the earl of Macclesfield and other authorities not mentioned in this passage; the letters received in response to these letters; and, most important, the pages from Fortescue Aland's *Reports* that we are reading here). Third, the final effect of this discursive production, despite the dissent of "two or three Judges," was to secure the authority of the dominant interpretation (here represented by Fortescue Aland and the Earl of Macclesfield) that "the words reach it, and the reason of the law reaches it," and that, therefore, the "majority of all Judges held it was sodomy both at the common and civil law." Finally, it is thus clear that sodomy was an elastic category capable of subsuming a variety of "species," whether or not those species were expressly enumerated or intended by the original "law-makers."

So certain was Judge Fortescue Aland of the urgency and importance of his victorious interpretation that he contravened the conventional directive toward reticence (*inter Christianos non nominandum*) in order to extend his analysis across eight pages of his 1748 trial *Reports*—a remarkable volubility that prompted William Eden in his *Principles of Penal Law* (1771) to chastise Fortescue Aland for "a very indelicate profusion of learning on the subject."[51] Out of this profusion of learning we need to isolate two aspects. First, Fortescue Aland's delineation of the types or "species" of intercourse that may be subsumed under the generic term "sodomy": "Sodomy is the genus, *rem veneream habere in ano* with a man is only a species and with a woman is another species, and so with a boy or girl, is another species, and with a beast another species." Second, his direct assertion that heterosexual rather than homosexual sodomy constitutes the greater offense: "Besides the unnatural abuse of a woman, seems worse than either that of a man or a beast; for it seems a more direct affront to the Author of Nature, and a more insolent expression of contempt of His wisdom condemning the provision made by Him, and defying both it and Him." When a woman and her "provision" (i.e., her vagina) are, as Fortescue Aland goes on to say, "at hand," then the "affront" to "natural" copulation is, because more proximate, therefore more extreme. Why go the wrong road when the right road is right there? It is clear from these passages that Fortescue Aland's desire to regulate "perverse" behaviors certainly includes, but equally certainly does not pivot upon, what we would call the homosexual difference; his central concern is not same-gender relations. If his moral valuations are the reverse of Bentham's, his taxonomic logic is much the same—specific as to act, inspecific as to desire and gender: heterosexual sodomy "is a crime exactly of the same nature, as well as it is the same action as if committed upon a male." Homosexuality is very clearly not the definitive object of Fortescue Aland's disciplinary pursuit.

It is necessary now that we qualify, without relinquishing, our initial assertion that sodomy does not refer to same-gender sexuality but points rather toward a more generalized and inclusive notion of the perverse, the deviant, the unnatural. Our basic contradistinction between "sodomy" and "homosexuality" still stands but requires now a more precise historical shading, for the recent historiographical and bibliographical work in gay studies is making it increasingly clear that the language of sodomitical deviance was being employed in eighteenth-century London to identify and condemn a growing, or at least an increasingly visible, urban gay male subculture.[52] Although much remains to be learned about this subculture, this much at least seems clear: that its most prominent institutionalized form was the molly house, usually an inn or tavern (or a room in same) where male sodomites could congregate and copulate in relative safety; that the molly houses were sites of an extravagant and self-conscious transvestism that had, as we shall see, large implications for the semiotics of gender; that the molly houses were the focus of considerable discursive attention in the form of popular tracts and broadsheets; and that within the dominant culture this subculture articulated a sodomitical role self-consciously counterposed to the norm of marital conjugality.

"The late proceedings in our Courts of Law," writes the anonymous author of the sensationalist pamphlet *Hell Upon Earth: or, the Town in an Uproar* (London, 1729), "have furnished us with ample Proofs that this Town abounds too plentifully with a sect of brutish Creatures called SODOMITES; a sect that ought to be excluded from all civil society and human conversation."[53] Despite the recommendation for exclusion from "conversation" (itself an ambiguous term), this passage continues at some length:

> They exceed the worst Beasts of the Field in the Filthiness of their Abominations. The Birds of the Air couple Male and Female to propagate Generation, and every Animal moves by a natural Instinct; but Man, exclusive of all others, forms Ideas destructive to himself, and grows fond of new Inventions which are repugnant to divine Institution and the fundamental Laws of Nature; he is grown hardened in Iniquity, having abandon'd himself to all manner of Vice, and is not ashamed to act Crimes which expose him to the severity of the Laws and the Contempt of the World. . . . The greatest Criminal has some People that may drop some pitying Expressions for his unhappy and untimely Fate and condole his dismal Circumstances; while those Persons who fall by the Laws for Sodomy, can expect neither Pity or Compassion. It would be a pretty Scene to behold them in their Clubs and Cabals.

This passage does double duty: it registers a certain disjunction between discursive and social practices, and it helps us trace the elusive historical transition between the sodomy and homosexuality paradigms. Indeed, the passage may be said to straddle the difference between those paradigms. The passage derives its lexicon of deviance ("brutish Creatures," "hardened in Iniquity," "all manner of Vice") from an available sodomy discourse, and yet it deploys that language to describe social practices and institutions—those of a newly established gay male subculture—for which the conceptual apparatus of the older paradigm would prove inadequate. Surely, the eighteenth-century "sect" of sodomites with "their Clubs and Cabals" adumbrates, without fully realizing, the modern notion of homosexual identity. Here we witness, from an alienated and phobic perspective, early social traces of that process of identity formation; as Bray writes, "There was now a continuing culture to be fixed on and an extension of the area in which homosexuality could be expressed and therefore recognized; clothes, gestures, language, particular buildings and particular public places—all could be identified as having specifically homosexual connotations."[54] It must have been the presence within the dominant culture of just such a continuing subculture that in part led the nineteenth century to articulate the concept and the language of homosexuality.

Although the existence of a sodomitical subculture in eighteenth-century London is now beyond question, the details of its operations and practices are rather more obscure. Furthermore, extant knowledge of this subculture has been largely derived from trial reports and popular satires, that is, from discursive sources that stand in a self-consciously alienated relation to the practices they describe. The following text, extracted from Edward Ward's *The Secret History of London Clubs* (London, 1709), provides one such account of life inside a molly house; if, as seems likely, the passage consists of a cross-coupling of reportorial fact and cultural fantasia, it nonetheless provides a contemporaneous instance of how the subculture was represented in popular discourse. Ward imagines a "pretty scene" in which we "behold them in their Clubs and Cabals":

> There are a particular Gang of *Sodomitical* Wretches, in this Town, who call themselves the *Mollies*, and are so far degenerated from all masculine Deportment; or manly Exercises, that they rather fancy themselves Women, imitating all the little Vanities that Custom has reconcil'd to the Female Sex, affecting to Speak, Walk, Tattle, Curtsy, Cry, Scold, and to mimick all Manner of Effeminacy, that ever has fallen within their several Observations; not omitting the Indecencies of lewd Women, that they may tempt one another by such immodest Freedoms to commit those odious Bestialities, that ought for ever to be without a Name. At a certain Tavern in the City, whose Sign I shall not mention, because I am unwilling to fix an Odium upon the House; where they have settl'd a constant Meeting every Evening in the Week, that they may have the better Opportunity of drawing unwary Youth into the like Corruption. When they are met together, it is their usual Practice to mimick a Female Gossiping, and fall into all the impertinent Tittle Tattle, that a merry Society of good Wives can be subject to, when they have laid aside their Modesty for the Delights of the Bottle. Not long since, upon one of their Festival Nights, they had cusheon'd up the Belly of one of their *Sodomitical* Brethren, or rather Sisters, as they commonly call'd themselves, disguising him in a Womans Night-Gown, Sarsnet-Hood, and Nightrale, who, when the Company were met, was to mimick the wry Faces of a groaning Woman, to be deliver'd of a joynted Babie they had provided for that Purpose, and to undergo all the Formalities of Lying in. The Wooden Off-Spring to be afterwards Christen'd, and the holy Sacrament of Baptism to be impudently Prophan'd, for the Diversion of the Profligates, who, when their infamous Society were assembl'd in a Body, put their wicked Contrivance accordingly into practice.

The critical interest of this passage lies in the way it conjoins counterconventional sexual practice to a language of hyperconscious mimesis; for in doing so it implicitly figures "deviant" sexuality, at least in this eighteenth-century English context, as a necessarily belated mode of gender parody, as a farcical and dangerous troping upon established gender codes. Here we have a parody of a parody, parody in the second degree, as Ward defensively travesties what is in fact already a travesty: the sodomite's improvisational transvestite theater, complete with costumes, props, and predictable narrative—a theater, not incidentally, that found itself on a metaphor of gender reversal that anticipates, with important differences, the nineteenth century's biological and psychological figurations of sexual inversion. As we will see in some detail, the medicalizing discourses of the nineteenth century worked to inscribe the inversion metaphor as a deep structure indistinguishable from the constitution of individual being, as a radical biological or psychological truth whose effects radiated from the center of being outward toward the peripheries of behavior. But here gender reversal has about it the relative ease of a costume change. To the degree that this passage represents gender less as a given of nature than as a product of "Deportment" or cultural "Exercise," it identifies masculinity and femininity as the subjective effects of a cultural inscription whose anatomical loci may be preposterously reversed, so that these biological males, farcically "imitating all the little Vanities that Custom has reconcil'd to the Female Sex," may "rather fancy themselves Women." As the lexical and scenic emphases upon imitation and mimicry make clear, the presumptive perversion travestied in this passage is neither sexual inversion nor homosexuality in the modern sense; it is rather a radical, and radically equivocal, mode of gender stylization and performance—a matter, in Ward's lexicon, of extravagant sexual "Manners." And of course, as Ward is correct to note, the aggressive, revisionist intention of the mollies' closet theater is "impudently" to "Prophane" the dominant heterosexual and procreative ideology that drove these men to the protective confines of this theatrical space, this site of "deviant" representation in which "the subculture could pose its meanings and practices over/against the larger culture."[55]

A useful narrative simplification: by the late nineteenth century, the new "discursive practice" of sexuality would authorize a totalizing problematic. Sex would not just signify, it would signify everywhere and everyhow; no domain of knowledge or feeling, no recess of culture or subjectivity, would be immune to its ramifying effects, its power of insinuation, its general and diffuse causality. Foucault: "The most discrete event in one's sexual behavior—whether an accident or a deviation, a deficit or an excess—was deemed capable of entailing the most varied consequences throughout one's existence; there was a scarcely a malady or physical disturbance to which the nineteenth century did not impute at least some degree of sexual etiology."[56] An individual's sexuality would increasingly be thought to constitute, in Havelock Ellis's words, the "central core of organic personality," the natural or material base upon which the "deep truth" of individuality would be grounded. Here is Ellis, writing in the general preface to the 1897 edition of *Sexual Inversion*:

> It is perhaps a mistake to show so plainly at the outset that I approach what may seem only a psychological question not without moral fervor. But I do not wish any mistake to be made. I regard sex as the central problem of life. And now that the problem of religion has practically been settled, and that the problem of labour has at least been placed on a practical foundation, the question of sex—with the racial questions that rest on it—stands before the coming generations as the chief problem for solution. Sex lies at the root of life, and we can never learn to reverence life until we know how to understand sex.—So at least, it seems to me.

The passage could not be more direct in its overdetermination of the sexual. Displacing "moral fervor" onto a "psychological question," Ellis pointedly exemplifies modernity's drive toward a new cognitive mastery over what he calls, in a representative hyperbole, "the central problem of life"—the problem, that is, of "how to understand sex." Both Ellis's sense of an outsized problem and the reverent gravity with which he confronts it are markers of the modern experience of sexuality.

Lying thus "at the root of life," sexuality would manifest itself problematically, in strange branchings, extravagant exfoliations. The perversions became the object of a special solicitation. "During the second half of the nineteenth century," Arnold Davidson writes, "there was a virtual explosion of medical discussions about the sexual perversions"—discussions that mark an epistemic shift, a trans-European refiguration of sexuality as a pathogenic force and therefore a medical and psychological topic. "These discussions saturated European and, eventually, American psychiatric concerns, resulting in an epidemic of perversion that seemed to rival the recent cholera outbreaks. Despite many differences between the loquacious psychiatrists, differences both theoretical and clinical, all shared the conception of perversion that underpinned these discussions—the perversions were a *shared object* of psychiatric discourse about which there were commonly recognized and fully standardized forms of reasoning." What had once been figured as a perverse potential residing in all beings would become a definitive singularity; inversion, masochism, fetishism, etc., would be classified as functional diseases of the "sexual instinct." "That is to say, the class of diseases that affected the sexual instinct was precisely the sexual perversions."[57] Hence Ellis's definition of "congenital sexual inversion" as "sexual instinct turned by inborn constitutional abnormality toward persons of the same sex."[58]

As Davidson stresses, the notions of instinct, function, and perversion are "inextricably connected"; they are part of the epistemic web that made the medicalization of sex possible. "Once one offers a functional characterization of the sexual instinct, perversions become a natural class of diseases; without this characterization there is really no conceptual room for this kind of disease." That is, the conceptual space of modern perversion presupposes the supplanting of the Christian hermeneutic of the flesh (pleasure, gratification, control) by the modern problematic of the "sexual instinct" and its "normal" operation within the biological sphere. Within this mode of reasoning, perversion would be determined by deviation from "normal" function. Davidson again: "Without knowing the normal function of the instinct, everything and nothing could count as a functional disturbance. There would be no principled criterion to include or exclude any behavior from the disease category of perversion."[59] What, then, constitutes this criterion? What is the "natural" or "normal" function of the "sexual instinct" presumed to be? The following passages from two preeminent sexological texts, Krafft-Ebing's influential *Psychopathia Sexualis* (twelve editions between 1886 and 1902) and Albert Moll's *Perversions of the Sex Instincts*, help answer this question. Krafft-Ebing:

> The procreation of the human race is not left to mere accident or the caprices of the individual, but is guaranteed by the hidden laws of nature which are enforced by a mighty, irresistible impulse.[60]

> During the time of the maturation of the physiological processes in the reproductive glands, desires arise in the consciousness of the individual which have for their purpose the perpetuation of the species (sexual instinct).[61]

And Moll:

> To understand the homosexual urge we should consider the genital instinct not as a phenomenon apart from other functions but rather as a

psychic function. . . . From a teleological point of view, that is from the point of view of the reproduction of the species, we consider natural the urge that the normal man feels for the woman.[62]

These passages enact the conceptual transformations so characteristic of modern discourses on sexuality. Simply put, they transpose the experience of the flesh onto a deeply sexualized subjectivity. The biologically derived notion of sexual or genital "instinct" refers not to the material body and its extravagances but rather to a morphologically unspecifiable "psychic function" whose invisible operations penetrate to the "central core of organic personality." Working less to regulate specific sexual acts than to incite and police a subjective domain of "urges" and "mighty, irresistible impulses," this emphasis upon psychic function redefines the domain of sexual "truth." No longer merely a relation between the body and the law, sexuality interrogates the very constitution of the "desires [that] arise in the consciousness of the individual." And, as Krafft-Ebing suggests, the very might of these desires would be deployed to "enforce" (his particular interpretation of) "the hidden laws of nature." In a subtle disciplinary infiltration, psychiatric discourses on homosexuality transfused the exteriority of the traditional procreative bias into the very recesses of being, into the constitution of the sexed subject and his or her desires: "procreation . . . is guaranteed by the hidden laws of nature which are enforced by a mighty, irresistible impulse," i.e., "the urge that the normal man feels for the woman." Operating within a heterosexist and masculist ideology, these discourses presume the heterosexual configuration of desire itself—a grounding belief that, as Davidson puts it, "the sexual instinct manifested itself in an attraction to members of the opposite sex and in a desire for sexual intercourse with them."[63] This monological belief, so different from the indiscriminate tropings of Thomas's *delectatio venereorum* or Bentham's "irregularities" of the venereal appetite, would enable what we may call, in Foucaldian shorthand, the homosexual implantation—the historical process by which homosexuality or sexual inversion inherits sodomy's place as the central paradigm for same-sex relations in the West.

In England the discursive history of this implantation begins in the last decades of the nineteenth century and continues into the first decades of the twentieth; during this time English writers produced a sustained private and public discourse about the variability of sexual desire, with a culturally typical androcentric emphasis upon male homoerotic love that had earlier received anxiogenic representation in Tennyson's *In Memoriam* and Whitman's "Calamus" poems. The pivotal texts contributing to this English discourse include John Addington Symonds's *A Problem in Greek Ethics*, written in 1873, privately printed in 1883, and included in a revised form as an appendix to the first published edition of Havelock Ellis's and Symonds's *Sexual Inversion* (1897); Sir Richard Burton's brilliant and coy "Terminal Essay," published in 1885 as an appendix to his *A Thousand and One Arabian Nights*; Symonds's excellent *A Problem in Modern Ethics*, printed privately in 1891, and more widely available in pirated editions of 1896 and 1901; Havelock Ellis's (and J. A. Symonds's) *Sexual Inversion*, certainly the most influential of these texts, published and suppressed in England in 1897, later to be published in America as volume two (despite the fact that it was written first) of Ellis's monumental *Studies in the Psychology of Sex* (1901); and Edward Carpenter's important *The Intermediate Sex*, published in book form in 1908, although shorter versions of his polemic in favor of "homogenic love" had appeared earlier. Admittedly apologetic and polemical, written by men whom, with the exception of Ellis, we would call gay or homosexual, these texts argued for the transvaluation of "sodomy" into "sexual inversion" (the preferred English taxonomic label) or "homosexuality" (a neologism against which Symonds, Ellis, and Carpenter protested) or "intermediate sexuality." Clearly inhabiting an ambivalent position, these texts are at once marginal and representative. Marginal in the sense that they represent a minority, even a radical opinion, as their troubled histories of printing, publication, suppression, and piracy suggest. And yet representative in two senses at least: first because they may stand metonymically for the scores of texts—novels, plays, poems, stories, essays—contributing to the inversion discourse in which our heterosexualizing academy has shown little or no interest (we are apparently nervous still); and second because they represent the English and trans-European need to formulate a new taxonomy for same-sex relations—a new way, that is, to begin speaking the unspeakable.

This new volubility provided the working medium through which some of the nineteenth century's most famous "sods" (one of Symonds's self-lacerating terms of self-reference) sought to transvalue themselves into "inverts" or "intermediates." The first tactical move in this refiguration of the sexual paradigm was the devaluation of the anus as the site of sexual signification; specifically this meant a denial of sodomy (here I *do* mean anal intercourse) as the definitive gay male activity. As part of their polemic for the decriminalization of sodomy, Symonds and Carpenter stressed the crucial distinction: an invert was not a sodomite. "It is a common belief that one, and only one, unmentionable act is what lovers seek as the source of their unnatural gratification. . . . Nothing can be more mistaken."[64] Symonds here tries to divest the anus of its inherited overdeterminations, thereby seeking to produce an account of gay male sexuality that does not revolve obsessively around the anus. When in *Modern Ethics* Symonds complains that he "can hardly find a name that will not seem to soil" his text "because the accomplished languages of Europe in the nineteenth century provide no term for this persistent feature of human psychology without importing some implication of disgust, disgrace, vituperation," he is trying to elude, at least discursively, the anxiogenic precincts of the anus. Symonds's double gesture here is definitive. In simultaneously pointing away from the anus ("disgust, disgrace, vituperation") and toward a morphologically imprecise center of desire ("this persistent feature of human psychology"), Symonds's sentence enacts a movement crucial to the inversion model: a turning away from the flesh with its economy of pleasures and toward the psyche with its economy of desires. Edward Carpenter concurred. In "homogenic love," as he preferred to call it, "the love sentiment" achieves "one of its most perfect forms—a form in which from the necessities of the situation the sensuous element, though present, is exquisitely subordinated to the spiritual."[65]

In its "exquisite subordination" of the sensuous to the spiritual, Carpenter's sentence does more than merely rehearse a conventional program of Christian sublimation; more importantly, it relays the tropological duplicity by which the inversion metaphor would articulate or incite (at the level of "sentiment" or subjective affect) the very homosexual desire it would also repress (at the level of act). Homosexual desire would be "perfected" in a precariously balanced, inverted subjectivity—a subjectivity characterized, in Foucault's terms, "less by a type of sexual relations than by a quality of sexual sensibility, a certain way of inverting the masculine or feminine in oneself."[66] Nor was this distinction between sexual act and sexual being the exclusive emphasis of gay polemicists championing the legitimacy or "naturality" of homosexual desire, for whom it provided a considerable argumentative lever. Rather, the distinction was constitutive of the inversion metaphor as such; Krafft-Ebing, for instance, regarded it as fundamental:

Perversion of the sexual instinct . . . is not to be confounded with perversity in the sexual act; since the latter may be induced by conditions other than psychopathological. The concrete perverse act, monstrous as it may be, is clinically not decisive. In order to differentiate between disease (perversion) and vice (perversity), one must investigate the whole personality of the individual and the original motive leading to the perverse act. Therein will be found the key to the diagnosis.[67]

Between mere "vice" ("perversity"/sodomy) and the clinical signification of "disease" ("perversion"/inversion), an explanatory limit intervenes. A "psychopathological" difference penetrates "the whole personality of the individual," disclosing itself as "the original motive" of a perverse act whose former taxonomic centrality is here erased: "the concrete perverse act . . . is clinically not decisive." In this account of being and origination (an account whose presuppositions were shared by both the psychiatrists and the gay revisionists), the specificity of the sodomitical act yields to the diffusion of the inverted condition.

In what precisely does the "decisive" difference consist? What is it, situated so deeply in the recesses of being, that counts as "the key in the diagnosis?" A truncated answer to this question is suggested by Foucault in the passage quoted above: "a certain way of inverting the masculine and the feminine." But a more carefully elaborated answer will have to acknowledge the historical process by which nineteenth-century writers would deploy severely dichotomized notions of gender—the categorical poles of male and female—in order to devise a new mechanism for the interpretation, production, and regulation of homosexual desire. For our purposes, the history of this process may be said to begin not with the medical community *per se*, but rather with an obscure Hanoverian legal official named Karl Heinrich Ulrichs (1825–1895), an "invert" or (as he called himself) an "Urning" who, having written in the 1860s and 1870s "a series of polemical, analytical, theoretical, and apologetic pamphlets,"[68] may be justifiably called both the father of modern gay activism and, by a familiar paradox, the author of the etiological account of gay desire that would prove, with slight modification, paradigmatic for subsequent medical definitions of homosexuality. As Ellis explains it, Ulrichs "regarded Uranismus, or homosexual love, as a congenital abnormality by which a female soul had become united with a male body—*anima muliebris in corpore virili inclusa*."[69] In Symonds's synopsis of Ulrichs's account, the etiology of this misalignment

between anatomy and desire is "to be found in physiology, in that obscure department of natural science which deals with the evolution of
sex." Nature's attempt to coordinate the differentiation of the "male
and female organs of procreation" with the subsequent differentiation
of the "corresponding male and female appetites" falls short of success:
"Nature fails to complete her work regularly and in every instance.
Having succeeded in differentiating a male with full-formed sexual organs from the undecided foetus, she does not always effect the proper
differentiation of that portion of the psychical being in which resides
the sexual appetite. There remains a female soul in a male body." The
utility of this account of inverted desire within the gay polemic is obvious: in holding nature responsible for "the imperfection in the process
of development," it relieves the individual of moral responsibility for
his or her anomalous development. "It is established that their appetites, being innate, are *to them* at least natural and undepraved; the
common appetites [i.e., heterosexuality], being excluded from their sexual scheme, are *to them* unnatural and abhorrent."[70] Inverts or Urnings
or homosexuals are therefore statistically "abnormal" but nonetheless
"natural beings." Symonds puts it succinctly in a letter to Carpenter:
"The first thing is to force people to see that the passions in question
have their justification in nature."[71]

But if this attempt to justify the ways of nature to man pointed with
one hand toward the decriminalization of sodomy, it simultaneously gestured with the other toward the medicalization of inversion—toward,
that is, a compensatory modality of regulation. Indeed, the liability of Ulrichs's inversion account to medical and psychological appropriation lay
in its essentially retrograde conceptual underpinnings. Precisely what the
inversion account does not do is deconstruct or radically disrupt the "heterosexual paradigm" that grounds sexual discourse in the nineteenth and
twentieth centuries; instead it merely shuffles conventional gender
norms, leaving the "microstructural heterosexual attitudes" intact.[72] The
argument's intrinsic doubleness—its insistence on the simultaneous inscription within the individual of two genders, one anatomical and one
not, one visible and one not—curiously betrays its own desire to elude
heterosexual regimentation. The individual "Urning" or "invert" may be
ambiguously reified by this confusion of antipodal genders, but the relationship between desire and gender remains, at the conceptual level, absolutely unambiguous; it is transfixed by an assumed foundational heterosexuality. A male's desire for another male, for instance, is from the

beginning assumed to be a feminine desire referable not to the sex of the body (*virili corpore*) but rather to an occulted "psychic function" controlled by the "opposite" gender (*anima muliebris*). Desire is thus always already enlisted under the regime of heterogender—to want a male cannot not be a feminine desire, and vice versa; and the body, having become an unreliable signifier, ceases to represent the invisible truth of desire, which itself never escapes heterosexual configuration. A truly homosexual embrace thus becomes an ontological impossibility since an interpolated principle of gender difference always intervenes to distantiate the sameness of bodies. Within the gender structure of the inversion trope, the categorical poles of male and female "remain distinct even in the compromise they accomplish."[73]

What we may now call the latent heterosexuality that grounds Ulrichs's account of Uranian desire provided the handle for the forthcoming medical/psychiatric appropriation. That appropriation began in 1870 when Carl Westphal, having read Ulrichs, published in *Archiv für Psychiatrie und Nervenkrankheiten* his seminal article "Die Conträre Sexuelempfindung" or "Contrary Sexual Instinct." In this article, which Ellis regarded as "the first to put the study of sexual inversion on an assured scientific basis," Westphal defines inversion or homosexuality or contrary sexual feeling as a congenital perversion in which "a woman is physically a woman and psychologically a man, and on the other hand, a man is physically a man and psychologically a woman."[74] This definition, which patently appropriates Ulrichs's etiological formula, subjects *anima muliebris virili corpore inclusa* to a double transformation: it transposes the mystified notion of *anima* or soul into a purely psychological register and then transvalues the Urning's presumptively benign developmental anomaly ("a sport of nature," Symonds sometimes called it) into a palpable sign of individual morbidity and hereditary degeneration (two specters that everywhere haunt the medical discourse on inversion). In thus revising Ulrichs's account, Westphal preferred the first psychological definition of homosexuality—a definition that would provide the conceptual schema for subsequent medical discourse on the subject.

The cultural work of disseminating Westphal's revised account throughout Europe and America began immediately. In the October 1871 issue of the English *Journal of Mental Science*, an anonymous reviewer provided a brief synopsis of Westphal's article and translated his title as "Inverted Sexual Proclivity"; here, it would seem, the language of sexual inversion was inaugurated. In 1878 an Italian article, "*Sull'inversione dell'instinto sensuale*," appeared, and by 1882, when Charcot and Magnan published their influential "*Inversion du sens genital*," the metaphorics of sexual inversion had been established as the dominant fiction for the constitution of homosexuality as a psychiatric disease characterized by gender dysfunction.[75] And of course Krafft-Ebing, "the great clinician of sexual inversion," as Ellis called him, worked assiduously to implant the new "truth" of a psychopathologically inverted sexuality.[76] Throughout the twelve editions of *Psychopathia Sexualis* that appeared between 1886 and 1902, the metaphorics of inversion remained intact:

> It is purely a psychical anomaly, for the sexual instinct does in no wise correspond with the primary and secondary physical sexual characteristics. In spite of the fully differentiated sexual type, in spite of the normally developed and active sexual glands, man is drawn sexually to the man because he has, consciously or otherwise, the instinct of the female toward him, or vice versa.[77]

Once Krafft-Ebing had identified this "psychical anomaly" as a "neuropathic taint," as nothing less than a "functional sign of degeneration," the nineteenth-century medical appropriation of Ulrichs's presumptively subversive gay polemic was substantially complete. The "reverse discourse" had itself been reversed.

But did not this normalizing reversal itself almost immediately suffer another peripety, nothing less than a fierce and irrecuperable deconstruction at the decisive hand of Freud when he published in 1905 *Three Essays on the Theory of Sexuality*, a text whose first movement is a study of the perversions generally and inversion specifically? In the first essay, Freud makes an epochal, a "revolutionary," scission or cut; he severs the heretofore presumed linkage between the sexual instinct and the sexual object ("the person [or thing] from whom sexual attraction proceeds"). Although the passage is well known, I quote at some length:

> It has been brought to our notice that we have been in the habit of regarding the connection between the sexual instinct and the sexual object as more intimate than it in fact is. Experience of the cases that are considered abnormal has shown us that in them the sexual instinct and the sexual object are merely soldered together—a fact which we have been in danger of overlooking in consequence of the uniformity of the normal

picture, where the object appears to form part and parcel of the instinct. We are thus warned to loosen the bond that exists in our thought between instinct and object. It seems probable that the sexual instinct is in the first instance independent of its object; nor is its origin likely to be due to its object's attractions.[78]

Davidson credits this passage with the power of devastation: "By claiming, in effect, that there is no natural object of the sexual instinct, that the sexual object and sexual instinct are merely soldered together, Freud dealt a conceptually devastating blow to the entire structure of nineteenth century theories of sexual psychopathology. . . . If the object is not internal to the instinct, then there can be no intrinsic clinico-pathological meaning to the fact that the instinct can become attached to an inverted object."[79]

Thus dissociated from an intrinsic object, Freud's *Sexualtrieb* (sexual instinct or drive) remains fundamentally ductile—open to a panoply of fusions, weldings, or "mere" solderings; no reliable law or principle advenes to govern the linkage between the subject's desire and that desire's object. "This gives us the hint," Freud says later in the same essay, "that perhaps the sexual instinct itself may be no simple thing, but put together from components which have come apart again in the perversions." As an unstable amalgam compounded out of diverse and even contradictory elements, "sexual instinct" for Freud signifies not just a plurivocal constituency but a dynamics of substitution and iterability. This indeed constitutes an epochal break with the logic of inversion. For once the "bond" between *Trieb* and *Objekt* has been thus severed, there can be no subsequent recourse to fantasies of a natural or instinctive sexuality, whether hetero, homo, or other-o. Without a definitive standard, how to measure, or even posit, a deviation? Given the theoretical schema Freud here advances, the perversions come virtually to epitomize "the normal picture," precisely because the sexual instinct is, *ab ovo*, "independent of its object." Perversion, then, *tout court*: the law of nature denatured.

It would thus seem that Freud emphatically submits the inversion metaphor to the vertiginous dispersions of metonymy. Does not Freud, like Sade before him, conceptualize desire as a gender-indifferent tropism liable to labile displacement, which in turn "opens the door," to recall Gallop's phrasing, "for a potentially unending series of paradigmatic equivalents"? And yet we know things are not so simple. The inversion metaphor, despite the "conceptually devastating blow" acknowledged above, nonetheless continued to operate with impressive immunity throughout Freud's subsequent writings on homosexuality. The machinery of inversion would whir on, as if chthonically. How, then, to account for the persistence of a "devastated" metaphor? A facile deconstruction might prefer to see the metaphor's vigorous afterlife as a kind of nonsignifying epistemic drag, the as-yet-undiscarded effluvia of a retrograde sexology. Davidson gestures toward a more interesting answer. While continuing to claim that Freud had delegitimated "the conceptual preconditions" for the employment of perversion and inversion, he also acknowledges that "Freud continued to use the idea of perversion, as if he failed to grasp the real import of his own work." "Freud in effect reintroduces, behind his own back, an identification that he has shown to be untenable."[80]

It is not possible here to launch a comprehensive critique of Freud's shifting account of homosexuality or of the ideas (narcissism, castration, Oedipal identification) that make his account intelligible and compelling. But it may be useful, in closing this chapter, to engage one of Freud's texts, the late essay "Female Sexuality" (1931), in which the inversion metaphor, "devastated" but still vigorous, continues to perform its work of normalization. Freud's topic in "Female Sexuality" is the problematic trajectory by which the developing female child assumes her adult femininity. By what "path," Freud asks, "does she reach the final normal female attitude, in which she takes her father as her object and so finds her way to the feminine form of the Oedipus complex?"[81] As Freud's language of heterosexual teleology implies, "final normal" femininity is not a given nature; it is, rather, a tortuous achievement governed, as we shall see, by a double displacement. Freud diagrams this developmental itinerary in his opening paragraph:

> During the phase of the normal Oedipus complex we find the child tenderly attached to the parent of the opposite sex, while its relation to the parent of its own sex is predominantly hostile. In the case of a boy there is no difficulty in explaining this. His first love-object was his mother. She remains so; and, with the strengthening of his erotic desires and his deeper insight into the relations between his father and mother, the former is bound to become his rival. With the small girl it is different. Her first object, too, was her mother. How does she find her way to her father? How, when, and why does she detach herself from her mother? We have long understood that the development of female sexuality is complicated by the fact that the girl has the task of giving up what was originally her leading genital zone—the clitoris—in favour of a new zone—

the vagina. But it now seems to us that there is a second change of the same sort which is no less characteristic and important for the development of the female: the exchange of her original object—her mother—for her father. The way in which the two tasks are connected with each other is not yet clear to us. (225)

The question, then, is this: given the female child's original homosexual identification with the mother, "how does she find her way to her father?" Freud answers this question by way of a vestigial bisexuality that functions, in Sarah Kofman's metaphor, as a double-edged sword: "it allows him both to break down the metaphysical opposition of 'pure' masculinity and femininity and to continue to keep masculinity in its traditionally privileged position."[82] Such ideological duplicity is especially clear, for instance, when Freud writes:

> First of all, there can be no doubt that the bisexuality, which is present, as we believe, in the innate disposition of human beings, comes to the fore much more clearly in women than in men. A man, after all, has only one leading sexual zone, one sexual organ, whereas a woman has two: the vagina—the female organ proper—and the clitoris, which is analogous to the male organ. We believe we are justified in assuming that for many years the vagina is virtually non-existent. . . . In women, therefore, the main genital occurrences of childhood must take place in relation to the clitoris. Their sexual life is regularly divided in two phases, of which the first has a masculine character, while only the second is specifically feminine. (227–28)

Freud's account of feminine development begins with an ideological bifurcation. In a single diacritical cut, he determines the female genitalia as the anatomical representative of gender difference itself: if the vagina is "proper" to the girl's femininity, the clitoris "with its virile character" definitionally is not (228). As miniaturized simulacrum, the clitoris has been subsumed under a phallic "analogy," one of whose chief historical operations is what Gayatri Spivak calls "the effacement of the clitoris"—that is, the denial of the clitoris as a "specifically feminine" property. With her body (and psyche) thus virilized *and* feminized, the little girl is disclosed to be both herself and her own "opposite," the little boy she must (suicidally) kill in order to assume the vaginal passivity that alone will establish what Freud calls her "definitive femininity" (232).

Once securely in place, this duplicitous gender structure enables the inversion metaphor to resume the work by which it keeps things straight.

In Freud's psychoanalytic itinerary, as in the simpler sexological articulations, a seemingly homosexual desire will disclose itself, willy-nilly, as inverted or displaced heterosexuality. For once it is given a priori that pre-Oedipal female sexuality is primarily clitoral (at this time, Freud defensively claims, "the vagina is virtually non-existent") and that the clitoris is possessed of (by) "a masculine character," then the possibility of originary lesbian desire is theoretically nullified. Under the sway of her puny simulacrum and its "characteristic phallic activity—masturbation of the clitoris" (232), the little girl desiring mother operates as a little boy doing same, the lesbian specificity of her desire thus returned, via inversion, to its familiar heterosexual base.

But Freud's question still remains unanswered: "how does she find her way to her father" and to "the feminine form of the Oedipus complex?" Theoretically at least, the answer is simpler than is sometimes admitted. Given the barely occluded heterosexual origin of her (only apparent) homosexual desire, all that is required to freeze female sexuality in its normalizing Oedipal frame is a diphasic "process of transition" in which the vagina, or "female organ proper," supplants the virilized clitoris as the female's "leading sexual zone." This fantasmatic genital transposition is axiomatically precipitated by "the influence of castration" (230); while still in the phallic phase, the female child is obliged to acknowledge "the fact of her castration, and with it, too, the superiority of the male and her own inferiority" (229). With this lacerating self-recognition in place, the "normally" developing female must then negotiate a double inversion. An inversion, first, in her subjectivity: a movement from her vestigial "masculine character" to "her final normal female attitude." This inversion in the subject entails a kind of psychosurgical complicity—in Spivak's term, "a symbolic clitoridectomy"[83]—by which the female completes the castration that "nature" has already only half performed. And to this inversion a second corresponds, an inversion in the gender of the object (from feminine/maternal to masculine/paternal): "at the end of her development, her father—a man—should have become her new love object" (228). The heterosexual presumption implicit in this inversion schema should be manifest; Freud himself puts it in the form of an axiom: "to the change in her own sex [i.e., from masculine to feminine] there must correspond a change in the sex of her object [i.e., vice versa]" (228).

In what is perhaps his oblique acknowledgment of the sheer violence of this "very circuitous" itinerary (230), Freud admits that it is subject to considerable deviation, in large part because the female "rebels" against "the fact" of her castration, which Freud (pseudo)sympathetically calls "this unwelcome state of affairs" (229). He specifies two perverse or abnormal "lines of development" in addition to the "normal" Oedipal "path" described above, each involving a presumptively "unnatural" protest against the finality of vaginal accommodation:

> The first leads to a general revulsion from sexuality. The little girl, frightened by the comparison with boys, grows dissatisfied with her clitoris, and gives up her phallic activity and with it her sexuality in general as well as a good part of her masculinity in other fields. The second line leads her to cling with defiant self-assertiveness to her threatened masculinity. To an incredibly late age she clings to the hope of getting a penis some time. That hope becomes her life's aim; and the phantasy of being a man in spite of everything often persists as a formative factor over long periods. This "masculinity complex" in women can also result in a manifest homosexual choice of object. (229–30)

Thus Freud's castration trope imposes upon the female three nonoptional options, each one teleologically determined: (1) the terminal vaginality of "normal" oedipal compliance, replete with the castration/clitoridectomy that alone situates the female in a "proper" relation to the phallus; (2) the absolute cessation of all sexuality consequent upon her "general revulsion" when confronted with "the fact" of her phallic effacement; and (3) a specifically butch "defiance" of feminine termination (i.e., her "masculinity complex") , as evidenced by, among other things, "a manifest homosexual choice of object."

This last "option" clearly discloses the vigorous psychoanalytic afterlife, the continuing hegemonic press, of the (presumably superseded) inversion metaphor, as a vigilant feminism has not failed to notice. Kofman: "We are to understand that constitutionally she is more masculine than feminine, and that therefore she cannot help persisting in this masculinity. She is by nature, as it were, a boy manqué who ends up taking herself to be a boy for real."[84] And Irigaray, more tersely: "As soon as she has any relationship with another woman, she is homosexual, and therefore masculine. . . . Not a word has been said here about *feminine* homosexuality."[85] Indeed, not a word *could* have been said. Not, that is, without a thorough dismantling of the sexist and heterosexist gender ideology that underwrites the inversion model, whose psychoanalytic deployment, however displaced or "circuitous," nonetheless betrays a palpable genealogical relation to the more reductive formulations of the sexologists.

What had been for Ulrichs and Krafft-Ebing a convenient fiction of origination (*anima muliebris virili corpore inclusa*, in the case of the male homosexual) becomes, in the subtler displacements of Freudian narrative, a teleological fiction whose terminus is governed by a now-familiar gender inversion. In the case of the lesbian, this is the story of an Oedipalization whose "failure" or incompletion locks the female in the perverse grip of an unexcised "masculinity" that dutifully inverts her desire even as it reasserts the primacy of the phallus at exactly the site where the penis has no place.

Predictably, the case with the male is vice versa. And there are no real surprises: Freud anatomizes male homosexual desire according to a developmental schema in which the "future invert" fails to arrive at *his* appointed terminus—that is, at the "final normal" masculine subjectivity for which heterosexual object choice alone will provide sufficiently convincing evidence. As with the lesbian in "Female Sexuality," this monitory narrative signals an unresolved Oedipal struggle; but because it is enacted from the other side of the gender divide, this story does not center upon unexcised masculinity but rather upon introjected femininity. Here is Freud writing in 1910 on heterosexual sons and homosexual lovers:

> It is true that psycho-analysis has not yet produced a complete explanation of the origin of inversion; nevertheless, it has discovered the psychical mechanism of its development, and has made essential contributions to the statement of the problems involved. In all the cases we have examined we have established the fact that the future inverts, in the earliest years of their childhood, pass through a phase of very intense but short-lived fixation to a woman (usually their mother), and that, after leaving this behind, they identify themselves with a woman and take themselves as their sexual object. That is to say, they proceed from a narcissistic basis, and look for a young man who resembles themselves and whom they may love as their mother loved them. Moreover, we have frequently found that alleged inverts have been by no means insusceptible to the charms of women, but have continually transposed the excitation aroused by women onto a male object. They have thus repeated all through their lives the mechanism by which their inversion arose. The compulsive longing for men has turned out to be determined by their ceaseless flight from women.[86]

Despite the formality of his hesitations ("psycho-analysis has not yet produced a complete explanation," etc.), Freud in this passage seems especially complacent about reconstituting homosexual desire as heterosexual mnemonic. In his definitive redaction of the inversion paradigm, Freud once again narrativizes—that is, temporalizes—the atemporal formulations of a precedent sexology. What had once been a static metaphor (*anima muliebris virili corpore inclusa*) becomes in Freud's writing a more complex psychodynamic itinerary, the unfolding of a "psychical mechanism" whose normalizing rhythms are readily scanned: originally, the male child is deeply fixated upon the interdicted mother; subsequently, he introjects the mother in a futile attempt to resolve his Oedipal dilemma; consequently, he inclines thereafter toward a homosexual practice that nonetheless continues to bespeak its Oedipal origins. So supervenient is the heterosexual presumption here that it operates equally in cases false and true: "alleged inverts," Freud tells us, "have continually transposed the excitations aroused by women onto a male object," thereby repeating "all through their lives the mechanism by which their inversion arose"; authentic inverts, meanwhile, "identify themselves with a woman and take themselves as their sexual object," ever after caught in a narcissistic search "for a young man . . . whom they may love as their mother loved them." In either case, in any case, in every case, Oedipal heterosexuality underwrites the truth of sex down to its deepest substrate: so much so that Freud's apotropaic myth of origins and termini will always disclose male homosexual desire as little more than an Oedipal chimera, a mere simulacrum whose gender dynamics continually relay and replay the son's heterosexual desire for the mother. Ultimately, then, Freud's redaction of the inversion metaphor enables him to proffer a definitive unmasking: peel away the veneer of male homosexual desire and you will disclose the paradigmatic Greek subject: just another motherfucker.

2

"Descend, and Touch, and Enter"

Tennyson's Strange Manner of Address

It is obvious that I am then in the process of fetishizing
a corpse.

—Roland Barthes, *A Lover's Discourse*

In the final chapter of *Sexual Inversion,* Havelock Ellis turns with
measured circumspection to the difficult problem of the correction and
consolation of the sexual invert. In the especially vexed case of the "congenital invert"—in the case, that is, of a person who is the "victim of abnormal [homosexual] impulses" that spring incorrigibly from "the central
core of organic personality"—consolation through sublimation provides
the only available palliation; and this because the invert's "inborn constitutional abnormality" remains, by definition, nonductile and fundamentally resistant to "psychotherapeutical [and] surgical treatment."[1] Still, the
impossibility of effective medical remediation did not legitimate an active
homosexual genitality. Instead, and for reasons less medical than political, Ellis prescribed the difficult consolation of a more than Penelopean
patience: "it is the ideal of chastity, rather than normal sexuality, which
the congenital invert should hold before his eyes."[2] Yet if the rigors of so
sustained a meditation upon "the ideal of chastity" were likely to produce
intense ocular strain, then perhaps this difficulty could be mitigated by
the implementation of a practical program of displacement and surrogate
satisfaction: a regimen of sublimation, a course of psychosexual exercises,
or, as Ellis cheerfully calls it, a "method of self-restraint and self-culture,
without self-repression."[3] A civilization, it would seem, without the burden of *much* discontent.

What does Ellis offer as his primary example of this "method of self-
treatment?" By what "psychic methods" may the invert "refine and spiritualize the inverted impulse"? How else than by a course of corrective

44

reading? And indeed Ellis proposes a list of books to read and imitate, a prophylactic mimesis. Such remedial homosexual reading, at once consolatory and disciplinary, would serve a double or ambivalent function: the verbal substitution would express the very desire it would also work to contain; the text would be at once the home of desire and the site of its exile. (*The Memoirs of John Addington Symonds,* as we have seen, narrates a personal history of this agonistic Victorian belief that "literary and imaginative palliatives" would double as both "the vehicle and the safety valve for [the] tormenting preoccupations" that beset the victims of "this inexorable and incurable disease.")[4] First among the exemplary texts listed in Ellis's curriculum of literary palliation are, predictably enough, the dialogues of Plato, which "have frequently been found a source of great help and consolation by inverts." The reading of Plato, especially the *Phaedrus* and the *Symposium,* often had for nineteenth-century gay males the force of a revelation. Symond's case history in *Sexual Inversion,* transcribed by Ellis into the third person, is representative: "It was in his 18th year that an event which A [Symonds] regards as decisive in his development occurred. He read the *Phaedrus* and *Symposium* of Plato. A new world opened, and he felt that his own nature had been revealed."[5] This topos of self-recognition via Platonic texts is of course a staple in the cultural construction of nineteenth-century male homosexual subjectivity. Second in order of emphasis in Ellis's itinerary of inverted reading is, again predictably, Whitman's *Leaves of Grass,* with "its wholesome and robust ideal" of "manly love," although Whitman's exuberant sensuality and aboriginal stance rendered his poetry "of more doubtful value for general use." Again, Symonds on Whitman has representative value: *Leaves of Grass* "became for me a kind of Bible. Inspired by 'Calamus' I adopted another method of palliative treatment, and tried to invigorate the emotion I could not shake off by absorbing Whitman's conception of comradeship. . . . The immediate result of this study of Walt Whitman was the determination to write the history of paiderastia in Greece [Symonds's *A Problem in Greek Ethics*] and to attempt a theoretical demonstration of the chivalrous enthusiasm which seemed to me implicit in comradeship."[6] Here, in the transposition of desire into sexual discourse and of sexual discourse into *more* sexual discourse, we may see a paradigmatic example of Ellis's program of disciplinary reading and writing, itself a striking confirmation of Foucault's assertion that the nineteenth century worked assiduously to "put sex into discourse."

Yet if Ellis felt the rhetorical need to demur at Whitman's anatomical insistence, his barely veiled genital reference, he also had the advantage of an absolutely canonical counterexample, a Victorian text whose passionate discursivity and sexual obliquity everywhere marked its constitutive submission to the agonistic Victorian imperative "to refine and spiritualize" so problematic a desire. He turned with confidence to *In Memoriam*:

> Various modern poets of high ability have given expression to emotions of exalted or passionate friendship towards individuals of the same sex, whether or not such friendship can properly be termed homosexual. It is scarcely necessary to refer to *In Memoriam*, in which Tennyson enshrined his affection for his early friend, Arthur Hallam, and developed a picture of the universe on the basis of that affection.[7]

Ellis's sentences here pivot on an ambivalence we may recognize as our own: it may be "scarcely necessary" to adduce *In Memoriam* in this homosexual context, so famous is it as a site of exalted friendship and erotic displacement, yet Ellis equivocates, as indeed he must, as to "whether or not such friendship can properly be termed homosexual." Ellis's verbal equipoise here—his dichotomous need to affirm the homosociality of Tennyson's poem while refusing to specify the homosexuality of Tennysonian desire—responds faithfully both to Ellis's own delicate discursive situation as a writer of suspect texts and to a certain strategic equivocation within *In Memoriam* itself, one accurately identified by Edward Carpenter when he described *In Memoriam* as being "reserved" and "dignified" "in [its] sustained meditation and tender sentiment" but as also "half revealing here and there a more passionate feeling."[8] Exactly this equivocation defines the critical and taxonomic problem of whether *In Memoriam* "can properly be termed homosexual." The issue here is not merely one of choosing specific terminologies, words like homosexual or heterosexual, but also of submitting (or refusing to submit) to the historically particular acts of conceptualization that make a taxonomic category like homosexuality intelligible at all. To make any definition is first to establish, and then to be governed by, a set of constitutive limits or boundaries. Obviously enough, this process of defining entails the inscription within specific vocabularies and discourses of the authorizing culture's signature, its particular impress of value and belief. Equally obviously, the category of homosexuality, with its inescapable residuary imputations of disease, dysfunction, and disorder, is manifestly incompetent to represent the complex, evasive, and beautiful manipulations that Tennyson's desire for Hallam receives in *In Memoriam*.

This is not to deny but rather to assume and affirm that *In Memoriam* revolves around Hallam as around "the centre of a world's desire."[9] Or, rather more accurately, around Hallam's absconded presence, for he is, as Carol T. Christ writes, "the absent center around which the poem moves."[10] But if Hallam is Tennyson's "central warmth diffusing bliss," the elegy negotiates its problematic desire less by a centering of its warmth than by the dispersion of its bliss, less by acts of specific definition than by strategies of deferral, truncation, and displacement, strategies that everywhere work to "refine and spiritualize" what otherwise would be "the wish too strong for words to name" (93). But *In Memoriam* is more than a machine for the sublimation, management, or transformation of male homosexual desire; it is, rather, the site of a continuing problematization: the problem not merely of desire between men, but also of the desire (very urgent in the elegy) to speak it.

A certain anxiety attends the reading of *In Memoriam* and always has. The first reviews were, of course, largely laudatory, but a palpable dis-ease haunts particular early responses. An anonymous review in *The Times* (28 November 1851), now usually attributed to Manley Hopkins, father of Gerard Manley Hopkins, specifically complained of the elegy's erotic metaphorics, its "strange manner of address to a man, even though he be dead."[11] A "defect," this reviewer noted, "which has painfully come out as often as we take up the volume, is the tone of—may we say so!—amatory tenderness." "Very sweet and plaintive these verses are," Hopkins the elder continued, "but who would not give them a feminine application? Shakespeare may be considered the founder of this style in English." Here the reviewer's palpable gender anxiety, his fear of the unhinged gender within Tennyson's poetic voice, reflects the bewildering ease with which Tennyson employs heterosexual desire and marriage as a trope to represent his passion for lost Hallam, a tropological indiscretion, the reviewer assumes, derived from "floating remembrances of Shakespeare's sonnets," which "present the startling peculiarity of transferring every epithet of womanly endearment to a masculine friend—his master-mistress, as he calls him by a compound epithet, harsh, as it is disagreeable." This homoerotic linkage of *In Memoriam* to Shakespeare's sonnets is hardly anomalous. In another review published anonymously, Charles Kingsley found in *In Memoriam* a descendant of "the old tales of David and Jonathan, Damon and Pythias, Socrates and Alcibiades, Shakespeare and his nameless friend, of 'love passing the love of woman'," although recently Christopher Ricks has charged Kingsley with "recklessness" and has balked at the allusion to 2 Samuel, calling it "that perilous phrase."[12] By the 1890s, when Tennyson's son Hallam wrote his biography-cum-hagiography *Alfred Lord Tennyson: A Memoir* (1897), the perils of what Ricks defensively calls the "homosexual misconstruction" incited Hallam to a prudential pruning of any material that might conduce to equivocal interpretation. For example, as Ricks's biography of Tennyson informs us, when Hallam quoted Benjamin Jowett regarding "the great sorrow of [Tennyson's] mind," he carefully elided anything suggesting what Jowett called, with discreet indirection, "a sort of sympathy with Hellenism." Jowett's comment on Tennyson's grief, that "it would not have been manly or natural to have lived in it always," succumbed to Hallam's editorial vigilance and was cut from the *Memoir*.[13]

Very much the same critical propensity to keep Tennyson "manly and natural" has governed more recent criticism of *In Memoriam,* although modern evasions of the poem's disturbing sexuality have generally demonstrated more cunning than Hallam Tennyson's. Perhaps the simplest of contemporary critical circumventions of *In Memoriam*'s homoerotic discourse are those, like Jerome Buckley's *Tennyson: The Growth of a Poet* (1960), that don't find sexuality pertinent at all to the elegy's recuperative desiring; we have here the simple elision of the homosexual subject. A more intriguing strategy for negotiating the problematics of same-gender desire can be found in Harold Bloom's early essay "Tennyson, Hallam, and Romantic Tradition" (1966), in which Bloom declares, with a false assurance, that it "need disturb no one any longer" that "Tennyson's Muse was (and always remained) Hallam." Bloom's poetic/sexual centering of Hallam is of course substantially correct, but his cosmopolitan poise would be more convincing did he not directly exculpate himself from further musing on homoerotic muses by saying, first, that "the sexual longings of a poet *qua* poet appear to have little relation to mere experience anyway" and second, that "the analytical sophistication in aesthetic realms that would allow a responsible sexual history of English poetry is not available to us."[14] There is therefore very little to say.

We may see in Bloom's passing acknowledgment of the homosexual subject an ambivalence characteristic of our tradition's reading of this poem. First, he specifies the inescapable homoerotics of *In Memoriam*'s elegiac desire, then precludes a sustained and detailed analysis of that desire by foreclosing critical access either to "mere experience" (which in the case of Tennyson and Hallam is unrevealing anyway) or to the "analytical sophistication" that would render such criticism "responsible." (Since 1966, of course, Bloom has been writing a brilliant and responsible "sexual history of English poetry": a history, not incidentally, in which a belated poet's creative potency—his power of speech as self-production or self-fathering—is tested not in a heterosexual embrace with a female muse but rather in a distinctly Oedipal tussle between men, during which the muscular ephebe may wrest from his father/precursor the power of seminal speech. It is precisely this gladiatorial wrestling—during which the ephebe, now giving what he had been forced to take, reverses the temporal hydraulics of influence—that enables his subsequently productive intercourse with the text-to-be, whose essentially "feminine" receptivity has been, until that moment, effectively forfended by the father's presence, by the Oedipal force of his prior inscriptions. In Bloom's agonistic reading, a text functions as an already inscribed mediatrix, an intervening distance or difference, between two competing familial male potencies whose displaced intercourse is poetry itself. The applicability of all this to *In Memoriam* is, to say the least, enticing, but as yet we have had from Bloom no revised misprision of Tennyson's elegy.)

But Bloom's blithe assurance in 1966 that Hallam's erotic centrality in *In Memoriam* "need disturb no one any longer" seems not to have had its pacifying effects, seems indeed to have gone unheeded, for in 1972 Christopher Ricks in his astute critical biography *Tennyson* paused for some ten pages to worry over precisely this issue. "But do we too," Ricks asks, "need to speak bluntly? Is Tennyson's love for Hallam a homosexual one?"[15] Ricks's answer—I doubt that I am betraying any suspense here—is no, although a number of equivocations beset this denial. His discussion of this anxiogenic question opens with a gesture that recalls Bloom's deferral of adequate discussion to that millennial day when analytic sophistication in aesthetic realms will enable intelligent discourse, but whereas Bloom's displacement is temporal, Ricks's is spatial. Disclaiming the authority of literary criticism altogether, Ricks invokes another professional discipline, and a predictable one: "the crucial acts of definition will have to be left to the psychologists and psychiatrists, though it should be said that literary historians usually vitiate their arguments by conveniently jumbling the old severely differentiating view with the newer 'something of it in everybody' one." Such recourse to psychiatry and psychology does double duty: in submitting poetry to pathology, the literary critic escapes ultimate responsibility for what must remain a literary-critical decision about the representational function of desire in the text, while simultaneously and inescapably situating that decision within an ideological economy of disease, dysfunction, and presumptively desirable remediation. Implicit in this gesture is the normalizing hope that Tennyson was not "bluntly" "homosexual" or, in Ricks's odd locution, "abnormally abnormal." More importantly still, the deferral of literary decision to medical authority quite simply misses the point. The question at issue is neither the history of Tennyson's genitalia (which Tennyson's most recent biographer suggests would yield a rather brief and tedious narrative) nor the potentially psychopathic trajectories of an obviously tortured psyche. Rather, as we shall see, the issue that matters here is the function of represented sexual desire within the verbal economy we call *In Memoriam* and within the larger tradition of representation from which the poem arises, the tradition to which it continues to direct its strange manner of address.

Ricks's extended "defense" (so to speak) "of Tennyson" against imputations of homosexuality remains sympathetic to certain Tennysonian notions of an orderly and conventional androgyny, an androgyny that perhaps mitigates but never subverts the disciplinary bifurcation of gender characteristics, as when Tennyson admonishes that "men should be androgynous and women gynandrous, but men should not be gynandrous nor women androgynous."[16] A transparent ambivalence informs Tennyson's sentence: a desire to escape the containments of gender engages a desire to contain the escape. Tennyson's precise marshalling of prefixes and suffixes, of fronts and backs, of (to borrow one of Ricks's metaphors) "heads" and "tails," bespeaks an anxiety of gender inversion strong enough to require careful regulation at the level of the signifier. (If signifiers can be compelled into remaining "jubilantly straight" [Ricks again], perhaps signifieds will follow suit.) The disciplinary punctilio of gender enacted by Tennyson's sentence suggests one reason for the obliquity of sexual representation in *In Memoriam,* and it certainly anticipates the disease circulating throughout Ricks's defense of Tennyson's (hetero)-sexuality. As a parting instance of this representative anxiety consider Ricks's response to the inclusion of selected stanzas of *In Memoriam* in an anthology of homosexual writing published by Brian Reade in 1970:

> Was Tennyson, so to speak, abnormally abnormal? A new anthology entitled *Sexual Heretics: Male Homosexuality in English Literature from 1850 to 1900* does not hesitate to quote extensively from ten sections of *In*

Memoriam; its editor, anxious to enlist or if necessary pressgang Tennyson, quaintly says "the fact that Tennyson evolved an emphatically
heterosexual image in later life does nothing to disqualify him as homosexual when he wrote *In Memoriam.*"

To read Ricks reading Reade is to disclose a confusion that in turn generates an anxiety: Reade's confusion is to fail to transcend the cultural
agon of a fixed, bipolar opposition between the homo and the hetero (despite the familiar compromise trope of temporal oscillation), while
Ricks's anxiety registers itself as a barely suppressed metaphor of homosexual rape by an editor "anxious to enlist or if necessary pressgang Tennyson" into a very dubious literary brotherhood. The rigors of such an
enlistment are presumably unbearable, but for a poet laureate to be
ganged upon and then pressed—perhaps im-pressed as well as em-
pressed—is to suffer at editorial hands the additional indignity of a
sodomitical intrusion. Better, obviously, to house *In Memoriam* in canonical—that is to say, heterosexual—anthologies.

   The foregoing reading of *In Memoriam* criticism, however fragmen-
tary, suggests the conceptual and imagistic burden suffered by our culture's discourse on same-sex eroticism. *In Memoriam* remains a pivotal
case in this regard precisely because the problematics of the poem's erotic
representations are indistinguishable from readerly problems of interpretation and feeling. To mouth the Tennysonian "I," as the reader of this
poem must repeatedly and obsessively do, is to bespeak (for the duration
of the reading at least) an anxiogenic identification with the poet's fierce
reparational longing, which regularly presses to a transgressive homosexual verge. But *In Memoriam* approaches this verge only when compelled by an incommensurate grief; homosexual desire, in other words, is
here constituted only elegiacally, once its object has been surpassed. Why,
we must now ask, does *In Memoriam* disclose homosexual desire as indissociable from death? As itself a mode of mourning? Why this constitutive linking of desire and death?

In *In Memoriam* death discovers desire, the latter arriving in and as the
wake of the former. The linkage between desire and death is not a casual
metaphorical articulation; it is a causal narrative one. For in the highly
personal erotic myth that *In Memoriam* so extensively develops, the

death of Hallam, when "God's finger touch'd him, and he slept" (85), initiates in the poet both a recuperational homosexual desire—a desire to restore to its preschismatic unity the "divided hal[ves] of such / A friendship as had master'd Time"—and, what is worse, a desperate need to speak this potentially philosophic "desire and pursuit of the whole" under the aegis of a transgressive erotics.[17] "Descend, and touch, and enter," Tennyson dangerously pleads, and "hear / The wish too strong for words to name" (93). The extremity of such expression, its desperate mode of erotic address, proceeds from the poet's belated recognition that no other human love will ever be "as pure and whole / As when he loved me here in Time" (43); correlative to this recognition of loss is the fear that "love for him [may] have drain'd / My capabilities of love" (85). Thus desire's duration, the temporal and spatial extensions of this very distended text's poetic wooing (compare 85, "I woo your love"), commences not with Arthur's desirable presence—for when Arthur is present desire and language are supernumerary—but rather with its opposite, with destitution: the poet recognizes that his "dear friend" has become in death's difference "my lost Arthur's loved remains" (129,9). In a figure whose murderous implications will concern us repeatedly in the present study, the language of active homosexual desiring discovers its origin in a death or terminus that disrupts an ontologically prior wholeness whose unitary gender remains emphatically, inescapably, male. In what we may now correctly call the "hom(m)osexual" economy of In Memoriam, death and not gender is the differential out of which longing is so painfully born; it is death that breaches the perfect male couple and opens it to the circulations of desire.[18]

This structure of desire entrains certain disciplinary relations that are coextensive with, indistinguishable from, the desire itself. Because it established homosexual desire as always already elegiac, as originally grounded in the destitution of its object, In Memoriam both incites and contains homosexual desire in a single cunning articulation. The elegiac mode constrains the desire it also enables: the sundering of death instigates an insistent reparational longing, yet it claustrates the object of this desire on the far side of a divide that interdicts touch even as it incites the desire for touching. An infinite desire is infinitely deferred, subject always to postponement, displacement, diffusion. Death works to inscribe a prophylactic distance, as Tennyson himself suggested in a related context. Commenting on the initial line of lyric 122 ("Oh, wast thou with me, dearest, then"), the poet said: "If anybody thinks I ever called him 'dear-

est' in his life they are much mistaken, for I never even called him 'dear.'"
Ricks finds this statement "naïve perhaps, but not tonally suggestive of
homosexuality."[19] Better to say that such "naïveté" marks Tennyson's perfectly Victorian strategy of linguistic displacement, precisely because it
embeds homosexual desire within an idealizing elegiac register. The elegy
insists that desire and death conjugate out of tropological necessity: "Let
Love clasp Grief lest both be drown'd" (1). What is "saved" in this embrace is a poetic logic that instantiates homosexual desire as already its
own distantiation. "My prime passion [is] in the grave," and "so hold I
commerce with the dead" (85).

Of course, as Victorian and modern readers have been quick to notice,
the formal solution to this problem is Christ. In a way that is so straight-
forward as to be transparent, Tennyson would master his unconventional
desire for Hallam by figuring it as a subspecies of a very conventional desire for "the Strong Son of God" (prologue). A perfectly conventional
trope of typological interpretation enables Tennyson to represent Hallam
as a "noble type / Appearing ere the times were ripe" (epilogue)—as, that
is, a medial character whose death repeats the ontologically prior sacrifice
of the other "He that died" (84), and whose earthly presence had pointed
to the superior consummation of a second coming. Yet simply to identify
Hallam and Christ as interpenetrated figures of erotic and religious devotion is to repeat what the criticism has already noticed. "*In Memoriam,*"
Gerhard Joseph writes, "describes the transformation of Hallam into an
analogue of Christ; to render this Hallam-Christ accessible Tennyson
eroticizes him, giving him female attributes."[20] Joseph's sentence is of
course summarily correct—correct, that is, as summary—but the pages
to follow will argue that a more capacious understanding of Tennyson's
fluent erotics demands that we pause at length to consider just how *In
Memoriam* articulates its analogy between Hallam and Christ, and how
that analogy operates to relieve the speaker's desperate erotic distress—a
distress, as I have said, indistinguishable from his grief. To rush to the
Christological or logocentric solution—to chant compliantly with Tennyson "Love is and was my lord and king" (126)—risks another terminological reduction, one that, in its leap to the available comforts of a conventional faith, fails to register the anxious and fluctuant interfusion of
sexual desire and religious faith in a poem justly more famous for the quality of its oscillations than for the force of its closural affirmation. *In
Memoriam,* Eliot was right to say, "is not religious because of the quality
of its faith, but because of the quality of its doubt."[21] If, making explicit

what Eliot in his essay leaves implicit, we recognize doubt as a figure of desire, as a mode of suspension poised between the loss of Hallam and the promise of his restoration in a Christological embrace, we will have begun to trace the homoerotic basis of the elegy's extensive yearning.

In its most orthodox articulation, Tennyson's typological strategy represents Hallam as a beautiful but fallen simulacrum of the ontologically prior archetype of Christ himself. The disciplinary and transferential trajectory of such a figural strategy is clear: a desire that would seem to begin in Hallam is discovered to begin and end in Christ, whose forgiving body safely absorbs, relays, and completes a fierce homoerotic cathexis. The elegy's sustained appeal to the "conclusive bliss" (85) of its Christological closure identifies apocalyptic death as the site of a deferred but certain erotic restoration. In the closural ecstasis of the "one far-off divine event / To which the whole creation moves," Christ will "take" the lovers' riven halves and restore them to a "single soul" (84). *In Memoriam* thus solves the problem of desire's divisiveness by fantasizing a dissolving incorporation:

> Dear friend, far off, my lost desire
>   So far, so near in woe and weal;
>   O loved the most, when most I feel
> There is a lower and a higher;
>
> Known and unknown; human, divine;
>   Sweet human hand and lips and eye;
>   Dear heavenly friend that canst not die,
> Mine, mine, for ever, ever mine. (129)

The intermediate qualities identified in these quatrains refer equally or indistinguishably to Hallam and to Christ; the blended might of erotic and religious devotion both facilitates and idealizes the poet's indefatigable longing for "that dear friend of mine who lives in God" (epilogue). In this transfiguration the conventional topoi of a reparational theology subsume and discipline the transgressive force of Tennyson's elegiac desire.

Faithful to its consolatory structure, *In Memoriam* begins and ends with an orthodox stress upon this Christological figuration; begins and ends, that is, with promises of transcendence for the unappeasable homosexual longing that drives the poem's extended middle. For as *In Memoriam* opens, the problematics of elegiac desire—of desire for the dead and desire for death as recuperated sameness—have already found their solution and resolution in Christ; or so at least the pietistic voice of the prologue suggests:

> Strong Son of God, immortal Love,
>   Whom we, that have not seen thy face,
>   By faith, and faith alone, embrace,
> Believing where we cannot prove;
>
> Thine are those orbs of light and shade;
>   Thou madest Life in man and brute;
>   Thou madest Death; and lo, thy foot
> Is on the skull which thou hast made.
>
> Thou wilt not leave us in the dust:
>   Thou madest man, he knows not why,
>   He thinks he was not made to die;
> And thou hast made him: thou art just.

That the prologue, which was written last and postdates the composition of the earliest lyrics by some seventeen years, should offer the image of a Christocentric "embrace" as the elegy's apparently originary gesture very well figures the evasive dislocations, both temporal and spatial, required to manage the anxieties generated by Tennyson's "lost desire."[22] Indeed, part of the disciplinary work of the prologue specifically, as of the Christological figuration generally, is thus belatedly to install a fantasized terminus (the promise of Christ's restorative embrace) in the place of the origin (the rift opened by Hallam's death) in order thereby to mask the apostacy intrinsic to a personal love that is, to borrow Bloom's apt phrase, "about as restrained and societal as Heathcliff's passion."[23]

Within the figural economy of *In Memoriam,* the Christocentric impulse works its consolatory changes largely through the extended trope by which Christ's hand comes to substitute for Hallam's own; the oft-repeated images of "clasp," "touch," and "embrace" are all local variations on this trope. Indeed, as the criticism has already noticed, *In Memoriam* is almost obsessive in its concern for the human hand and in its desire for a restored male touch. Noting correctly that "Tennyson's love for Hallam is the overriding subject of *In Memoriam,*" John D. Rosenberg continues: "Indeed, Tennyson's unending speculation on immortality is rooted in his inexhaustible impulse to visualize and to *touch* Hallam. Hence the ubiquitous image of the hand."[24] Ubiquitous indeed, Hallam's "sweet human hand" (129) is at once this text's primary synecdoche for presence ("hands so often clasp'd in mine"; 10); for absence ("A hand that can be clasp'd no more"; 7); and for the medial condition between these two (that crepuscular state of "dreamy touch" during which the poet is left "waiting for a hand"; 44, 7). Nor is it surprising that "one of the great love poems in English," as Rosenberg correctly calls it, should identify the hand as a site of passional interchange, since the elegy's explicit recommendation that "Love clasp Grief lest both be drown'd" specifically cathects the hand with an erotic charge that oscillates obscurely between the homosocial and the homosexual. At times the poet's desire that Hallam "should strike a sudden hand in mine" (14) takes on a startling sexual configuration:

> Tears of a widower, when he sees
>   A late-lost form that sleep reveals,
>   And moves his doubtful arms, and feels
> Her place is empty, fall like these;
>
> Which weep a loss for ever new
>   A void where heart on heart reposed;
>   And, where warm hands have prest and closed,
> Silence, till I be silent too. (13)

Tennyson's specification of the squeeze of the hand as a multivalent site of male homosocial communion is anything but anomalous in Victorian literature, although the extraordinary repetitiousness in his use of this figure may well be so. The utility of the hand as at once an overdetermined and unstable signifier is, I take it, manifest and obvious: on the one hand, the "manly" handshake and the "fraternal" embrace are respectable, disciplined, and sexually innocent gestures of Victorian male homosociality (imagine, for instance, counting the handshakes in Dickens); on the other hand, such gestures, given a slightly altered social context, readily take on the heat and the pressure of the sexual. A mobile figure, the hand ranges dexterously across the entire male homosocial spectrum. Consider what happens when fingers wander:

> I stripped him naked, and fed sight, touch and mouth on these things.
> Will my lips ever forget their place upon his breast, or of the tender satin
> of his flank, or on the snowy whiteness of his belly? Will they lose the
> nectar of his mouth—those opened lips like flower petals, expanding
> neath their touch and fluttering? Will my arms forget the strain of his
> small fragile waist, my thighs the pressure of his yielding thighs, my ears
> the murmur of his drowsy voice, my brain the scent of his sweet flesh

and breathing mouth? Shall I ever cease to hear the metallic throb of his mysterious heart—calm and true—ringing little bells beneath my ear?

I do not know whether, after all, the mere touch of his fingers as they met and clasped and put aside my hand, was not of all the best. For there is a soul in the fingers. They speak. The body is but silent, a dumb eloquent animated work of art made by the divine artificer.[25]

The ambivalent gesture that dominates this passage from *The Memoirs of John Addington Symonds* very well figures the cloven subjectivity of sexual inversion while it also tellingly exercises the ambivalence at hand here. "For [if] there is a soul in the fingers" and if "they speak," then what they bespeak is a rivenness so integral to soul that soul must celebrate its own alienation. The touch that repels touch touches fulfillment; to have one's hand "put aside" is indeed "all the best." As a self-nominated "invert" who understood himself to be "a compound of antagonistic impulses" and whose sexual praxis certainly included mutual masturbation, Symonds repeatedly inclined toward the hand as a figure, and a mode, of self-expression:

I knew that my right hand was useless—firmly clenched in the grip of an unconquerable love, the love of comrades. But they [i.e., those who criticized "the languor of my temperament"] stung me into using my left hand for work, in order to contradict their prognostications [of failure].[26]

When one hand is busy at pleasure, the other may be stung by criticism into the compensation of good work. Clearly enough, the heterosexualizing semiotics of Victorian masculinity inscribe a developmental trajectory by which the boy's hand of pleasure must pass into the mature hand of work (a trajectory, obviously, that Symonds never quite mastered). What is understood to happen between boys in the dormitories of Harrow ("onanism, mutual masturbation, the sport of naked boys in bed together")[27] must not happen, as Wilde was to discover, between men in the private dining rooms of, say, the Savoy Hotel. Hence the maturing boy's growing hand must be lifted from the specific genitality of an institutionalized homosexual pedagogy and carefully steered forth into the businesslike and sterilizing grip of a radically homophobic male homosociality. Handsome is as handsome does; fingers must not wander.[28]

If, as I have suggested, these passages from Symonds's *Memoirs* present genitally specific analogues to *In Memoriam*'s fetishizing of the hand, then it is also clear that large differences of tact and tactility distinguish the two discourses. Part of *In Memoriam*'s rhetorical finesse lies in its articulation of a desire whose intensities are sexual but whose modalities have already superseded the genital placement that Symonds's autobiography works to justify and explain. Indeed, the elegy's typological figuration works against the "deviations" that Symonds so breathlessly charts, especially so since *In Memoriam* curbs the longing of its hands by transfiguring Hallam's hands into Christ's own "shining hand." By way of a "metamorphosis of Hallam's hands into those of divinity,"[29] *In Memoriam* devises a trajectory by which a desire to touch Hallam is satisfied in Christ, as when late in the poem "out of darkness came the hands / That reach thro' nature moulding men" (124). And in turn these consoling hands point to the closural embrace in which Christ's outstretched apocalyptic hand will redeem—or, more literally, re-member (restore the hand to)—the interrupted secular embrace between the poet and Hallam. In that good moment the poet and his beloved will

> Arrive at last the blessed goal,
> And He that died in Holy Land
> Would reach us out the shining hand,
> And take us as a single soul. (84)

The singular virtue of Christ's apocalyptic hand is that its finishing touch finishes everything, and not the least of what it finishes—completes and erases—is the constitutive ambivalence about intermasculine union that the metonymy of hands so ambidextrously conveys. In the rapture that comes at his second coming, the handy interchangeability of Hallam and Christ insures a taking so complete that it leaves nothing—no one—to be desired.[30]

But now we must clarify what Tennyson's orthodox typology works to obscure: this Christocentric embrace—which should at once be originary, medial, and terminal—is in fact secondary and irreducibly belated; only by a strategic misspeaking may such fulfillment be termed Christocentric at all. For the consoling pieties of a conventional typological reading cannot diminish the elegy's strong impression that Christ arrives as a belated lover who functions as the devotional succedaneum of which Hallam is the great original. Christ's otherwise redundant presence is fathered by Hallam's absence, since it is the loss of Hallam's hand and Hallam's embrace that alone motivates the re/pair/ational touch of Christ, whose hand must "shine" in order to obscure its transparent second-handedness. T. S. Eliot, who understood the anamorphic optics of Christological displacement well enough not to be blinded by the light, caught Tennyson at his sleight of hand. In what remains the best essay ever written on *In Memoriam,* Eliot handles this subject with characteristic and knowing finesse:

> [Tennyson] was desperately anxious to hold to the faith of the believer, without being very clear about what he wanted to believe: he was capable of illumination which he was incapable of understanding. "The Strong Son of God, immortal Love," with an invocation of whom the poem opens, has only a hazy connection with the Logos, or Incarnate God. Tennyson is distressed by the idea of a mechanical universe; he is naturally, in lamenting his friend, teased by the hope of immortality and reunion beyond death. Yet the renewal craved for seems at best but a continuance, or a substitute for the joys of friendship upon earth. His desire for immortality never is quite the desire for eternal life; his concern is for the loss of man rather than the gain of God.[31]

Eliot's circumspection here constitutes a brilliant tactical response to the failure of tact in Tennyson's account of Christological tactility. Gently reproving Tennyson for dubious or eccentric theology, Eliot clearly recognizes that the elegy's desire for Christ is "at best but a continuance, or a substitute for the joys of friendship upon earth." A stylistic chastisement is also implicit here. Consider, for instance, the revisionary subtlety with which Eliot redeploys Tennyson's language of desperate and anxious "holding," of "teasing," of "craving," and finally of "desiring." Performing a kind of postmortem refinement upon *In Memoriam*'s language of desire, Eliot effectively chastens the precursor poet for the startling clarity of his longing to fill the "void where heart on heart [had once] reposed/ And, where warm hands have prest and closed" (13). Eliot's tact inherits and then reproves Tennyson's passionate failure of it.

In the opening pages of "Mourning and Melancholia," Freud explicates the libidinal work that mourning performs:

> Reality-testing has shown that the loved object no longer exists, and it proceeds to demand that all libido shall be withdrawn from its attachments to the object. This demand arouses understandable opposition—it is a matter of general observation that people never willingly abandon a libidinal position, not even, indeed, when a substitute is already beckoning to them. This opposition can be so intense that a turning away from

reality takes place and a clinging to the object through the medium of hallucinatory wishful psychosis. Normally, respect for reality gains the day. Nevertheless its orders cannot be obeyed at once. They are carried out bit by bit, at great expense of time and cathectic energy, and in the meantime the existence of the lost object is psychically prolonged. Each single one of the memories and expectations in which the libido is bound to the object is brought up and hypercathected, and detach-ment of the libido is accomplished in respect of it. Why this comprom-ise by which the command of reality is carried out piecemeal should be so extraordi-narily painful is not at all easy to explain in terms of eco-nomics. It is re-markable that this painful unpleasure is taken as a matter of course by us. The fact is, however, that when the work of mourning is completed the ego becomes free and uninhibited again.[32]

In this compact synopsis of a libidinal dilemma that recalls Tennyson's own, Freud delineates the process of "normal" mourning: an excruciat-ing, fluctuant, and piecemeal process through which the mourner is com-pelled by the reality of loss to abandon one object cathexis for another. "A substitute," after all, "is already beckoning." But this cruel process of abandonment and substitution is sometimes impeded by an intractable resistance, as the mourner refuses to abandon his attachment to the beloved object. An ambivalent memorialization ensues. "Each single one of the memories and expectations in which the libido is bound to the ob-ject is brought up and hypercathected." As Freud carefully stresses, this work of remembering performs a double or ambivalent function, a bind-ing and an unbinding. The beloved object is revived and made present, even by "hallucinatory wish," to consciousness; in this way "the existence of the lost object is psychically prolonged." Conversely, and by way of an operation whose workings Freud leaves obscure, the same labor of re-membering accomplishes "detachment of the libido" in respect to the lost beloved; somehow the "hypercathected" repetition unbinds or decathects desiring subject and desired object. Every act of vivifying memory, Freud seems to imply, entrains a corresponding death, a terminal forgetting, if only because the desiring subject cannot, short of psychosis, sustain the fantasmatic presence of the beloved. The lost object thus suffers a thou-sand posthumous deaths at the now-murderous hands of the mourner. Hence the duplicitous work of mourning: to "prolong" in order to "de-tach," to give birth in order to kill. Once this "work of mourning is com-pleted"—once detachment overmasters prolongation—"the ego becomes free and uninhibited again." Free, that is, to become bound to a substi-tute object.

It is unnecessary, I think, to belabor the striking symmetries between Freud's account of mourning and Tennyson's elegy; each of Tennyson's lyrics operates like a hypercathected memory, working at once to prolong Hallam's presence and to facilitate his substitution in Christ. Freud's intuition regarding the ambivalence of memorialization may be employed to interrogate the divided work of *In Memoriam*'s homosexual figuration, to suggest, that is, the ways in which *In Memoriam* resists its own ideology of recuperative substitution, Christological or otherwise, and the ways in which this resistance ensures the intractable circulation of male homosexual desire. For *In Memoriam* works to postpone the conclusive bliss it also wants to complete. Thus at odds with its own desire to end desiring, the elegy wards off, even as it employs, an (eroto)logic of efficient surrogation. Until that far-off and divine event enfolds the poet and his beloved in its closural embrace, the poet must endure the empty and passive space of grief, the same space in which "the existence of the lost object is psychically prolonged." It is, finally, this medial space of unclosed longing that *In Memoriam* memorializes. But there is compensation here too. Because disseminated Hallam inseminates everything, Tennyson as desiring subject partakes of an equivocal expansion that helps him endure his subjection to desire:

> Thy voice is on the rolling air;
> I hear thee where the waters run;
> Thou standest in the rising sun,
> And in the setting thou art fair.
>
> What art thou then? I cannot guess;
> But tho' I seem in star and flower
> To feel thee some diffusive power,
> I do not therefore love thee less:
>
> My love involves the love before;
> My love is vaster passion now;
> Tho' mix'd with God and Nature thou,
> I seem to love thee more and more. (130)

Not the least beauty of *In Memoriam,* nor its least cultural utility, can be traced in these lines, which very well enact the equivocal process of substitution that Freud anatomizes in "Mourning and Melancholia." Hallam is prolonged even as he is dispersed into simulacra whose "more and more," Tennyson says, involves and extends "the love before." This ambivalent procedure subjects male homosexual desire to an almost sanitizing mediation. An intense desire for another male submits itself, or is taught by privation to submit, to a mediating force, or "diffusive power," that generates the difference of a "vaster passion" whose very differences will in turn recondense (if Tennyson's promise of the good moment holds) into the closural bliss of an absolutely androcentric embrace. From sameness to sameness, then, but only *through* difference. If this is a disciplinary trajectory (and of course it is), its particular strength resides in the quality of its ambivalence: on the one hand a startling and sometimes abrupt acknowledgment of intermasculine desire and its right to bliss; on the other, the submission of this desire to mediation by substitutes that bespeak a more conventional erotics of difference.

Of course the most obvious instance of such differentiating substitution is what Ricks aptly calls "the reiterated metaphor of man and wife,"[33] which both sexualizes and heterosexualizes the perduring grief whose extreme painfulness seems to have neutralized whatever disciplinary anxiety would otherwise have forestalled the use of an even heterosexually figured homosexual desire. Perhaps the sheer straightforwardness of the requisite gender inversion is this figure's most disarming quality:

> Two partners of a married life—
>   I look'd on these and thought of thee
>   In vastness and in mystery
> And of my spirit as of a wife. (97)

As *In Memoriam* repeats this swerve toward heterosexual (only sometimes marital) figuration, the gender assignments within the figure vary. In lyric 13, "Tears of a widower," which specifically recalls Milton's sonnet on the seeming return of his dead wife, Tennyson identifies himself as a male, though a weeping one; but it is more characteristic, given both the passivity of his grief and the feminization of passivity within Victorian gender codes, that Tennyson should feminize his longing for Hallam as a "perpetual maidenhood" that expects "no second friend" (6). Like Marianna, who fixedly grieves for the arrival of a male lover who "cometh not," Tennyson, as the speaker of *In Memoriam,* can only yearn in a perpetual—and here "heterosexual"—stasis.

Yet the metaphor of heterosexual embrace remains—at least for Tennyson and Hallam—a figure of separation, interdiction, distance. In *In Memoriam* woman indeed "exists only as an occasion for mediation, transaction, transition, transference, between man and his fellow man, indeed between man and himself."[34] The very presence of woman signifies the rift or gap in sameness that the hetero, by definition, cannot heal, or perhaps even help. Hence the elegy most characteristically represents the heterosexual embrace as always already interrupted, and therefore as a sign or structure whose primary service is painfully to repeat loss without ever recuperating loss into gain. Of course to say even this much is to refute the recuperative or reparational value of the thumpingly symbolic heterosexual marriage that so famously and unconvincingly closes—or almost closes—the elegy. Tennyson himself made the point didactically enough: "the poem," he said, "concludes with the marriage of my youngest sister [to Edward Lushington]. It was meant to be a kind of *Divina Commedia,* ending with happiness."[35] If Tennyson's argument for this particular variety of terminal bliss seems a little forced—more formal than felt—this is because the overweighted marriage quite obviously leaves the elegy's two central lovers still halved by desire, still unwed, the distantiated participants (Hallam's spirit, Tennyson conjectures, is present as a silent "stiller guest") at a wedding whose symbolic recompense quite openly ignores the poem's primary erotic schism. Even Tennyson himself seems unconvinced by this account of heterosexual closure; his "posture in the closing epithalamium is mannered and false."[36] When the poem quite correctly dismisses the newlyweds ("But they must go . . . and they are gone"; epilogue) and Tennyson "retire[s]" to his enduring loss, he must then dream (or dream up) the abundant recompense of this poem's other dream of closure: its prolepsis of the "one far-off divine event" whose Christocentric erotics we have already examined. In a very linear way, therefore, the epilogue repeats the elegy's double or contrary relations to longing: its desire to put an end to desire and its countervailing desire to exceed all such endings. Hence the epilogue goes on to supersede its own account of satisfactory heterosexual closure, requiring its speaker once again to fantasize the conclusive bliss that is offered only by—and only in the deferral of—that divine embrace with the compound "Christ that is to be" (106). A promise, then, of homosexual closure rather than the thing itself. Or better: a promise indistinguishable from its own deferral.

In Memoriam may be Victorian poetry's preeminent example of this aesthetic regime of hygenic deferral, but it is hardly the only one. Consider, for instance, the febrile equivocations of Coventry Patmore's little-noted poem "The Unknown Eros" (1878), a text that obliquely narrates both the advent of pedophilic desire and its subsequent sublimation. Consisting largely of an extended series of interrogatives, Patmore's seventy-five-line poem nervously questions the meaning of the "blind and unrelated joy" that seizes the poet/speaker when he is unexpectedly subject to the descent of an "Unknown Eros"—that is, of an insufficiently celebrated homoerotic Cupid ("which not a poet sings") whose promise of "rumour'd heavens" provokes in Patmore an otherwise "unguess'd want" "to lie / Between those quivering plumes that thro' fine ether pant."[37] Teased into an anxious sentience by the flirtations of this fluttering boy-god, the speaker begins his speculation upon the problem of homosexual desire by presenting, coyly but recognizably, his genital response to the unknown deity's (semi)divine bottom:

> O, Unknown Eros, sire of awful bliss,
> What portent and what Delphic word,
> Such as in the form of snake or bird,
> Is this?
> In my life's even flood
> What eddies thus?
> What in its ruddy orbit lifts the blood
>
> Like a perturbed moon of Uranus
> Reaching to some great world in ungauged darkness hid;
> And whence
> This rapture of the sense
> Which, by thy whisper bid,
> Reveres with obscure rite and sacramental sign
> A bond I know not of nor dimly can divine?

If the obliquity with which the lifted blood of the poet's genitalia (itself figured, by way of an astronomical pun, as "a perturbed moon of Uranus") stands and tracks the hovering boy's "ruddy orbit" seems more than a little comic, it is clear that Patmore intended no laughter. The gravity of tone and diction in these lines implicitly counterspeak the indignity of their latent anal implications. Indeed the nervously, or even unconsciously, embedded pun on "your anus" accurately figures the poet's anxious oscillation between the exalted pedophilia, or Aphrodite Uranos, as encomiastically described by Pausanias in Plato's *Symposium,* and the specifically anal desire to reach into "some great world in ungauged darkness hid."

If one hears a residually Satanic resonance in the temptation of a great world in darkness hid, it will come as no surprise that the speaker renounces the boy-god's body as a "compulsive focus" that must lead to

"Nought." The poet's errant and culturally transgressive desire to gauge this darkness yields, not unexpectedly, to a conventional fear of the anus as a site of decreation; and this fear in turn moves the poet to refuse or renounce his "meaningless desire." But, by way of a familiar paradox whose ideological investments still require unpacking, this act of renunciation is said to entail a benefit, a recompense, in the form of an enabling sublimation. In the poem's closing lines, Patmore discloses the "enigma," or constitutive ambivalence, that structures this representative Victorian renunciation (the quotation marks are Patmore's):

> "There lies the crown
> "Which all thy longing cures.
> "Refuse it, Mortal, that it may be yours!
> "It is a spirit, though it seems red gold;
> "And such may no man, but by shunning, hold.
> "Refuse it, though refusing be despair;
> "And thou shalt feel the phantom in thy hair."

As in the more subtle and beautiful example of *In Memoriam,* these programmatic lines deploy a compensatory logic of substitution that both excites and curtails homosexual desire by identifying renunciation as itself a deferred mode of possession: "Refuse it, Mortal, that it may be yours!" And in a substitution too funny to be intentional, the poet renounces "the Crown / Which all thy longing cures" in return for the endless tickle of a heady sublimation: "And thou shalt feel the phantom in thy hair."

But any desire that must be shunned in order to be held might indeed be occasion for despair. The extreme personal cost inherent in Patmore's phantom logic has already been registered for us by a self-declaredly "complete and undoubtedly congenital" homosexual who discovered in Patmore's verse a copytext for the conversion of his own "inverted nature" into "transcendental interpretations." The individual to whom I refer is "R.S., aged 31, American of French descent," also known as "History IX" in Ellis's *Sexual Inversion.*[38] As is typical of these case histories, which seem to have been patterned after a questionnaire developed by John Addington Symonds, R.S. begins his narrative with a personal genealogy ("Upon the question of heredity I may say that I belong to a reasonably healthy, prolific, and long-lived family . . . my father was a very masculine man."); moves next to a history of childhood and adolescence ("It was always the *prince* in fairy tales who held my interest or affection."); and then expatiates at some length upon the process that "stirred me to a full consciousness of my inverted nature." In this context and in a striking parallel to the erotic situation in *In Memoriam,* R.S. describes the self-revelatory effects of a passionate but nongenital friendship that is prematurely terminated by the death of the friend:

> It was now that I felt for the first time the full shock of love. He returned my affection but both of us were shy of showing our feelings or speaking of them. Often when walking together after nightfall we would put our arms about each other. Sometimes, too, when sleeping together we would lie in close contact, and my friend once suggested that I put my legs against his. He frequently begged me to spend the night with him; but I began to fear my feelings, and slept with him but seldom. We neither of us had any definite ideas about homosexual relations, and, apart from what I have related above, we had no further contact with each other. A few months after our amorous feelings had developed my friend died. His death caused me great distress, and my naturally religious temperament began to manifest itself quite strongly. At this time, too, I first read some writings of Mr. Addington Symonds, and certain allusions in his work, coupled with my recent experience, soon stirred me to a full consciousness of my inverted nature.

After the passage of some years, during which he continued to "couple" his "recent experience" with his "allusive" reading, an anguished R.S. developed "what, for lack of a better name, I term my homosexual Patmorean ideal":

> Three or four years ago a little book by Coventry Patmore fell into my hands, and from its perusal resulted a strange blending of my religious and erotic notions. The desire to love and be loved is hard to drown, and, when I realized that homosexually it was neither lawful nor possible for me to love in this world, I began to project my longings into the next. By birth I am a Roman Catholic, and in spite of a somewhat skeptical temper, manage to remain one by conviction.
>
> From the doctrines of the Trinity, Incarnation, and Eucharist, I have drawn conclusions which would fill the minds of the average pietist with holy horror; nevertheless I believe that (granting the premises) these conclusions are both logically and theologically defensible. The Divinity of my fancied paradise resembles in no way the vapid conceptions of Fra Angelico, or the Quartier St. Sulpice. His physical aspect, at least, would be better represented by some Praxitilean demigod or Flandrin's naked, brooding boy.
>
> While these imaginings have caused me considerable moral disquietude, they do not seem wholly reprehensible, because I feel that the

chief happiness I would derive by their realization would be mainly from the contemplation of the loved one, rather than from closer joys.

If R.S. circumspectly omits the title of that "little book by Coventry Patmore," we may with reasonable certainty identify it, a little belatedly, as *The Unknown Eros,* the 1878 volume whose title Patmore derived from the coyly pedophilic poem we have already read. Like *In Memoriam,* it is a volume preeminent for its "strange blending of religious and erotic notions," a process in which the considerable work of homosexual deferral can be completed only by a diffusion of these otherwise inadmissible erotics into a Christocentric "Desire of Him whom all things love."[39] As we have seen, this implicitly disciplinary process is not without its agonistic benefits, as when in the volume's final poem, "The Child's Purchase," Patmore deploys an elaborate trope of feminine mediation in order himself to share, with Christ, "the spousal rapture of the sharp spear's head." But even as a way of forestalling "closer joys," these pleasures are not innocent of individual expense. "To project [one's] longing into the next [world]" may itself constitute a project of self-dessication. These are the last sentences of History IX:

> Since the birth and development within me of what, for lack of a better name, I term my homosexualized Patmorean ideal, life has become, in the main, a weary business. I am not despondent, however, because many things still hold for me a certain interest. When that interest dies down, as it is wont from time to time, I endeavor to be patient. God grant that after the end here, I may be drawn from the shadow, and seemingly vain imaginings into the possession of their never-ending reality hereafter.

Displacement may have its place, but it also has its costs.

But what is the place of displacement, short of that "never-ending reality hereafter"? Exactly this question intervenes between R.S.'s finally disheartened account of the bleak housing offered to desire by the "homosexualized Patmorean ideal" and Tennyson's altogether more bullish accounting of the compensatory economics that fund *In Memoriam*'s strategy of erotic deferral. *In Memoriam* more deeply invests, and is more deeply invested in, the practices of postponement and sublimation. The sheer extensiveness of Tennyson's discourse of desire (no one ever wished the poem longer) writes against desire's own desire to end. And if it is true that *In Memoriam* concludes with one of Victorian poetry's most famous promises of satisfaction—that "one far-off divine event / To which the whole creation moves"—it is conversely true that it is this movement, rather than this event, that the whole creation of *In Memoriam* memorializes. For the very medium of Tennyson's spoken desire to embrace Hallam in Christ and Christ in Hallam depends upon the same enabling rupture or scission that this desire also wants rapturously to terminate; the very desire to speak the end leaves one stranded in the desiring middle, where "[a] use in measured language lies" (5). This paradoxical condition can be readily measured into orthodox uses: a potentially transgressive desire is obsessively evoked in order that it may be just as obsessively repeated in words that "half reveal / And half conceal the soul within" (5). The desiring subject is thus held back, by language as by death, from his proper place, but in some sense he loves that displacement:

> O days and hours, your work is this
>   To hold me from my proper place,
>   A little while from his embrace,
> For fuller gain of after bliss:
>
> That out of distance might ensue
>   Desire of nearness doubly sweet;
>   And unto meeting when we meet,
> Delight a hundredfold accrue,
>
> For every grain of sand that runs,
>   And every span of shade that steals,
>   And every kiss of toothed wheels,
> And all the courses of the suns. (117)

Here, in a totalizing eroticism that would be difficult to exceed, Tennyson submits all things to desire in order thereby to achieve the submission of desire itself. As Hallam had once been "the centre of a world's desire," its "central warmth diffusing bliss" (84), so in these lines he becomes diffusion itself, as Tennyson dutifully deploys the whole of creation—every grain, every span, all suns—to facilitate the good Victorian work of interdicting the homoerotic embrace that is nonetheless acknowledged to be "my proper place." It may have been death alone that set Tennyson to his specifically reparational wooing, but these lines suggest the poet's own complicity with the duty of differentiation; for just as it is the "work" of the world both to separate and remember lovers by incarnating difference, so it is the poet's work to distribute his desire as meaning—indeed, as the most overdetermined of meanings—through the differentiae of an otherwise blank scape. The diffusive power of imagination thus perfectly fetishizes the world: where Hallam emphatically is not, Hallam therefore everywhere is.

In a strategically double way, then, Tennyson retains the ontological primacy of his desire for Hallam while simultaneously dispersing the perils of gender sameness into the prophylactic difference of an absolute heterocosm; the inescapable residuum of this process is that "every kiss" of this therefore secondary hetero remains but the disfigured memorial of a banished originary homo. The erotics of such a substitutive structure are irreducibly ambivalent: since the homo is lost or banished only to be rediscovered in and as the hetero, all longing remains longing for the homo even as it submits to the differences intrinsic to mediation. Difference itself thus bespeaks a desire for sameness—speaks, like the poet, in memoriam. No surprise, then, that the work of mediation is double: time ("O days and hours") and "distance" "work" to "hold" the poet "a little while" from his proper "embrace", yet this deferral recenters and heightens the desire for that "meeting when we meet." Within this transparently compensatory structure, distance (here the aporia of death) is said to double the sweetness of desire, even as the postponement of desire's closural embrace yields, in due time, that "fuller gain of afterbliss."

It was, I think, to this strategic ambivalence that Ellis alluded when he recommended *In Memoriam* as a primary literary exemplar of how "by psychic methods to refine and spiritualize the inverted impulse." In the extremity of his grief, Tennyson had authored a virtual copytext for the recognition and articulation of a homosexual desire whose subjective effects were palpable in their intensity, but whose distantiated object had always already been exiled to a realm beyond touch if not beyond the desire for touching. In figuring Hallam's death as the terminus in which desire discovers its origin, Tennyson's discourse of homosexual longing instructs the desiring subject in the affined Victorian virtues of heroic patience and active surrogation, virtues that alone make it possible to endure a desire otherwise impossible of fulfillment. (They also serve who only stand and wait.) And in his figuration of the hetero as the diffused or encoded expression of the homo, as in his subsumption of erotic privation within an economy of symbolic reparation, Tennyson had in effect devised a translation machine for the conversion of the desire otherwise too strong for words to name; by 1850 he had provided a personal and exacting version of what Ellis, more than fifty years later, was still struggling to formulate: "a method of self-restraint and self-culture, without self-repression." Revaluing the easy optimism of Ellis's last phrase, we may say that Tennyson transvalued his passionate grief into a semiotics of homosexual desire in which the painful but presumably liberating work of recognition and accommodation blends indistinguishably into the work of discipline and containment; incitement and repression are complicit and coeval here.

But to have said even this much is already to have overvalued the disciplinary register at the expense of its revisionary or oppositional complement; and it would be wrong to leave *In Memoriam* with so compliant an acceptance of its normalizing significations, important as it is for criticism to acknowledge these. For Tennyson's elegy retains much of the transgressive force that so unsettled some of its first readers. Whatever bliss or agony the poem owns it owes to its insuperable desire for Hallam; nor can the manifold dispersions of that "vaster passion" displace Hallam as the affective center of *In Memoriam*'s world of desire. In this sense, *In Memoriam* refuses to complete its work of mourning; refuses, that is, the work of normal, and normalizing, substitution. Thus, in the sheer ferocity of its personal loss, as in the extreme extensiveness of its reparational hungering, Tennyson's elegy manages to counterspeak its own submission to its culture's heterosexualizing conventions. In this view, our departing view, *In Memoriam* remains at its end what it had been at its beginning: a desiring machine whose first motive is the restitution of lost Hallam. As such *In Memoriam* continues to do what it has always done best: it keeps its desire by keeping its desire desiring.

3

Just Another Kiss

Inversion and Paranoia in Bram Stoker's Dracula

Blood is not at all a sealed biological element, strictly belonging
to this or that person who possesses his blood as he might possess eyes or legs. It is a cosmic element, a unique and homoge-
neous substance which traverses all bodies, without losing, in
this accidental individuation, anything of its universality. Itself
a transformation of the earth (of bread and of the fruits that we
eat), it has the immensity of an element.

—Roland Barthes, *Michelet*

When Joseph Sheridan Le Fanu observed in *Carmilla* (1872) that "the
vampire is prone to be fascinated with an engrossing vehemence resem-
bling the passion of love" and that vampiric pleasure is heightened "by
the gradual approaches of an artful courtship," he identified clearly the
analogy between monstrosity and sexual desire that would prove, under
a subsequent Freudian stimulus, paradigmatic for future readings of
vampirism.[1] Modern critical accounts of *Dracula* almost univocally agree
that vampirism both expresses and distorts an originally sexual energy.
That distortion, the representation of desire under the defensive mask of
monstrosity, betrays the fundamental psychological ambivalence identified by Franco Moretti when he writes that "vampirism is an excellent
example of the identity of desire and fear."[2] This interfusion of sexual
desire and the fear that the moment of erotic fulfillment may occasion
the erasure of the conventional and integral self informs both the central
action in *Dracula* (1897) and the surcharged emotion of the characters
about to be kissed by "those red lips."[3] So powerful an ambivalence, generating both errant erotic impulses and compensatory anxieties, demands a strict, indeed an almost schematic formal management of
narrative material. In *Dracula* Stoker borrows from Mary Shelley's

Frankenstein, Robert Louis Stevenson's *Dr. Jekyll and Mr. Hyde,* and Le Fanu's *Carmilla* a narrative strategy characterized by a predictable, if variable, triple rhythm. Each of these texts first invites or admits a monster, then entertains and is entertained by monstrosity for some extended duration, until in its closing pages it expels and repudiates the monster and all the disruption that he/she/it brings.[4]

Obviously enough, the first element in this triple rhythm corresponds formally to the text's beginning or generative moment, to its desire to produce the monster, while the third element corresponds to the text's terminal moment, to its desire both to destroy the monster it had previously admitted and to close the narrative in which the monster has come to life. Interposed between these antithetical gestures of admission and expulsion lies a narrative space marked by fundamental equivocation: in its prolonged middle,[5] the Gothic novel affords its ambivalence a degree of play sufficient to sustain a pleasurable, indeed a thrilling anxiety. Within this extended middle, the Gothic novel entertains its resident demon—is, indeed, entertained by it; and the monster, now ascendent in its strength, seems for a time potent enough to invert the "natural" order and overwhelm the comforting closure of the text. That threat, of course, is effectively dismissed by the narrative requirement that the monster be repudiated and the world of normal relations restored; thus the gesture of expulsion brings the play of monstrosity to its predictable close, thereby compensating for the original irruption of deviance. This tripartite cycle of admission/entertainment/expulsion diachronically enacts an essentially synchronic psychological equivocation; in doing so, it both excites and manages the irreducible ambivalence that drives these texts and our reading of them. Or, rather, our rereading and (in the case of the film versions) our reviewing of them. The very impulse to repeat (in) these texts—an impulse that joins reader, monster, writer in a shared fantasia— subverts the very closure that it will also programmatically enact over and over again. Reading the Gothic—perhaps reading in any case—is itself a mode of repetition compulsion, an attempt at mastery that always bespeaks the condition of already having been mastered by trauma.

Thus to speak in the language of mastery and submission, of agency and passivity, is implicitly to have succumbed, however self-consciously or ironically, to the asymmetrical dimorphism of gender (masculine/feminine) and desire (homosexual/heterosexual) that structure the Gothic generally and *Dracula* specifically. For what *Dracula* more than melodramatically stages is a violent contest for proprietorship of gender and sex roles: Who (which gender) shall be active and who passive? Who shall kiss and who shall not? Who shall penetrate and with what devices? The simple displacement of the vampire metaphor enables Stoker to problematize these questions and thereby to repeat, with a monstrous difference, a pivotal anxiety of late Victorian culture. Jonathan Harker, whose diary opens the novel, provides *Dracula*'s most precise articulation of this anxiety. About to be kissed by the "weird sisters" (64), the incestuous vampiric daughters who share Castle Dracula with the Count, a supine Harker thrills to a double passion:

> All three had brilliant white teeth, that shone like pearls against the ruby of their voluptuous lips. There was something about them that made me uneasy, some longing and at the same time some deadly fear. I felt in my heart a wicked, burning desire that they would kiss me with those red lips. (51)

Immobilized by the competing imperatives of "wicked desire" and "deadly fear," Harker awaits an erotic fulfillment that entails both the dissolution of the boundaries of the self and the thorough subversion of conventional Victorian gender codes, which constrained the mobility of sexual desire and the varieties of genital behavior by according to the more active male the right and responsibility of vigorous appetite while requiring the more passive female to "suffer and be still." John Ruskin, concisely formulating Victorian conventions of sexual difference, provides a useful synopsis: "The man's power is active, progressive, defensive. He is eminently the doer, the creator, the discoverer, the defender. His intellect is for speculation and invention; his energy for adventure, for war, and for conquest." Woman, predictably enough, bears a different burden: "She must be enduringly, incorruptibly, good; instinctively, infallibly wise— wise, not for self-development, but for self-renunciation . . . wise, not with the narrowness of insolent and loveless pride, but with the passionate gentleness of an infinitely variable, because infinitely applicable, modesty of service—the true changefulness of woman."[6] Stoker, whose vampiric women exercise a far more dangerous "changefulness" than Ruskin imagines, anxiously inverts this conventional pattern, as a virile Harker enjoys a "feminine" passivity and awaits a delicious penetration from a woman whose demonism is figured as the power to penetrate. A swooning desire for an overwhelming penetration and an intense aversion to the demonic potency empowered to gratify that desire: this is the ambivalence that motivates action and emotion in *Dracula*.

This ambivalence, always excited by the imminence of the vampiric kiss, finds its most sensational representation in the image of the Vampire Mouth, the central and recurring image of the novel: "There was a deliberate voluptuousness which was both thrilling and repulsive ... I could see in the moonlight the moisture shining on the red tongue as it lapped the white sharp teeth" (52). That is Harker describing one of the three vampire women at Castle Dracula. Here is Dr. Seward's description of the Count: "His eyes flamed red with devilish passion; the great nostrils of the white aquiline nose opened wide and quivered at the edges; and the white sharp teeth, behind the full lips of the blood-dripping mouth, champed together like those of a wild beast" (336). As the primary site of erotic experience in *Dracula,* this mouth equivocates, giving the lie to the easy separation of the masculine and the feminine. Luring at first with an inviting orifice, a promise of red softness, but delivering instead a piercing bone, the vampire mouth fuses and confuses what Dracula's civilized nemesis, Van Helsing and his Crew of Light,[7] works so hard to separate—the gender-based categories of the penetrating and the receptive, or, to use Van Helsing's language, the complementary categories of "brave men" and "good women." With its soft lips barred by hard bone, its red crossed by white, this mouth swallows oppositions in order to announce a compelling (because phobic) disturbance of sexual difference. And it asks some disquieting questions. Are we male or are we female? Do we have penetrators or orifices? And if both, what does *that* mean? What about our bodily fluids, red and white? What are the fluent relations between blood and semen, milk and blood? Furthermore, this mouth is the mouth of all vampires, male and female. It—and they—are both both.

Yet we must remember that the vampire mouth is first of all Dracula's mouth, and that all subsequent versions of it (in *Dracula* all vampires other than the Count are female)[8] merely repeat as diminished simulacra the desire of the great original, the "father or furtherer of a new order of beings" (360). Dracula himself, calling his children "my jackals to do my bidding when I want to feed," specifies the systematic creation of female surrogates who enact his will and desire (365). This should remind us that the narrative's originary anxiety, its first articulation of the vampiric threat, derives from Dracula's hovering interest in Jonathan Harker; the sexual threat that this novel first evokes, manipulates, sustains, but never finally represents, is that Dracula will seduce, penetrate, drain another male. The suspense and power of *Dracula*'s opening section, of that phase of the narrative we have called the invitation to monstrosity, proceeds precisely from this unfulfilled sexual ambition. Dracula's desire to fuse with a male, most explicitly evoked when Harker cuts himself shaving, subtly and dangerously suffuses this text. Always postponed and never directly enacted, this desire finds evasive fulfillment in an important series of heterosexual displacements.

Dracula's ungratified desire to vamp Harker is represented through his three vampiric daughters, whose anatomical femininity permits, because it masks, the silently interdicted homoerotic embrace between Harker and the Count. Here, in a displacement typical both of this text and the gender-anxious culture from which it arose, an implicitly homosexual desire achieves representation as a monstrous heterosexuality, as a demonic inversion of normal gender relations. Dracula's daughters offer Harker a feminine form but a masculine penetration:

> Lower and lower went her head as the lips went below the range of my mouth and chin and seemed to fasten on my throat. . . . I could feel the soft, shivering touch of the lips on the supersensitive skin of my throat, and the hard dents of two sharp teeth, just touching and pausing there. I closed my eyes in a languorous ecstasy and waited—waited with a beating heart. (52)

This moment, constituting the text's most direct and explicit representation of a male's desire to be penetrated, is governed by a double deflection: first, the agent of penetration is nominally and anatomically (from the mouth down, anyway) female; and second, this dangerous moment, fusing the maximum of desire and the maximum of anxiety, is poised precisely at the brink of penetration. Here the "two sharp teeth," just "touching" and "pausing" there, stop short of the transgression that would unsex Harker and toward which this text constantly aspires and then retreats: the actual penetration of the male.

This moment is interrupted, this penetration denied. Harker's swooning pause at the end of the paragraph ("waited—waited with a beating heart"), which seems to announce an imminent piercing, in fact anticipates not the completion but the interruption of the scene of penetration. At precisely this point, Dracula himself breaks into the room, drives the women away from Harker, and admonishes them: "How dare you touch him, any of you? How dare you cast eyes on him when I had forbidden it? Back, I tell you all! This man belongs to me" (53). Dracula's intercession here has two obvious effects: by interrupting the scene of penetration, it suspends and disperses throughout the text the desire maximized

at the brink of penetration, and it repeats the threat of a more direct libidinous embrace between Dracula and Harker. Dracula's taunt, "This
man belongs to me," is suggestive enough, but at no point subsequent to
this moment does Dracula kiss Harker, preferring instead to pump him
for his knowledge of English law, custom, and language. Dracula, soon
departing for England, leaves Harker to the weird sisters, whose final penetration of him, implied but never represented, occurs in the dark interspace to which Harker's journal gives no access—if it occurs at all.

Hereafter *Dracula* will never represent so directly a male's desire to be
penetrated; once in England, Dracula observes a decorous heterosexuality and vamps only women, in particular Lucy Westenra and Mina
Harker. The novel, nonetheless, does not dismiss homosexual desire and
threat; rather it submits a conventionally unspeakable intermasculine sexuality to a fierce heterosexual itinerary that compels women to mediate
between men in an otherwise forfended "circuit of male transactions."[9]
Late in the text, the Count himself lucidly explicates this phobic circuitry
when he admonishes the Crew of Light thus: "My revenge is just begun.
I spread it over the centuries, and time is on my side. Your girls that you
all love are mine already; and through them you and others shall yet be
mine" (365). In thus specifying the triangular structure of substitution by
which "the girls that you all love" mediate and displace a more direct communion among males, *Dracula* in fact offers a remarkably condensed synopsis of the critical schema we now so usefully call the "traffic in women"
or "between men" paradigm. Derived in part from feminist/lesbian reval-
uations of the insights of Freud, Lévi-Strauss, and Girard, this critical
schema has evinced an impressive explanatory power. Here is Eve Kosofsky Sedgwick's précis of Girard's notion of "triangular desire":

> René Girard's early book, *Deceit, Desire, and the Novel,* was itself some-
> thing of a schematization of the folk-wisdom of erotic triangles. Through
> readings of major European fictions, Girard traced a calculus of power
> that was structured by the relation of rivalry between the two active
> members of an erotic triangle. What is most interesting for our purposes
> in his study is its insistence that, in any erotic rivalry, the bond that links
> the two rivals is as intense and potent as the bond that links either of the
> rivals to the beloved: that the bonds of "rivalry" and "love," differently as
> they are experienced, are equally powerful and in many senses equiva-
> lent. For instance, Girard finds many examples in which the choice of
> the beloved is determined in the first place, not by the qualities of the
> beloved, but by the beloved's already being the choice of the person who

has been chosen as a rival. In fact, Girard seems to see the bond between rivals in an erotic triangle as being even stronger, more heavily determinant of actions and choices, than anything in the bond between either of the lovers and the beloved. And within the male-centered novelistic tradition of European high culture, the triangles Girard traces are most often those in which two males are rivals for a female; it is the bond between males that he most assiduously uncovers.[10]

It is such bonds between males that *Dracula,* too, most assiduously covers and uncovers. Intermasculine "rivalry" and "love" are not merely interfused in this text, they are literally *transfused* in a perverse exchange of bodily fluids whose anatomical locus is the traduced body of a somnolent woman. For once Van Helsing begins his series of presumptively therapeutic transfusions, the blood that Dracula withdraws from Lucy is no longer hers, but is rather that already transferred from the veins of the Crew of Light. Van Helsing himself explicates the perverse exchange: "even we four who gave our strength to Lucy it also is all to him [*sic*]" (244). Here, emphatically, is another instance of the heterosexual displacement of a fluid, homosexual desire. Everywhere in this text such desire seeks a strangely deflected heterosexual distribution; only through women may men touch.

In its patently overdetermined insistence that male homosexual desire be channeled or filtered through a defensive heterosexual mask, *Dracula* submits, very excitedly, to Victorian culture's imperative that desire for the same represent itself as "in fact" a desire for the different or the "other"—with the other of course figured as a species or version, however displaced, of the feminine. *Dracula* replays, in other words, the essentially homophobic metaphorics of sexual inversion, of *anima muliebris virili corpore inclusa.* As demonstrated at length in Chapter 1, sexual inversion explains homosexual desire as a physiologically misplaced heterosexuality; a principle of gender dimorphism is insinuated within desire in order to distantiate the sameness of bodies. A male's desire for another male, according to this account, is a priori assumed to be a feminine desire referable not to the sex of the body (*virili corpore*) but rather to a psychologized sexual center characterized by the "opposite" gender (*anima muliebris*). If this argument's intrinsic doubleness—its insistence on the simultaneous inscription within the individual of two genders, one anatomical and one not, one visible and one not—provided polemicists like Ulrichs, Symonds, and Ellis with a conceptual lever for the decriminalization of homosexual activity, it nonetheless reinstated the ideological presumption of the heterosexist norm. Precisely what this account of same-sex eroticism cannot imagine is that sexual attraction between members of the same gender may be a reasonable and "natural" articulation of a desire whose excursiveness is simply indifferent to the distinctions of gender, that desire may not be intrinsically sexed as the body is, and that desire seeks its objects according to a complicated set of conventions that are culturally and institutionally determined.

Significantly, the inversion account's displaced repetition of heterosexual gender norms contains within it the undeveloped germ of a radical redefinition of Victorian conventions of feminine desire. The interposition of a feminine soul between erotically associated males inevitably entails a certain feminization of desire, since the very site and source of desire for males is assumed to be feminine (*anima muliebris*). Implicit in this argument is the submerged acknowledgment of the sexually independent woman, whose erotic empowerment refutes the conventional assumption of feminine passivity. Nonetheless, this nascent redefinition of notions of feminine desire remained largely unfulfilled. Symonds and Ellis did not escape their culture's phallocentrism, and their texts predictably reflect this bias. Symonds, whose sexual and aesthetic interests pivoted around the "pure & noble faculty of understanding and expressing manly perfection,"[11] seems to have been largely unconcerned with feminine sexuality; his seventy-page *A Problem in Greek Ethics,* for instance, offers only a two-page "parenthetical investigation" of lesbianism. Ellis, like Freud, certainly acknowledged sexual desire in women, but nevertheless accorded to masculine heterosexual desire an ontological and practical priority: "The female responds to the stimulation of the male at the right moment just as the tree responds to the stimulation of the warmest days in spring."[12] (Nor did English law want to recognize the sexually self-motivated woman. The Labouchere Amendment to the Criminal Law Amendment Act of 1885, the statute under which Oscar Wilde was convicted of "gross indecency," simply ignored the possibility of erotic behavior between women.) In all of this we may see an anxious defense against recognition of an independent and active feminine sexuality. A submerged fear of the feminization of desire precluded these polemicists from fully developing their own argumentative assumption of an already sexualized feminine soul.

A historical complicity would thus seem to subsist between the inversion account of homosexuality and the occlusion of independent feminine sexuality. D. A. Miller, commenting on Ulrichs's formulation of *anima muliebris virili corpore inclusa,* provides a compact delineation of precisely this complicity:

> For if what essentially characterizes male homosexuality in this way of putting it is the woman-in-the-man, and if this "woman" is *inclusa,* incarcerated or shut up, her freedoms abridged accordingly, then homosexuality would be by its very nature homophobic: imprisoned in a carceral problematic that does little more than channel into the homosexual's "ontology" the social and legal sanctions that might otherwise be imposed on him. Meant to win a certain intermediate space for homosexuals, Ulrichs's formulation in fact ultimately colludes with the prison or closet drama—of keeping the "woman" well put away—that it would relegate to the unenlightened past. And homosexuals' souls are not the only ones to be imprisoned in male bodies; Ulrichs's phrase does perhaps far better as a general description of the condition of nineteenth-century women, whose "spirit" (whether understood as intellect, integrity, or sexuality) is massively interned in male corporations, constitutions, contexts. His metaphor thus may be seen to link or condense together 1) a particular fantasy about male homosexuality; 2) a homophobic defense against that fantasy; and 3) the male oppression of women that, among other things, extends that defense.[13]

What Miller so efficiently anatomizes here—the interlocking violence of a pervasive cultural homophobia, the subjugation of women, and certain disciplinary fantasies about homosexuality—is played out with a fatal and almost totemic simplicity in *Dracula,* a text in which the excitations of male homosexual desire must suffer a detour through the image of a mobile and hungering woman who has usurped the "masculine" prerogative of penetration. As we are about to see, the very inversion that requires intermasculine desire disclose itself in and as a feminine locus also guarantees, if we may adapt a phrase of Hardy's, that the woman will pay.

Our strong game will be to play our masculine against
her feminine.
   —Bram Stoker, *The Lair of the White Worm*

To make a dead body of woman is to try one last time to overcome her enigmatic and ungraspable character, to fix in a definitive and immovable position instability and mobility themselves.
   —Sarah Kofman, *The Enigma of Woman*

The portion of Gothic novel that I have called the prolonged middle, during which the text allows the monster a certain dangerous play, corresponds in *Dracula* to the duration beginning with the Count's arrival in England and ending with his flight back home; this extended middle constitutes the novel's prolonged moment of equivocation, as it entertains, elaborates, and explores the very anxieties it must later expel in the formulaic resolution of the plot. The action within this section of *Dracula* consists, simply enough, in an extended battle between two evidently masculine forces, one identifiably good and the other identifiably evil, for the allegiance of a woman (two women actually—Lucy Westenra and Mina Harker née Murray).[14] This competition between alternative potencies has the apparent simplicity of a black-and-white opposition. Dracula ravages and impoverishes these women, Van Helsing's Crew of Light restores and "saves" them. As Dracula conducts his serial assaults upon Lucy, Van Helsing, in a pretty counterpoint of penetration, responds with a series of defensive transfusions; the blood that Dracula takes out Van Helsing then puts back. Dracula, isolated and disdainful of community, works alone; Van Helsing enters this little English community, immediately assumes authority, and then works through surrogates to cement communal—that is, patriarchal and homosocial—bonds. As critics have noted, this pattern of opposition distills readily into a competition between antithetical fathers. "The vampire Count, centuries old," Maurice Richardson writes, "is a father figure of huge potency" who competes with Van Helsing, "the good father figure."[15] The theme of alternate paternities is, in short, simple, evident, unavoidable.

This oscillation between vampiric transgression and medical correction exercises the text's ambivalence toward those fundamental dualisms—life and death, spirit and flesh, male and female, activity and passivity—that have served traditionally to constrain and delimit the excursions of desire. As doctor, lawyer, and sometimes priest ("The Host. I brought it from Amsterdam. I have an Indulgence."), Van Helsing stands as the protector of the patriarchal institutions he so emphatically represents and as the guarantor of the traditional dualisms his religion and profession promote and authorize (252). His largest purpose is to reinscribe the dualities that Dracula would muddle and confuse. Dualities require demarcations, inexorable and ineradicable lines of separation, but Dracula, as a border being who abrogates demarcations, makes such distinctions impossible. He is *nosferatu,* neither dead nor alive but somehow both, mobile frequenter of the grave and boudoir, easeful communicant of exclusive realms, and as such he toys with the separation of the living and the dead, a distinction crucial to physician, lawyer, and priest alike. His metaphoric power derides the distinction between spirit and flesh, another of Van Helsing's sanctified dualisms. Potent enough to ignore death's terminus, Dracula has a spirit's freedom and mobility, but that mobility is chained to the most mechanical of appetites: he and his children rise and fall for a drink and for nothing else, for nothing else matters. This confusion or interfusion of spirit and appetite, of eternity and sequence, produces a madness of activity and a mania of unceasing desire. Dracula lives an eternity of sexual repetition, a lurid wedding of desire and satisfaction that parodies both.

But the traditional dualism most vigorously defended by Van Helsing and most subtly subverted by Dracula is, of course, sexual: culture's division of being into gender, either masculine or feminine. Indeed, as we have seen, the vampiric kiss excites a sexuality so mobile, so insistent, that it threatens to overwhelm the distinctions of gender, and the exuberant energy with which Van Helsing and the Crew of Light counter Dracula's influence represents the text's anxious defense against the very desire it also seeks to liberate. In counterposing Dracula and Van Helsing, Stoker's text simultaneously threatens and protects the line of demarcation that insures the intelligible division of being into gender. This ambivalent need first to invite the vampiric kiss and then to repudiate it defines exactly the dynamic of the battle that constitutes the prolonged middle of this text. The field of this battle, of this equivocal competition for the right to define the possible relations between desire and gender, is the infinitely penetrable body of a somnolent woman. This interposition of a woman between Dracula and Van Helsing should not surprise us; in England, as in Castle Dracula, a violent wrestle between males is mediated through a feminine form.

The Crew of Light's conscious conception of women is, predictably enough, idealized—the stuff of dreams. Van Helsing's concise description of Mina may serve as a representative example: "She is one of God's women fashioned by His own hand to show us men and other women that there is a heaven we can enter, and that its light can be here on earth" (226). The impossible idealism of this conception of women deflects attention from the complex and complicitous interaction within this sentence of gender, authority, representation. Here Van Helsing's exegesis of God's natural text reifies Mina into a stable sign or symbol ("one of God's women") performing a fixed and comfortable function within a masculist sign system. Having received from Van Helsing's exegesis her divine impress, Mina signifies both a masculine artistic intention ("fashioned by His own hand") and a definite didactic purpose ("to show us men and other women" how to enter heaven), each of which constitutes an enormous constraint upon the significative possibilities of the sign or symbol that Mina here becomes. Van Helsing's reading of Mina, like a dozen other instances in which his interpretation of the sacred determines and delimits the range of activity permitted to women, encodes woman with a "natural" meaning composed according to the textual imperatives of anxious males. Precisely this complicity between masculine anxiety, divine textual authority, and a fixed conception of femininity—which may seem benign enough in the passage above—will soon be used to justify the destruction of Lucy Westenra, who, having been successfully vamped by Dracula, requires a corrective penetration. To Arthur's anxious importunity "Tell me what I am to do," Van Helsing answers: "Take this stake in your left hand, ready to place the point over the heart, and the hammer in your right. Then when we begin our prayer for the dead—I shall read him; I have here the book, and the others shall follow—strike in God's name." (258). Here four males (Van Helsing, Seward, Holmwood, and Quincey Morris) communally read a masculine text (Van Helsing's mangled English even permits Stoker the unidiomatic pronominalization of the genderless text: "I shall read him")[16] in order to justify the fatal correction of Lucy's dangerous wandering, her insolent disregard for the sexual and semiotic constraint encoded in Van Helsing's exegesis of "God's women."

The process by which women are construed as signs determined by the interpretive imperatives of authorizing males had been brilliantly identified over a quarter of a century before the publication of *Dracula* by John Stuart Mill in *The Subjection of Women* (1869). "What is now called the nature of women," Mill writes, "is an extremely artificial thing—the result of forced repression in some directions, unnatural stimulation in others."[17] Mill's sentence, deftly identifying "the nature of women" as an "artificial" construct formed (and deformed) by "repression" and "unnatural stimulation," quietly unties the lacings that bind something called "woman" to something else called "nature." He subtly devastates any claim to the "natural" authority of gender by asserting that the significatory difference between male and female is available to consciousness only as it is subjected to cultural interpretation: "I deny that anyone knows, or can know, the nature of the two sexes, as long as they have only been seen in their present relation to one another." Mill's agnosticism regarding "the nature of the sexes" suggests the societal and institutional quality of all definitions of the natural, definitions that ultimately conspire to produce "the imaginary and conventional character of women."[18] This last phrase, like the whole of Mill's essay, underscores and criticizes the authoritarian nexus that arises when a deflected or transformed desire ("imaginary"), empowered by a gender-biased societal agreement ("conventional"), imposes itself upon a person in order to create a "character." "Character" of course functions in at least three senses: who and what one "is," the role one plays in society's supervening script, and the sign or letter that is intelligible only within the constraints of a larger sign system. Van Helsing's exegesis of "God's women" creates just such an imaginary and conventional character. Mina's body/character may indeed be feminine, but the signification it bears is written and interpreted solely by males. As Susan Hardy Aiken has written, such a symbolic system takes for granted "the role of women as passive objects or signs to be manipulated in the grammar of privileged male interchanges."[19]

Yet exactly the passivity of this object and the ease of this manipulation are at issue in *Dracula*. Dracula, after all, kisses these women out of their passivity and so endangers the stability of Van Helsing's symbolic system. Both the prescriptive intention of Van Helsing's exegesis and the emphatic methodology (hypodermic needle, stake, surgeon's blade) he employs to insure the durability of his interpretation of gender suggest the potential unreliability of Mina as signifier, an instability that provokes an anxiety we may call fear of the mediatrix. If, as Van Helsing admits, God's women provide the essential mediation ("that [heaven's] light can be here on earth") between the divine but distant patriarch and his earthly sons, then God's intention may be distorted by its potentially changeable vehicle. If woman as signifier wanders, then Van Helsing's whole cosmology, with its founding dualisms and supporting texts, collapses. Van Helsing works to avert this catastrophe by imposing an a priori constraint upon the significative possibilities of "Mina." Such an authorial gesture, intended to forestall the semiotic wandering that Dracula inspires, indirectly acknowledges woman's dangerous potential. Late in the text, while Dracula is vamping Mina, Van Helsing will admit, very uneasily, that "Madam Mina, our poor, dear Madam Mina is changing" (384). The potential for such a change demonstrates what Nina Auerbach has called this woman's "mysterious amalgam of imprisonment and power."[20]

Dracula's authorizing kiss, like that of a demonic Prince Charming, triggers the release of this latent power and excites in these women a sexuality so mobile, so aggressive, that it thoroughly disrupts Van Helsing's compartmental conception of gender. Kissed into a sudden sexuality,[21] Lucy grows "voluptuous" (a word used to describe her only during the vampiric process), her lips redden, and she kisses with a new interest. This sexualization of Lucy, metamorphosing woman's "sweetness" to "adamantine, heartless cruelty, and [her] purity to voluptuous wantonness" (252–53), terrifies her suitors because it entails a reversal or inversion of sexual identity; Lucy, toothed now like the Count, usurps the function of penetration that Van Helsing's moralized taxonomy of gender reserves for males. *Dracula,* in thus figuring the sexualization of woman as phallic deformation, parallels exactly some of the more extreme medical uses of the idea of inversion. Late Victorian accounts of lesbianism, for instance, superscribed conventional gender norms upon sexual relationships to which those norms were anatomically irrelevant. Again the heterosexual norm proved paradigmatic. The female "husband" in such a relationship was understood to be dominant, appetitive, masculine, and "congenitally inverted"; the female "wife" was understood to be quiescent, passive, only "latently" homosexual, and, as Havelock Ellis argued, unmotivated by genital desire. Extreme deployment of the heterosexual paradigm approached the ridiculous, as George Chauncey explains:

> The early medical case histories of lesbians thus predictably paid enormous attention to their menstrual flow and the size of their sexual organs. Several doctors emphasized that their lesbian patients stopped menstruating at an early age, if they began at all, or had unusually difficult and irregular periods. They also inspected the woman's sexual organs, often claiming that inverts had unusually large clitorises, which they said inverts used in sexual intercourse as a man would his penis.[22]

This rather pathetic hunt for the penis in absentia denotes a double anxiety: first, that the penis shall not be erased, and if it is erased, that it shall be reinscribed in a perverse simulacrum; and second, that all desire repeat, even under the duress of deformity, the heterosexual norm that the metaphor of inversion always assumes. Medical professionals had in fact no need to pursue this fantasized Amazon of the clitoris, this "unnatural" penetrator, so vigorously, since Stoker, whose imagination was at least deft enough to displace that dangerous simulacrum to an isomorphic orifice, had by the 1890s already invented her. His sexualized women are men too.

Stoker emphasizes the monstrosity implicit in such abrogation of gender codes by inverting a favorite Victorian maternal function. His New Lady Vampires feed at first only on small children, working their way up, one assumes, a demonic pleasure thermometer until they may feed at last on full-blooded males. Lucy's dietary indiscretions evoke the deepest disgust from the Crew of Light:

> With a careless motion, she flung to the ground, callous as a devil, the child that up to now she had clutched strenuously to her breast, growling over it as a dog growls over a bone. The child gave a sharp cry, and lay there moaning. There was a cold-bloodedness in the act which wrung a groan from Arthur; when she advanced to him with outstretched arms and a wanton smile, he fell back and hid his face in his hands.
>
> She still advanced, however, and with a languorous, voluptuous grace, said:
>
> "Come to me Arthur. Leave those others and come to me. My arms are hungry for you. Come, and we can rest together, Come, my husband, come!" (253)

Stoker here gives us a *tableau mordant* of gender inversion: the child Lucy clutches "strenuously to her breast" is not being fed, but is being fed upon. Furthermore, by requiring that the child be discarded that the husband may be embraced, Stoker provides a little emblem of this novel's anxious protestation that appetite in a woman ("My arms are hungry for you") is a diabolic ("callous as a devil") inversion of natural order, and of the novel's fantastic but futile hope that maternity and feminine sexuality be divorced.

The aggressive mobility with which Lucy flaunts the encasement of gender norms generates in the Crew of Light a terrific defensive activity, as these men race to reinscribe, with a series of pointed instruments, the line of demarcation that enables the differentiation of gender. To save Lucy from the mobilization of desire, Van Helsing and the Crew of Light counterpose to Dracula's subversive series of penetrations a "therapeutic" series of their own, that sequence of transfusions intended to provide Lucy with the "brave man's blood," which is, as the text affirms, "the best thing on earth when a woman is in trouble" (180). There are in fact four transfusions, beginning with Arthur, who as Lucy's accepted suitor has the right of first infusion, and including Lucy's other two suitors (Dr. Seward, Quincey Morris) and Van Helsing himself. One of the established observations of *Dracula* criticism is that these therapeutic penetrations represent displaced marital (and martial) penetrations; indeed, the text is emphatic about this substitution of medical for sexual penetration. After the first transfusion, Arthur feels as if he and Lucy "had been really married and that she was his wife in the sight of God" (209); and Van Helsing, after his donation, calls himself a "bigamist" and Lucy "this so sweet maid . . . a polyandrist" (212). These transfusions, in short, are displaced seminal infusions[23] and constitute, in Auerbach's phrase, "the most convincing epithalamiums in the novel."[24]

As such, these transfusions mark the text's first anxious reassertion of the conventionally masculine prerogative of penetration; as Van Helsing tells Arthur before the first transfusion, "You are a man and it is a man we want" (148). Countering the dangerous mobility excited by Dracula's kiss, Van Helsing's penetrations restore to Lucy both the stillness appropriate to his sense of her gender and "the regular breathing of healthy sleep," a necessary correction of the loud "stertorous" breathing, the animal snorting, that the Count inspires. In this regard, the transfusions begin as the first repetitions of the hypertrophic phallic exercises through which the text seeks to secure its rigid schematization of difference. This work of differentiation both affirms a schematic bifurcation of gender and labors intensively to deny—to keep cloven—"the potential unbrokenness of a continuum between [the] homosocial and homosexual."[25] The novel's violent homosociality, its blaring thematics of heroic or chivalric male bonding, forfends against (even as it also inadvertently foretells) a specifically homosexual identification. The obvious male bonding in *Dracula* is precipitated by action—a good fight, a proud ethic, a great victory. Dedicated to a falsely exalted conception of woman, men combine fraternally to fulfill the collective "high duty" that motivates their "great quest" (261). Van Helsing, always the ungrammatical exegete, provides the apt analogy: "Thus we are ministers of God's own wish. . . . He have allowed us to redeem one soul already, and we go out as the old knights of the Cross to redeem more" (381). Van Helsing's chivalric analogy establishes this homosociality within an impeccable lineage signifying both moral rectitude and adherence to the limitation upon desire that this tradition encodes and enforces.

Yet beneath this screen or mask of sanitized fraternity a more libidinal bonding occurs, as male fluids find a protected pooling place in the body of a woman. We return to those serial transfusions that pretend to serve and protect "good women" while actually enabling the otherwise inconceivable interfusion of the blood that is semen too. The Crew of Light's penetration therapy only too schematically mirrors the vampiric method, as puncture for puncture Van Helsing counters the Count. Van Helsing's doubled penetrations, first the morphine injection that immobilizes the woman and then the infusion of masculine fluid, repeat Dracula's spatially doubled penetrations of Lucy's neck. And that morphine injection, which subdues the woman and improves her receptivity, curiously replicates the Count's strange hypnotic power; both men immobilize a woman before risking a penetration.[26] Moreover, each penetration bespeaks this same sense of danger. Dracula enters at the neck, Van Helsing at the limb; each evades available orifices and escapes the dangers of vaginal contact. The shared displacement is telling: to make your own holes is an ultimate arrogance, an assertion of penetrative prowess that nonetheless acknowledges, in the flight of its evasion, the threatening power imagined to inhabit woman's available openings, those secret places that no boy can fill. Woman's body readily accommodates masculine fear and desire, whether directly libidinal or culturally refined. We may say that Van Helsing and his tradition have polished teeth into hypodermic needles, a cultural refinement that masks violation as healing. Yet precisely this cultivation of violence, at once gynephobic and homophobic, ensures a heterosexually displaced homosexual identification. Displacement (this is a woman's body) and sublimation (these are "therapeutic" penetrations) enable the otherwise interdicted exchange of bodily fluids, just as in gang rape men share their semen in a location displaced sufficiently to divert the anxiety excited by a more direct union. *Dracula* again employs an apparently rigorous heterosexuality to represent anxious desire for a less conventional communion. The parallel here to Dracula's taunt ("Your girls that you all love are mine already; and through them you . . . shall be mine") is inescapable; in each case Lucy, the woman in the middle, connects libidinous males. The sheer fungibility here of violence and desire, of blood and semen, very eloquently bespeaks the homosexual agon driving—and driving mad—this text's heterosexual and homosocial mediations.

This repetitive contest (penetration, withdrawal; penetration, infusion) continues to be waged upon Lucy's accommodating body until Van Helsing exhausts his store of "brave men," whose generous gifts of blood ultimately fail to save Lucy from the mobilization of desire. But even the loss of this much blood does not enervate a male homosocial energy as indefatigable as the Crew of Light's, especially when it stands in the service of a tradition of "good women whose lives and whose truths may make good lesson [*sic*] for the children that are to be" (222). In the name of those good women and future children (very much the same children whose throats Lucy is now penetrating), Van Helsing will repeat, with an added emphasis, his assertion that penetration is a masculine prerogative. His logic of corrective penetration demands an escalation; the failure of the hypodermic needle motivates the stake. A woman, apparently, is better still than mobile, better dead than sexual:

> Arthur took the stake and the hammer, and when once his mind was set on action his hands never trembled nor even quivered. Van Helsing opened his missal and began to read, and Quincey and I followed as well as we could. Arthur placed the point over the heart, and as I looked I could see its dint in the white flesh. Then he struck with all his might.
>
> The Thing in the coffin writhed; and a hideous, blood-curdling screech came from the opened red lips. The body shook and quivered and twisted in wild contortions; the sharp white teeth champed together till the lips were cut and the mouth was smeared with a crimson foam. But Arthur never faltered. He looked like the figure of Thor as his untrembling arm rose and fell, driving deeper and deeper the mercy-bearing stake, whilst the blood from the pierced heart welled and spurted up around it. His face was set, and high duty seemed to shine through it; the sight of it gave us courage, so that our voices seemed to ring through the little vault.
>
> And then the writhing and quivering of the body became less, and the teeth ceased to champ, and the face to quiver. Finally it lay still. The terrible task was over. (258–59)

Here is the novel's real—and the woman's only—climax, its most violent and misogynistic moment, displaced roughly to the middle of the book so that the sexual threat may be repeated but its ultimate success denied: Dracula will not win Mina, second in his series of English seductions. The murderous phallicism of this passage clearly punishes Lucy for her transgressions of Van Helsing's gender code, even as it reassures the threatened homosociality of these very anxious males. Violence against the sexual woman here is intense, sensually imagined, ferocious in its detail. Note, for instance, the terrible dimple, the "dint in the white flesh," that recalls and completes Jonathan Harker's swoon of passivity at Castle Dracula ("I could feel . . . the hard dents of two sharp teeth, just touching and pausing there") and anticipates the technicolor consummation of the next paragraph. That paragraph, masking murder as "high duty," completes

Van Helsing's penetrative therapy by "driving deeper and deeper the mercy-bearing stake." One might question a mercy this destructive, this fatal, but Van Helsing's actions, always sanctified by the patriarchal textual tradition signified by "his missal," manage to "restore Lucy to us as a holy and not an unholy memory" (258). This enthusiastic correction of Lucy's monstrosity provides the Crew of Light with a double reassurance, effectively exorcising the threat of a mobile and hungering feminine sexuality while also countering the "passive" homosexual desire latent in the vampiric threat. The line dividing the male who penetrates from the woman who receives is literally reinscribed upon Lucy's chest. By disciplining Lucy and restoring to each gender its "proper" function, Van Helsing's pacification program at once paralyzes the female, disperses a specifically homosexual threat, and consolidates the male homosocial community. Here indeed is a process "wherein male rivals unite, refreshed in mutual support and definition, over the ruined carcass of a woman."[27]

The vigor and enormity of this penetration (Arthur driving the "round wooden stake," itself "some two and a half or three inches thick and about three feet long," resembles "the figure of Thor") do not bespeak Stoker's merely personal or idiosyncratic anxiety, but suggest as well a whole culture's uncertainty about the fluidity of gender roles. Consider, for instance, the following passage from Ellis's approximately contemporaneous *Studies in the Psychology of Sex.* Ellis, writing on "The Mechanism of Detumescence" (i.e., ejaculation and its mollifying effects), employs a figure that Stoker would have recognized as his own:

> Detumescence is normally linked to tumescence. Tumescence is the piling on of the fuel; detumescence is the leaping out of the devouring flame whence is lighted the torch of life to be handed on from generation to generation. The whole process is double yet single; it is exactly analogous to that by which a pile is driven into the earth by the raising and the letting go of a heavy weight which falls on the head of the pile. In tumescence the organism is slowly wound up and force accumulated; in the act of detumescence the accumulated force is let go and by its liberation the sperm-bearing instrument is driven home.[28]

Both Stoker and Ellis need to imagine so homely an occurrence as penile penetration as an event of mythic, or at least seismic, proportions. Ellis's pile driver, representing the powerful "sperm-bearing instrument," may dwarf even Stoker's already outsized member, but both serve to channel and finally "liberate" a tremendous "accumulated force." Employing a

Darwinian principle of interpretation, Ellis reads woman's body (much as we have seen Van Helsing do) as a natural sign—or, perhaps better, as a sign of nature's overriding reproductive intention:

> There can be little doubt that, as one or two writers have already suggested, the hymen owes its development to the fact that its influence is on the side of effective fertilization. It is an obstacle to the impregnation of the young female by immature, aged, or feeble males. The hymen is thus an anatomical expression of that admiration of force which marks the female in her choice of a mate. So regarded, it is an interesting example of the intimate manner in which sexual selection is really based on natural selection.[29]

Here evolutionary teleology supplants divine etiology as the interpretive principle governing nature's text. As a sign or "anatomical expression" within that text, the hymen signifies a woman's presumably natural "admiration of force" and her invitation to "the sperm-bearing instrument." Woman's body, structurally hostile to "immature, aged, or feeble males," simply begs for "effective fertilization." Lucy's body, too, reassures the Crew of Light with an anatomical expression of her admiration of force. Once fatally staked, Lucy is restored to "the so sweet that was." Dr. Seward describes the change:

> There in the coffin lay no longer the foul Thing that we had so dreaded and grown to hate that the work of her destruction was yielded to the one best entitled to it, but Lucy as we had seen her in her life, with her face of unequalled sweetness and purity. . . . One and all we felt that the holy calm that lay like sunshine over the wasted face and form was only an earthly token and symbol of the calm that was to reign for ever. (259–60)

This postpenetrative peace[30] denotes not merely the final immobilization of Lucy's body but also the corresponding stabilization of the dangerous signifier whose wandering had so threatened Van Helsing's gender code. Here a masculine interpretive community ("One and all we felt") reasserts the semiotic fixity that underwrites Lucy's function as the "earthly token and symbol" of eternal beatitude, of the heaven we can enter. Penetration, finally, is efficacious: a single stroke satisfies both the sexual and the textual needs of the Crew of Light.

Despite its placement in the middle of the text, this scene corresponds formally to the scene of expulsion that usually signals the end of the Gothic narrative. Here, of course, this scene signals not the end of the story but its continuation, since Dracula will now repeat his assault on another woman. Such displacement of the scene of expulsion requires explanation. Obviously this displacement subserves the text's anxiety about the direct representation of eroticism between males: Stoker simply could not represent so explicitly a violent phallic interchange between the Crew of Light and Dracula. In a by now familiar heterosexual mediation, Lucy receives the phallic correction that Dracula deserves. Indeed, as readers regularly note, the actual expulsion of the Count at novel's end is a disappointing anticlimax. Two rather perfunctory knife strokes suffice to dispatch him, as *Dracula* simply forgets the elaborate ritual of correction that vampirism had previously required. And the displacement of this scene performs at least two other functions: first, by establishing early the ultimate efficacy of Van Helsing's corrective technology, it reassures everyone—Stoker, his characters, the reader—that vampirism may indeed be vanquished, that its sexual threat, however powerful and intriguing, may be expelled; and second, by establishing this reassurance it permits the text to prolong and repeat its flirtation with vampirism, its ambivalent petition of sexual threat. In short, the displacement of the scene of expulsion provides a heterosexual locus for Van Helsing's demonstration of compensatory phallicism, even as it also extends the text's ambivalent homosexual play.

This extension of the text's fascination with monstrosity—during which Mina is threatened by but not finally recruited into vampirism—includes the novel's only explicit scene of vampiric seduction. Important enough to be twice presented, first by Seward as spectator and then by Mina as participant, the scene occurs in the Harker bedroom, where Dracula seduces Mina while "on the bed lay Jonathan Harker, his face flushed and breathing heavily as if in a stupor." The Crew of Light bursts into the room; the voice is Dr. Seward's:

> With his left hand he held both Mrs. Harker's hands, keeping them away with her arms at full tension; his right hand gripped her by the back of the neck, forcing her face down on his bosom. Her white nightdress was smeared with blood, and a thin stream trickled down the man's bare breast, which was shown by his torn-open dress. The attitude of the two had a terrible resemblance to a child forcing a kitten's nose into a saucer of milk to compel it to drink. (336)

In this initiation scene Dracula compels Mina into the pleasure of vampiric appetite and introduces her to a world where gender distinctions collapse, where male and female bodily fluids intermingle terribly. For

Mina's drinking is double here, both a "symbolic act of enforced fella-tion"[31] and a lurid nursing. That this is enforced fellation is made even clearer by Mina's own description of the scene a few pages later; she adds the graphic detail of the "spurt":

> With that he pulled open his shirt, and with his long sharp nails opened a vein in his breast. When the blood began to spurt out, he took my hands in one of his, holding them tight, and with the other seized my neck and pressed my mouth to the wound, so that I must either suffo-cate or swallow some of the—Oh, my God, my God! What have I done? (343)

That "Oh, my God, my God!" is deftly placed: Mina's verbal ejaculation supplants the Count's liquid one, leaving the fluid unnamed and en-couraging us to voice the substitution that the text implies—this blood is semen too. But this scene of fellation is thoroughly displaced. We are at the Count's breast nursing, encouraged once again to substitute white for red: "The attitude of the two had a terrible resemblance to a child forc-ing a kitten's nose into a saucer of milk." Such fluidity of substitution be-speaks a confusion of Dracula's sexual identity, or an interfusion of mas-culine and feminine functions, as Dracula here becomes a demonic mother offering not a breast but an open and bleeding wound. But if the Count's gender identification is (at least) double, then the open wound must be another displacement (the reader of *Dracula* must be as mobile as the Count himself). We are back in the genital region, this time a woman's, and we have the suggestion of a bleeding vagina. As William Veeder writes: "That Dracula makes Mina drink not from the nipple but from a slit gives a vaginal orientation to the moment and a menstrual cast to the blood."[32] The image of red and voluptuous lips, with their slow trickle of blood, has, of course, always harbored this potential.

In this scene anatomical displacement and the conflation of bodily flu-ids forcefully erase the demarcation separating the masculine and the fem-inine; here is *Dracula*'s most explicit representation of the anxieties ex-cited by the vampiric kiss. Fluidity of desire and mobility of gender identification are at once released and arrested in a fierce tableau of pre-Oedipal orality that recalls the text's earlier, barely liminal acknowledg-ment of a more immediate homosexual fellation. Recalling the prehistory of their homosocial/pederastic bonding, Van Helsing says to Seward:

> Tell your friend [Arthur] that when that time you suck from my wound so swiftly the poison of the gangrene from the knife that our other

friend, too nervous, let slip, you did more for him when he wants my
aids and you call for them than all his great fortune could do [*sic*]. (138)

Veeder convincingly reads these lines as a subliminal indication of "an
originary ritual intercourse" in which "no woman need constitute a con-
duit of male desire." As "the lips of the willing male assure the continuity of patriarchy," Veeder continues, intermasculine fellation is disclosed
as "the ultimate origin of male bonding in *Dracula.*" Acknowledging the
perspicacity of this observation, we need only remark that it is precisely
this vestigial origin that *Dracula* continues to closet through its insistent
heterosexual mediations. But this great drinking scene marks Dracula's
last moment of empowerment, his final demonstration of dangerous potency; after this, he will vamp no one. The narrative now moves mechanically to repudiate the pleasures that have generated so much text; after a hundred tedious pages of pursuit and flight, *Dracula* perfunctorily
expels the Count.

Sentences with an as yet unspecified subject: "One morning while still in
bed (whether still half asleep or already awake I cannot remember), I had
a feeling which, thinking about it later when fully awake, struck me as
highly peculiar. It was the idea that it really must be rather pleasant to be
a woman succumbing to intercourse. This idea was so foreign to my
whole nature that I may say I would have rejected it with indignation if
fully awake; from what I have experienced since I cannot exclude the possibility that some external influences were at work to implant this idea in
me."[33] These autobiographical sentences, written in 1900 about a certain
male patient's psychic events of 1894 and years following, resonate deeply
with *Dracula.* The strident pseudo-opposition between a dangerously
permeable crepuscular consciousness and an indignantly foreclosed fully
conscious state; the pleasurable insertion into the former of a conventionally inverted desire, and a fierce repudiation from the latter of the already entertained (and always entertaining) "submission"; the haunting
sense that "external influences [are] at work" in one's being—all of this
corresponds with provocative exactitude to the ingenious delusional
structure of Stoker's perduring Gothic fantasy. A specifically "feminine"
desire to "succumb to intercourse" arouses a specifically "masculine"
protest, all within a single schismatic subject. Recall Jonathan Harker on

his back at Castle Dracula: "I could feel . . . the hard dents of two sharp teeth, just touching and pausing there. I closed my eyes in a languorous ecstasy and waited—waited with a beating heart." Recall as well the terrible defensive activity—needle, lancet, stake—that ensues in the wake of this desire to "succumb."

The sentences adduced above derive not from Stoker's *Dracula* but rather from the *Memoirs* of Daniel Paul Schreber, that famously paranoid "homosexual" judge whose case history inspired Freud to write a particularly brilliant version of his totalizing Oedipal narrative.[34] Freud never met, knew, or psychoanalyzed Schreber; like the reader of *Dracula,* Freud must ground his "Attempts at Interpretation" upon already written and assembled texts, primarily the 1903 German edition of Schreber's *Memoirs of My Nervous Illness,* an astonishing document whose spacious appendices include clinical reports composed by the director of the Sonnenstein Asylum (where Schreber was incarcerated), Schreber's own "Statement of his Case" (July, 1901), and the Court Judgment of July, 1902 that restored to Schreber his civil rights; Freud also seems to have had an unacknowledged correspondence with one Dr. Stegmann of Dresden, who conveyed to Freud personal information not available in the published texts. "How these papers have been placed in sequence," the headnote to *Dracula* begins, "will be made clear in the reading of them. All needless matters have been eliminated, so that a history at variance with the possibilities of latter-day belief may stand forth as simple fact." Something very like this prophylactic editorial strategy, which presents the "simple fact" of monstrosity as someone else's perceptual achievement, governed Freud's rearticulation of the Schreber documents. "Since paranoics cannot be compelled to overcome their internal resistances, and since in any case they only say what they choose to say, it follows that this is precisely a disorder in which a written report or a printed case history can take the place of personal acquaintance with the patient" (PN, 9). Even if we concede to Freud the sheer critical and analytic convenience of this statement—which quite obviously affords him a priori protection against the turbulence of homosexual transference and countertransference, even as it also forfends against the indignity of a Dora-like "No"—we must nonetheless demur, if only in passing, at Freud's claim about the paranoid's self-authenticating transparency—that "in any case they only say what they choose to say." Schreber, after all, was "not there to associate,"[35] and what Freud presents in "Psycho-Analytic Notes" is not quite what Schreber "himself" chose to say but rather a formidable condensation of Schreber's narrative material—his fierce trans-sexual millennialism, his delusional subjection to the "Rays of God," his obsessive anality, his perverse redaction of the Christ story. During Freud's renarrativizing, which submits all possibilities to the "latter-day belief" of psychoanalysis, the errancies of Schreber's desire are carefully inserted and circulated within the familiar triangular frame: Narcissus everywhere is stepson to Oedipus.

A skeletal recapitulation of the Schreber "facts" is in order. Daniel Paul Schreber: born in Leipzig on 25 July 1842; married in 1878, a childless marriage; in 1893 appointed *Senatspräsident* (a judge presiding over a court of appeals) at Dresden; institutionalized, both voluntarily and involuntarily, for much of his adult life (about fifteen years total) in various psychiatric clinics and asylums (Dosen, Leipzig, Lindenhof, Sonnenstein); attended at Leipzig by Dr. Paul Emil Flechsig (1847–1929), eminent professor of psychiatry, for whom Schreber developed a deep libidinal attachment that Freud would specify as the precipitating cause of the patient's para-noid delusion; wrote *Memoirs* from 1900 to 1902, published them in 1903; on 14 July 1902 the Royal Superior Country Court of Dresden granted Schreber's appeal for rescission of involuntary tutelage at Sonnenstein; af-ter his release Schreber withdrew into his delusional condition, "an ex-tremely disordered and largely inaccessible state [that lasted] until his death, after gradual physical deterioration, in the spring of 1911—only a short time before the publication of Freud's paper."[36] Besieged by an in-tractable delusion of Byzantine intricacy, Schreber's sanity was overcome by the belief that his (anatomically male) body was being compelled by God (or the "nerves" or "rays" of God) to suffer a prolonged and painful transsexualization, a piecemeal conversion into woman for reproductive millennial purposes. Working entirely from texts, Freud diagnosed Schreber's illness as a delusional paranoia (*dementia paranoides*) of ho-mosexual origin, the paranoia or "persecution-complex" being the in-verted or reversed image of Schreber's unappeasable homosexual longing (for his dead father, for his dead brother, for the paternal imago as em-bodied by the psychiatrist Flechsig).

How was it, then, that Schreber "entered into peculiar relations with God" (*M*, 43) and his minion Flechsig? Through an inescapable discourse of the "nerves," which for Schreber constitute the material base of all "voluptuousness" and of which his bifurcated God (one higher, one lower) is entirely composed: "Apart from normal human language there is also a kind of *nerve-language* of which, as a rule, the healthy human being is not aware. . . . In my case, however, since my nervous illness took the above-mentioned critical turn, my nerves have been set in motion *from without* incessantly and without any respite. . . . I myself first felt this influence as emanating from Professor Flechsig. . . . This influence has in the course of years assumed forms more and more contrary to the Order of the World and to man's natural right to be master of his own nerves" (*M*, 69–70; italics and capitalization original). The penultimate result of this nervous invasion is what Schreber terms "unmanning," or *entman-nung*, by which he indicates neither emasculation nor castration precisely, but rather his own becoming-woman at the hands of God: "During that time [November 1895] the signs of a transformation into a woman became so marked on my body, that I could no longer ignore the imminent goal at which the whole development was aiming. In the immediately preced-ing nights my male sexual organ might actually have been retracted had I not resolutely set my will against it. . . . Soul-voluptuousness had be-come so strong that I myself received the impression of a female body, first on my arms and hands, later on my legs, bosom, buttocks, and other parts of my body" (*M*, 148).

As might reasonably be expected, Schreber's involuntary "unmanning" generates a stupendous panoply of subject-effects, of which the following must concern us here. God's imperative effeminization of the male man-dates and justifies an absolute "voluptuousness," an erotic condition that for Schreber corresponds to the feminine: "An excess of voluptuousness would render man [i.e., the male] unfit to fulfil his other obligations; it would prevent him from ever rising to higher mental and moral perfec-tion . . . [but] *For me such moral limits to voluptuousness no longer exist, in-deed in a certain sense the reverse applies.* In order not to be misunderstood, I must point out that when I speak of my duty to cultivate voluptuous-ness, I *never mean any sexual desires towards other human beings (females) least of all sexual intercourse,* but that I have to imagine myself as man and woman in one person having intercourse with myself" (*M*, 208; italics original). Despite the ethical release implicit in this, Schreber's "manly honour" stages a ferocious masculine protest, not least because Schreber regards his transsexualization as a biological and spiritual regression. ("The male state of Blessedness [is] superior to the female state" because the latter consists "mainly in an uninterrupted state feeling of volup-tuousness" [*M*, 52].) Hence, the patient argues, "one may imagine how my whole sense of manliness and manly honour, my entire moral being, rose up against" this transformation (*M,* 76). Conversely, however, once Schreber is convinced of the absolute invincibility of the process (*God's will be done*), he is then free to celebrate the woman he has resisted becoming: "I consider it my right and in a certain sense my duty to cultivate feminine feelings which I am able to do by the presence of nerves of voluptuousness. . . . As soon as I am alone with God, if I may so express myself, I must . . . strive to give the divine rays the impression of a woman in the height of sexual delight" (*M,* 207–8). Finally, Schreber's consciousness is tormented by anxiety over the ultimate fate of his newly feminized body. Will "Miss Schreber" (*M,* 119) simply be handed over "in the manner of a female harlot" (*M,* 77) to some unidentified "human being for sexual misuse" and then "left to rot" (*M,* 75)? Or will the anguish that has overwhelmed the patient jurist finally be redeemed by an abundant compensation: say, perhaps, "fertilization by divine rays for the purpose of creating new human beings" (*M,* 148)?

The uncanny affinities conjoining *Dracula* and Schreber's delusional narrative do not derive merely from the (probably) transhistorical fantasy of "passive homosexual" intercourse, whether anally, orally, or "vaginally" enacted; rather, they proceed from the specifically gynephobic and homophobic itinerary to which nineteenth-century European culture subjected such desire. Within this itinerary, the erotic activation of the male body's orifices, its portals of "voluptuousness," entrains an intolerable corollary: the relinquishment of a "natural" and upright masculine privilege and the assumption of an axiomatically degraded femininity. Such is the castrating logic of the inversion metaphor, to which Schreber submitted with an unexampled, an almost parodic, rigor. In this regard Schreber's persecutory paranoia may be said to have been absolutely lucid: given the configurations of gender and desire at his disposal, Schreber recognized fantasmatically that he would have to submit, even at the expense of his own sanity, to a compulsory transsexualization in order thereby to ground or legitimate his desire for "passive" homosexual intercourse. And so, as if to embody the severity appropriate to his profession, Schreber assumed his castration with a gusto indistinguishable from disgust. Listen, for instance, to the "Rays of God" as they deride the very being they are in the process of feminizing: "So *this* sets up to have been a Senatspräsident, this person who lets himself be f---d!" Or again: "Don't you feel ashamed in front of your wife?" (PN, 20). Here the derogation of civil and familial masculine authority—the derogation, that is, of the Name and the Law of the Father—proceeds from Schreber's exquisite recognition of what Freud would acknowledge only thereafter to deny: the ineradicable presence within the male body of other than phallic drives. The very irreducibility of the "component instincts," themselves a radical Freudian insight, ensures that the male body too must remain a "sex which is not one."

Of course, as I have been stressing, the phallocratic order has an explanation ready to hand for what it must regard as the disastrous invagination of the male: somewhere, however occulted, a woman is lurking, interned in the body or soul or psyche of "the homosexual." *Anima muliebris virili corpore inclusa* is only the most transparently formulaic instance of this carceral strategy; another is represented by the all-too-familiar arguments for a vestigial "bisexuality" whose theoretical function is to shunt errant homosexual desire back onto straight heterosexual tracks; but the subtlest manifestation of this strategy is the developmental etiology through which Freud constructs the male homosexual as a gender-poor subject who, having adored the mother without sufficient Oedipal interdiction, thereafter introjects her image into his own being, thus ensuring both the femininity of his identification and the fundamental heterosexuality of his nonetheless homosexual practice. In each of these instances, phallocratic interpretation deploys a misogynistic notion of "the feminine" to remand male homosexuality to the shadow realm of the *pseudo,* the *almost,* the *not quite;* for no matter how you cut the figure, you will disclose the operations of an axiomatic heterodynamism in which a feminized subject is always seeking—can only seek—a masculine subject. Guy Hocquenghem has provided the definitive blueprint of this disciplinary machinery: "The perversity of homosexual desire is rooted in the fact that it constitutes the caricature or negative of the heterosexual object choice; it acts as a feedback to the latter, as if testifying to the strength of the [heterosexual] connection between sexual desire and sexual object."[37]

It was the peculiar "genius" of Schreber's delusional paranoia, just as it was of Stoker's more productively deranged imagination, to have made manifest the sheer brutalizing artifice implicit in this feminizing mechanism—a mechanism that appropriates a particularly hostile definition of woman in order to forfend the homosexual embrace. Just as Stoker's fantasy deploys a monstrous femininity in order to mediate an otherwise unrepresentable desire for sameness, Schreber's "ingenious delusional system" (PN, 14) requires the interposition—literally, the piecemeal fabrication, nerve by nerve—of a woman whose modesty of service is hetero-sexually to enable Schreber's otherwise homosexual desire. But whereas Stoker's narrative dispenses its mediations of desire through character dif-ference (through Lucy, Mina, the weird sisters), Schreber's perverse and rigorous condensation interns the mediatrix within the limits of his own fantasmatic but very sentient body. So convinced is Schreber of his trans-formation that he "calls for a medical examination, in order to establish the fact that his whole body has nerves of voluptuousness dispersed over it from head to foot, a state of things which is only to be found, in his opinion, in the female body, whereas, in the male, to the best of his knowledge, nerves of voluptuousness exist only in the sexual organs and their immediate vicinity." (PN, 17, 33). Freud reads Schreber's delusion, no doubt correctly, as perverse wish fulfillment: it is "clear beyond a doubt that his delusion of being transformed into a woman was nothing else than a realization of the content of [the] dream" that, in Schreber's words, "it really must be very nice to be a woman submitting to the act of copulation" (PN, 33). But what Freud does not read is just how Schre-ber's delusion "realizes," not a transhistorical truth about "passive" ho-mosexuality, but rather the gender enforcements of the cultural itinerary that identifies homosexual desire with femininity and femininity with castration, or "unmanning."

Precisely because "passive" desire is at once intolerable given an inter-nalized ideology of masculine inviolability and inescapable given the very porousness of all, even male bodies, Schreber must reconstitute homo-sexual desire as a kind of generative castration. "I became clearly aware that the Order of Things imperatively demanded my emasculation, whether I personally liked it or no, and that no *reasonable* course lay open to me but to reconcile myself to the thought of being transformed into a woman. The further consequence of my emasculation could, of course, only be my impregnation by divine rays to the end that a new race of men might be created" (PN, 20–21; italics original). Pressing his "emascula-tion" to its furthest consequence ("my impregnation"), Schreber's delu-sion reconstitutes his obsessive anality as millennial reproduction, thereby submitting his errant desire to a compulsory "Order of Things" that is homosexual in its origin, heterosexual in its method, and procreative in its telos. This, it should be clear, is very much the same order of things that governs the perverse erotic distributions of *Dracula,* where homo-sexual desire also suffers the violence of heterosexual enforcement, where a luxuriously passive desire also provokes an emphatic inscription of gender difference, and where an overwhelming parent figure also threatens to become the "father or furtherer of a new order of beings" (360). But Schreber, whose fantasy of passivity and transformation outstrips even Stoker's, pushed the limits of culture *into* his own being and body, which thereafter enacted both a literalist repetition and a fantasmatic critique of heterosexist ideology and its mechanisms of enforcement.

And what of Freud? Where do his recognitions lie? Somewhere, we might say, in the same bed with Schreber, sharing the paranoid's knowledge, repeating his ambivalences. Without doubt Freud must be credited with the radical insight into "the mechanism of paranoia," the recognition that *in heterosexist culture* persecutory paranoia and "homosexuality" stand in a reciprocating, mutually identifying relation. But of course Freud's analysis does not admit the phrase I have just italicized: in a classic, transhistoricizing articulation of his notions of fixation, repression, and projection, Freud identifies Schreber's delusional paranoia as the inverted precipitate of the libido's homosexual component: "The exciting cause of his illness, then, was an outburst of homosexual libido; the object of this libido was probably from the very first his doctor, Flechsig; and his struggles against the libidinal impulse produced the conflict which gave rise to the symptoms" (PN, 43). If Freud's agonistic language here ("outbreak," "struggle," "conflict") very well captures the exigent press of Schreber's condition, it nonetheless fails to acknowledge the historical and cultural dimensions of that distress. The "conflict" here seems securely grounded in an essential antithesis of (all) culture and (any) homosexual libido; Freud has foreclosed the possibility of reading Schreber's delusion as a fierce and self-destructive critique of dominant culture. Some pages later, extrapolating from the Schreber case, Freud continues:

> We should be inclined to say that what was characteristically paranoid about the illness was the fact that the patient, as a means of warding off a homosexual wishful phantasy, reacted precisely with delusions of persecution of this kind.
>
> These considerations therefore lend an added weight to the circumstance that we are in point of fact driven by experience to attribute to homosexual wishful phantasies an intimate (perhaps an invariable) relation to this particular form of disease. (PN, 59)

Certainly it is hard to argue with the clarity of Freud's perception here, at least as it regards Schreber's "particular form of disease," and certainly lines like these corroborate Sedgwick's claim that Freud's analysis of

Schreber discloses paranoia as "the psychosis that makes graphic the mechanisms of homophobia."[38] Sedgwick's cagey insertion of the post-Freudian neologism "homophobia" is apposite here, for it is precisely within the conceptual space opened by the lexical shift from "homosexuality" to "homophobia" that we must situate our critique of Freud's analysis of the homosexual psychogenesis of persecutory paranoia. Strictly speaking, of course, Freud nowhere promulgates an ideological critique of "the mechanism of homophobia"; rather he presents a discourse that can trace or "make graphic" a constitutive homophobia precisely because his discourse so unselfconsciously incorporates the very mechanisms it would also seem to be on the verge of disclosing and deconstructing. Nowhere in "Psycho-Analytic Notes," for instance, does Freud problematize the essentialist linkage of femininity and male homosexual desire; indeed, his analysis of the homosexual (as opposed to the homophobic) etiology of persecutory paranoia presupposes the correctness of this linkage. Similarly his uncritical adoption of the cruelly cathected language of "perversion" to designate presumably "neutral" psychoanalytic categories very well exemplifies the discursive ambivalence that must obtain when culturally specific phallocentric assumptions are put in the service of so extreme a transhistoricizing ambition as Freud's.[39] Oedipus of course is the large example. The declension of desire itself from the Oedipal schema tautologically ensures that all desires will recirculate within the triangle, however preposterous or displaced the versions of the triangle may be. (The uncanny, as Freud observed elsewhere, *always* comes home.) Hence the ready genealogical tracing of Schreber's psychosis: symptom formation (God's transsexualizing intervention) → (repressed and tertiary) desire for Flechsig → (repressed and secondary) desire for dead elder brother → (repressed and originary) desire for Father. The very collapsibility of desires within this regressive trajectory, their inescapable reference to the family romance, returns us to *Dracula,* where the vampire is about to be formally expelled, but not before being reintegrated within the domestic economy as, precisely, "one of us."

As heir to the narrative's ambivalence, the reader should leave *Dracula* with a troubled sense of the differences separating the forces of darkness and the forces of light. In its closing pages, *Dracula* deploys the venerable "paranoid Gothic" trope of reversing the roles of pursuer and pursued, of desiring (or murderous) subject and desired (or murdered) object, in order to implicate both in a specifically homosexual (and homophobic) identification; the homosexualization of persecutory paranoia is, as we have seen, the psychoanalytic redaction of this trope. Of course the closure of *Dracula,* in granting ultimate victory to Van Helsing and a dusty death to the Count, emphatically ratifies the simplistic opposition between the competing conceptions of force and desire, but even Dracula's final dessication suggests his dispersal or infiltration into the forces of light. Where monstrosity had once been, there normality shall be. But surely this impulse toward a baffled identification, anxious as it is, comes as no surprise within a text whose relation to its resident monster(s) has been ambivalently cathected all along, characterized at once by an obsessive overdetermination of difference and a transgressive desire for sameness. In a justly famous tableau, *Dracula* speculates upon such anxiogenic identification. Jonathan Harker, standing before his shaving glass, puzzles over a certain absence in an image:

> This time there could be no error, for the man was close to me, and I could see him over my shoulder. But there was no reflection of him in the mirror! The whole room behind me was displayed; but there was no sign of a man in it, except myself. (37)

Caught here in the uncanny interchange of the same and the different, Harker literally reflects the text's disturbing power of ambiguation. The very (non)image of Dracula's difference ("no reflection of him in the mirror") "displays" an identification that Harker himself can see and speak, but not understand: "no sign" of man or vampire "except myself."

So insistently does *Dracula* inscribe this trope of baffled identification that it repeats the pattern on its final page. Harker, writing in a postscript clearly meant to compensate for his assumption at Castle Dracula of a "feminine" passivity, announces his—and the text's—last efficacious penetration:

> Seven years ago we all went through the flames; and the happiness of some of us since then is, we think, well worth the pain we endured. It is an added joy to Mina and to me that our boy's birthday is the same day as that on which Quincey Morris died. His mother holds, I know, the secret belief that some of our brave friend's spirit has passed into him. His bundle of names links all our little band of men together; but we call him Quincey. (449)

As Veeder remarks, Harker's terminal note "recapitulates the story that patriarchs want to hear"; it "provides both a tableau of domestic unity and a story which shapes the future by organizing the past." And thus to shape the future requires a line of succession. As the "legitimate" offspring of Jonathan and Mina Harker, Little Quincey may arrive as little more than a name, a coded patronym, but his appearance on the scene has the force of an annunciation: the "natural" order has been restored, conventional gender roles have been rectified. Little Quincey's official genesis, then, is "obviously" heterosexual, and his arrival resoundingly affirms the reproductive order. But this is a reproductive heterosexuality whose larger cultural burdens include male homosocial articulation, here materialized at the level of the polyandrous signifier: "His bundle of names links all our little band of men together." In this text the linking of names also points retrospectively to the bundling of male bodies, specifically to an extravagant blood bond of the kind Lawrence would later call *Blutbrüdershaft*. On this reading, Little Quincey comes to represent the very excess that the reproductive order sponsors but refuses to affirm outright: he is the fantasy child of those sexualized transfusions, son of an illicit and closeted homosexual union that the text now underhandedly admits in the form of an almost farcically homosocial patronym "link[ing] all our little band of men together." Little Quincey's densely saturated name thus constitutes this text's last and subtlest articulation of its "secret belief" in homosexual insemination: its belief that "a brave man's blood," sublimated into "our brave friend's spirit," may then "pass into" the Oedipalized son whose filial obligation is to remember the Name(s) of the Father(s) even as he forgets the homosexual desire that he must hereafter continue to relay.

The other telling feature here is the novel's last prophylactic displacement—its substitution of Mina, who ultimately refused sexualization by Dracula, for Lucy, who was sexualized, vigorously penetrated, and consequently destroyed. We may say that Little Quincey was luridly conceived in the veins of Lucy Westenra and then deftly transposed into the purer body of Mina Harker. Here, in the last of its many displacements, *Dracula* ratifies the double postulate that governs its representation of eros: first, the matriphobic postulate that successful filiation requires the expulsion of all "monstrous" (that is, of any) sexuality in woman; second, the affined homophobic postulate that all desire, however mobile or polyvalent it may secretly be, must subject itself to heterosexual configuration. In this regard, Stoker's fable repeats in passive, ventriloquial fashion the heterosexualizing ideology of his age. As we have seen, even revisionists of same-sex desire like Ellis and Symonds could not reconfigure such desire without replicating, at whatever level of metaphor, the basic structure of the heterosexual paradigm; and surely Schreber, despite the heroic magnitude of his conflict, could not elude the alienating enforcements either of the inversion model or its later psychoanalytic redaction. In the parallel "cases" of Schreber and *Dracula,* male homosexual desire, whatever its inclinations to cruise, is compelled to stay home and assume an essentially heterosexual, familial definition.

In his reading of Schreber's paranoia, Freud even fantasizes that a specific reproductive failure, a break or rupture in the line of Oedipal succession, stands as the proximate cause of the "outbreak" of Schreber's homosexual libido:

> His marriage, which he describes as being in other respects a happy one, brought him no children; and in particular it brought him no son who might have consoled him for the loss of his father and brother and upon whom he might have drained off his unsatisfied homosexual affections. His family line threatened to die out, and it seems that he felt no little pride in his birth and lineage. . . . Dr. Schreber may have formed a phantasy that if he were a woman he would manage the business of having children more successfully; and he may thus have found his way back into the feminine attitude towards his father which he had exhibited in the earliest years of his childhood. If that were so, then his delusion that as a result of his emasculation the world was to be peopled with "a new race of men, born from the spirit of Schreber"—a delusion the realization of which he was continually postponing to a more and more remote future—would also be designed to offer him an escape from his childlessness. (PN, 57)

No passage could limn more precisely the triangular recirculations of homosexual desire, whose "correct" pedophilic object, the son, must inherit and transmit (but never enjoy) a structurally inescapable homosexual flux; the Schrebers' failure to complete the Oedipal triangle, to engender its necessary third member, requires in turn that Schreber stage the entire drama as intrapsychic agon—as, that is, the fantasmatic history of his own millennial "unmanning." Stoker's novel of course closes with a more conventional Oedipal "reconciliation," dutifully providing for the Crew of Light a son "upon whom [they] might have drained off [their] unsatisfied homosexual affections." But in *Dracula,* this normalizing Oedipal itinerary yields a truly perverse telos in Little Quincey, a child whose conception remains curiously immaculate yet disturbingly lurid: son of his fathers' violations. Never quite "naturally" engendered, Little Quincey descends from and into violence; the pleasures of his homosexual engendering "may be inferrable, but only from the forms of violence that surround them."[40]

4

Alias Bunbury

Desire and Termination in The Importance
of Being Earnest

No living word relates to its object in a *singular* way: between
the word and its object, between the word and the speaking
subject, there exists an elastic environment of other, alien
words about the same object, the same theme, and this is an
environment that is often difficult to penetrate. It is precisely in
the process of living interaction with this specific environment
that the word may be individualized and given stylistic shape.
—Mikhail Bakhtin, "Discourse in the Novel"

Besides, now that I know you to be a confirmed Bunburyist I
naturally want to talk to you about Bunbury. I want to tell you
the rules.
—Algernon to Jack in *The Importance of Being Earnest*

A vampire's is not the only kiss to initiate a metamorphosis in appetite.
Consider the influential kiss both "suffered" and enjoyed by "H.C.,
American, aged 28, of independent means, unmarried, the elder of two
children." As case history XXVII in Havelock Ellis's *Sexual Inversion,*
H.C.'s autobiographical narrative tells the story of what H.C. calls "my
developing inversion," a process whose early stages witness his puzzle-
ment before the dawning recognition that women are to him "as likable
as ever, but no longer desirable." H.C.'s equivocation here is historically
poised:

> Soon after this the Oscar Wilde case was bruiting about. The newspaper
> accounts of it, while illuminating, flashed upon me no light of self-reve-
> lation; they only amended some idle conjectures as to certain mystic
> vices I had heard whispered of. Here and there a newspaper allusion still
> too recondite was painstakingly clarified by an effeminate fellow-student,

who, I fancy now, would have shown no reluctance had I begged him to adduce practical illustration. I purchased, too, photographs of Oscar Wilde, scrutinizing them under the unctuous auspices of this same emasculate and blandiloquent mentor. If my interest in Oscar Wilde arose from any other emotion than the rather morbid curiosity then almost universal, I was not conscious of it.

Erotic dreams, precluded hitherto by coition, came now to beset me. The persons of these dreams were (and still are) invariably women, with this one remembered exception: I dreamed that Oscar Wilde, one of my photographs of him incarnate, approached me with a buffoon languishment and perpetrated *fellatio,* an act verbally expounded shortly before my oracle. For a month or more, recalling this dream disgusted me.[1]

Wilde comes to this dreamer, as to his readers, neither as "himself" nor even quite as his own simulacrum. Situated from the beginning within (indeed, as) an oscillating exchange of representations, "Oscar Wilde" surfaces in H.C.'s narrative as a precariously overdetermined signifier. He emerges both as the dominated subject of "the Oscar Wilde case," the very public object of political subjugation, his body disciplined and his name appropriated as a new alias for those nameless "mystic vices I had heard whispered of," and as the volatizing subject of those uncannily "clarifying" photographs, themselves the object of a bewildered "scrutiny" whose dreaming eye finally discloses an agent provocateur bringing liminal homosexual self-recognition to oracular crisis. In either case, each the palpable obverse or complement of the other, the signifier "Wilde" encodes not homosexual desire *per se* but rather a whole history of tendentious citation: "newspaper accounts," anonymous whisperings, "idle conjectures," "unctuous" explications by that "emasculate and blandiloquent mentor," those fetishized photographs. Caught from the beginning in a reciprocating exchange of repudiation and identification, of desire and disgust, of ignorance and "self-revelation," Wilde's discursively appropriated body circulates in H.C.'s text as "the inscribed surface of events (traced by language and dissolved by ideas)" and "the locus of a dissociated self."[2] Thus the scene of fellation, as a kind of flickering homosexual anagnorisis, marks H.C.'s assumption of, and insertion into, his culture's available narrative of "self"-disclosure. In "falling heir to inversion," H.C. inherits not so much the occulted truth of homosexual being (the "incubation," as he calls it, "of my perverse instinct") as he does access to a historically specific narrative trajectory. Soon after his dream

The antipodes of the sexual sphere turned more and more toward the light of my tolerance. Inversion, till now strained with a slight repugnance, became esthetically colorless at last, and then delicately retinted, at first solely with pity for its victims, but finally, the color deepening, with half-conscious inclination to attach it to myself as a remote contingency. This revolution, however, was not without external impetus. The prejudiced tone of a book I was reading, Krafft-Ebing's *Psychopathia Sexualis,* by prompting resentment, led me on to sympathy. My championing, purely abstract though it was to begin with, none the less involved my looking at things with eyes hypothetically inverted—an orientation for the sake of argument. After a while, insensibly and at no one moment, hypothesis merged into reality: I myself was inverted. That occasional and fictitious inversion had never, I believe, superposed this true inversion; rather a true inversion, those many years dormant, had simply responded finally to a stimulus strong and prolonged enough, as a man awakens when he is loudly called.[3]

This passage is remarkable for its equivocal appeal to rhetoric and nature as modes of identification; we may even say that the work of the passage, as of the inversion metaphor generally, is to subsume the former under the latter. On the one hand, a revisionist or "reverse" reading of dominant discourse (here represented by Krafft-Ebing) yields a rhetorical or tropological "inversion"—a conscious political recognition that subjects "the antipodes of the sexual sphere" to a chromatic slide, a cognitive unanchoring motivated by reason, reading, "pity," "sympathy." This inversion, or "revolution," implicitly figures sexual identity as tropologically grounded—and, therefore, as abstractable, manipulable, traversable: "it involved my looking at things with eyes hypothetically inverted—an orientation for the sake of argument." But on the other hand, the remainder of the paragraph dismantles this very emphasis upon tropological inversion, or "sympathetic" transformation, and displaces it with a counterfiction of authentic origination, the circumstantial "incubation" of a naturally inscribed "perverse instinct." Imperceptibly and "at no one moment," H.C. claims, "that occasional and fictitious inversion" miraculously opens onto a deeper ontological ground, an occulted or closeted "reality": his "true inversion, these many years dormant, had simply responded . . . as a man awakens when he is loudly called." In this transition, the vertigo of tropological sexuality yields to the enforcing call of a new name, a transfixing univocality, a singular identity: "I myself was inverted." Ellis, whose analytic commentary frames this and the other case

histories in *Sexual Inversion,* is quick to affirm this essentializing interpretation: "a critical reading of this history suggests that the apparent control over the sexual impulse by reason is merely a superficial phenomenon. Here, as ever, reason is but a tool in the hands of the passions. The
apparent causes are really the result; we are witnessing here the gradual
emergence of a retarded homosexual impulse."[4]

Wilde of course did not live long enough to savor the inadvertent
splendor of that "tool in the hands of the ["retarded"] passions." Had he
survived, and once his rippling laughter had subsided, he would no doubt
have renewed the merriment by parodying, as only he could, the dehis-
toricizing move that Ellis and H.C. find so reassuring, so fundamental to
the stabilization of inverted identity. He would have recalled to H.C. the
same displacement that H.C. had stressed in his scene of fellation: the displacement that "grounds" experience and identity not in nature, not in
the disclosure or discovery of absolute origin, but rather in the dizzying
oscillation of persons and representations, of identities and signifiers, as
when, in *The Importance of Being Earnest,* baby Jack is "quite literally exchanged for writing in the cloakroom of Victoria Station, his absent-
minded governess having substituted for his person a three-volume novel
'of more than usually repulsive sentimentality.' "[5] In this farcical exchange
of being and text, of self and writing, the authority of the origin is punningly abrogated, preposterously reversed, as the sober Lady Bracknell
makes deliriously clear: "Until yesterday," she says as she pauses before
the scandal of Jack's nonoriginary origins, "I had no idea that there were
any families or persons whose origin was a Terminus." Like a decon-
structionist before her time, a proper Derrida in late-Victorian drag, Lady
Bracknell exposes the irreducible secondariness of an origin that, in coming first, should but cannot authorize all that comes after. In Derrida's id-
iom, it is the nonorigin that is originary: "the origin did not even disap-
pear . . . it was never constituted except reciprocally by a nonorigin, the
trace, which thus becomes the origin of the origin."[6]

Lady Bracknell's joke (which is, as we shall see, cognate with the pun
governing the verbal slippage in the play's title) delegitimates any claim
of ontological authority or natural reference: first because it punningly in-
stalls a death or termination at the origin of male subjectivity, as when,
to cite only the most emphatic tragic instance, Oedipus murders his father at a crossroads or terminus in order thereby to inherit the opportunity of a plagued adulthood; and second because, punningly again, it
insinuates into the origin not a datum or a truth but rather the self-

conscious play of terms and terminologies, discourses and palpable fictions, of which Miss Prism's sentimental triple-decker is only the most
ponderous instance. Once the origin has been terminated in this way, its
grave solemnities mockingly redistributed as the "trivial" pleasure tra-
versing a pun on death and writing, no "serious" appeal can be made to
natural reference or natural ground.[7] The very possibility of a "true inversion," whose ontology must be grounded not in trope but in nature,
is laughingly dismissed by a pun—and a play—whose deepest insistence
is that individual and collective identities, especially sexual ones, are based
upon and secured by arbitrary and "unnatural" constructs: terms, terminations, termini, terminologies.

The difference between Wilde and H.C. may be put schematically as
follows: writing against all essentialist notions of being, inverted or otherwise, Wilde refuses to identify subjectivity and sexuality, insisting instead
on the irreducible difference between. That difference *is* the object of
Wildean desire; for what Wilde seeks in desire is not, as in H.C.'s narrative, the earnest disclosure of a single and singular identity, the deep truth
of sex. What Wilde wants is both something less and something more:
the vertigo of substitution and repetition. "The Creeds are believed,"
Wilde writes in "The Critic as Artist," "not because they are rational, but
because they are repeated. . . . Do you wish to love? Use Love's Litany,
and the words will create the yearning from which the world fancies that
they spring."[8] Nor would Wilde curtail this plastic power of language and
repetition; he actively recommended the modification of the flesh. "I do
not like your lips," he told a transfixed Gide, "they are quite straight, like
the lips of a man who has never told a lie. I want you to learn to lie so that
your lips may become beautiful and curved like the lips of an antique
mask."[9] Speaking and kissing with such false, beautiful lips (lips, alas, that
his physiogomy belied), Wilde explores the erotic velleities of "the secret
that Truth is entirely and absolutely a matter of style."[10] Hence, I suggest,
Wilde would have been thrilled to find that H.C. should experience his
first flash of homosexual recognition in a dream that directly thematizes
repetition, a dream in which H.C. is fellated by a labile—not to say a
labial—representation: by, we might say, the picture of Dorian Gray gone
Wilde, "one of my photographs of him incarnate." Whatever the annun-
ciatory energy of this fantasmatic experience, and however clearly the
dream bespeaks a watershed in H.C.'s narrative of self-disclosure, the fellation itself arrives as a "buffoon" enactment of a prior description. It arrives "originally" as an instance of repetition, as a re-presentation of the

"act expounded shortly before by my oracle." Years before H.C. wrote, Wilde had already explicated the erotics of repetition; in a beautiful letter of 1886, the first of his to thematize directly "the love of things impossible," he writes: "Sometime you will find, even as I have found, that there is no such thing as romantic experience; there are romantic memories, and there is the desire of romance—that is all. Our most fiery moments of ecstasy are merely shadows of what somewhere else we have felt, or of what we long someday to feel. So at least it seems to me."[11] Thus, *pace* Pater, even the most immediate shocks of sensation ("our most fiery moments of ecstasy") arrive in and as the wake of their own nativity, arrive already mediate, caught from the beginning in the dreamy interstices of power, discourse, repetition.

The text is (or should be) that uninhibited person who shows his behind to the *Political Father.*
       —Roland Barthes, *The Pleasure of the Text*

If it goes without saying that *The Importance of Being Earnest* is straight farce, conversely it has never been said that the object of Wilde's derision is heterosexual representation itself, which is first taken hostage and then subjected to a fierce, irrecuperable, but almost invisible transvaluation. Positioned at the latter end of a great tradition and written (1894–95) during the apex of Wilde's joint career as heterosexual dramatist and sodomitical poseur, written, that is, on the precipice of what Yeats called "the catastrophe," *Earnest* is a self-consciously belated text in which the venerable topoi of comedy—the dispersion of lovers and their ultimate distribution into cross-gender couples, the confusion and then the restoration of identities, the confrontation with and the expulsion of errant desire, the closural wedding under the aegis of the Name of the Father (here, specifically, Ernest John Moncrieff)—are repeated, inverted, finely perverted, set finally to spin. In the revolving door of Wildean desire, the counters of comedic representation are disclosed as formal ciphers, the arbitrarily empowered terms whose distribution schedules and enforces heterosexual diegesis.

As Wilde stages it, this narrative entails not just points of departure (a "social indiscretion" in "a cloak-room at a railway station") and termination (heterosexual conjunction under the paternal signifier), but also the irreducible necessity of preposterous excurses, sidelines of pseudonymous desire, here farcically dubbed "serious Bunburyism." Bunbury, to be sure, will be "quite exploded" by play's end, but this "revolutionary outrage," as Lady Bracknell calls it, will have only ensured his fragmented dissemination throughout the text. In a complete and completely parodic submission to heterosexist teleology, Wilde does indeed formally dismiss his lovers to the presumptive closure of marital bliss, but not until he has insinuated into his play what should, by law and convention, have been exiled as *non nominandum:* not merely a jubilant celebration of male homosexual desire, not merely a trenchant dissection of the duplicities that constitute the "legitimate" male heterosexual subject, but a withering critique of the political idea, exigent in the 1890s, that anyone's sexuality, inverted or otherwise, could be natural or unnatural at all.

That Wilde achieves these critical effects without the slightest breach in heterosexual decorum—that *Earnest* remains for "our" critical tradition a readily consumable straight play—is not the least measure of a genius whose wile it was to broadcast homosexual critique into the gay interspace of a pun. Here the play of occultation and display, slippage and spillage, could be conveniently housed, as is Ernest John, in two oppositional domiciles—or, as in a bedroom farce, two closets—between which a great deal of shuttling would be required. Wilde understood with a criminal clairvoyance that the inscription of the emergent binarism heterosexual/homosexual would ensure that, as in the inversion metaphor, homosexual desire would stand as the secondary, punning other of a dominant signification, thereby alternately boosting and subverting the authority of the norm. The inescapable duplicity of this procedure is historical in at least two senses: first because it plays with and against the tradition of interdiction, both implicit and explicit, by which celebration of the homosexual possibility had been silenced, and second because it plays with and against contemporaneous discourses on (as H.C. puts it) "true inversion," which repeatedly formulated homosexual desire as heterosexual desire manqué: in the case of the male, *anima muliebris virili corpore inclusa.*

Recent critical work by Ed Cohen and Jonathan Dollimore has made it possible to discern the homosexual countervalences in Wilde's transparently heterosexual texts. In a crucial essay on *Dorian Gray,* Cohen explores the ways in which Wilde "produce[d] new discursive strategies to express concerns unvoiced within the dominant culture." Examining

"Wilde's novel [as it] moves both with and athwart late Victorian ideological practices that naturalized male heterosexuality," Cohen indicates just how an ambidextrous Wilde maintains a protective heterosexual patina even as he also "inscribes the male body within the circuits of male desire."[12] And in a parallel essay on Wilde's anti-essentialism, Dollimore explicates the transgressive power of the Wildean text, which, he asserts, operates within the structures of legitimation and domination in order to release deviant vectors of desire, transverse lines of critique: "Deviant desire reacts against, disrupts and displaces from within; rather than seeking to escape the repressive ordering of the sexual, Wilde reinscribes himself within and relentlessly inverts the binaries upon which that ordering depends. Inversion . . . defines Wilde's transgressive aesthetic."[13] As Dollimore's phrasing suggests, Wilde deploys inversion not as an occulted truth of effeminated being but as a tropological strategy whose primary devices are reversal and repetition, a turning over and a turning around; in this way, the most upright of heterosexual norms could be brought to preposterous conclusion.

Hence the extreme formalism of heterosexual desire in *Earnest,* its inspired submission to the rigor of the conjugal mandate. As the effect of prior performances, heterosexuality for Wilde was both the a priori and the sine qua non of dramatic representation; he could neither stage nor publish an uncloseted gay play. But it was his genius in *Earnest* to transform this delegitimation into a mode of enablement; for if the heterosexual alignment of desires and bodies was prerequisite to representation, then Wilde could foreground and expose it as such, as a deus ex machina coming home to roost in a pun. The heterosexualizing machinery of Wilde's plot is too familiar to need much diagramming; clipped synopsis will do. The play opens on two exuberant bachelors, John Worthing (the eponymous hero of the play's eponymous pun) and Algernon Moncrieff, each living a "double life" of undefined specificity. ("I hope," says Cecily to Algy, "you have not been leading a double life, pretending to be wicked and being really good all the time. That would be hypocrisy.") John is Jack in the country (where he is respectable) and his own dissolute brother, Ernest, in the city (where he is not); concurrently Algy takes curious pleasure cruises to the country to visit Bunbury, about whom we know nothing except that his "permanent invalid[ism]" elicits from Algy a continuous succoring. Our heroes are schematically aligned with respective heroines: Jack with Gwendolen, who believes him in fact to be

Ernest and will only marry a man so named, and Algy with Cecily, who likewise will only marry an Ernest. "There is something in that name that seems to inspire absolute confidence," as Cecily explains to a bewildered Algy. And Gwendolen's explanation, which concurs with Cecily's, suggests access to a more than nominal rapture: "It is a divine name. It has a music of its own. It produces vibrations." The sheer arbitrariness of this "feminine" desire for E(a)rnest-ness underscores the formality of the play's manifest heterosexuality; it requires not so much that the heroes seek women as that they seek access to women, legitimacy, and wealth through the earnest assumption of an overdetermined signifier, a magical term or terminal identity whose power lies in its capacity to trigger the "vibrations" appropriate to a fetish.

The conventional work of the plot consists first in the obstruction and then in the facilitation of the two impending marriages, and the securing of the marriages turns upon the elimination of two impediments. The first is Lady Bracknell's objection to the scandal of Jack's origins and to the as yet illegible inscription of the Name of the Father; and the second is John Worthing's (very patriarchal, very hypocritical) insistence that Algy relinquish the incomparable pleasures of "serious Bunbury- ism." Wilde's great third act farcically achieves both conditions: in an offstage parody of tragic *sparagmos* Bunbury is "quite exploded" ("I killed Bunbury this afternoon," says Algy murderously and casually), just as at play's end the dispersions of Jack's identity are "properly" inte- grated within the (splayed) unity of the paternal signifier. When Jack discovers that indeed he "naturally is Ernest," this is a nature whose au- thority is farcically grounded in letters, terms, texts, in a genealogical ap- peal to writing, and not just any writing, but "the Army Lists of the last forty years"—the book, very simply, of the Names of the Fathers. Con- sulting this august text, and reading there for the first time both his own and his father's name, Jack discovers that his denatured nature is repeti- tion, quotation, division:

> JACK. The Army Lists of the last forty years are here. These delightful
> records should have been my constant study. (*Rushes to bookcase and
> tears the books out.*) M. Generals . . . Mallam, Maxbohm, Magley—what
> ghastly names they have—Markby, Migsby, Mobbs, Moncrieff! Lieu-
> tenant 1840, Captain, Lieutenant-Colonel, Colonel, General 1869,
> Christian names, Ernest John. (*Puts book very quietly down and speaks
> quite calmly.*) I always told you, Gwendolen, my name was Ernest,
> didn't I? Well, it is Ernest after all. I mean it naturally is Ernest.

In these lines Jack inherits as his proper or natural identity the very same pair of signifiers that all along had structured the oscillation of his "double life." As if in reward for the earnestness of his lying, Jack discovers himself to be, as indeed he had always been, both himself and his own fictive other. No longer split between "Jack" and "Ernest," the split "Ernest"/"John" now inscribed as the law of his being, Jack inherits himself "after all" as his "own" difference from himself. In thus inheriting what Joel Fineman has aptly called "the unity of his duplicity,"[14] Jack's now "natural" being is introjected with the same oscillation that the play had just ritually expelled by "quite explod[ing]" Bunbury. Condensing these figures, and acknowledging their more than casual relation, we may say that the murder of Bunbury enables the pseudo-integration of an irreducibly divided male subject.

Wilde's farce thus discloses heterosexual closure as itself the function of two fatally interlocked figures: the formal expulsion of Bunbury, with whatever unspeakable pleasures "serious Bunburyism" entails, and the "integration" of the "heterosexual" male subject under the aegis of the Name of the Father. At once crucial and arbitrary, these predicates structure the heterosexual alignment of genders; they alone enable the marriage that will presumably close the otherwise open circuits of desire. (I say "presumably" because early in the first act Algy refutes this dream of closure: "You don't seem to realize," he tells Jack, "that in married life three is company and two is none.") And yet these predicates seem, as they have always seemed, ridiculous or (in Wilde's preferred term) "trivial." What, we now need to ask, is the meaning of this overdetermined triviality, itself finally indistinguishable from the equivocal pleasure of the play's titular pun? Who is "Bunbury" and what are his filiations—familial, erotic, conceptual—with "Ernest John?" Why must desire submit to such arbitrary terms and terminations? To begin answering these questions, we must now confront this play's phantom self, himself actually no self but rather a gnomic signifier—a name, that is, without a being. I mean of course the nonexistent but omnipresent Mr. Bunbury, upon whom (but there is no whom) so much so curiously depends.

Like all works of art, it [*The Importance of Being Earnest*] drew
its sustenance from life, and, speaking for myself, whenever I
see or read the play I always wish I did not know what I do

about Wilde's life at the time he was writing it—that when, for instance, John Worthing talks of going Bunburying, I did not immediately visualize Alfred Taylor's establishment. On rereading it after his release, Wilde said, "It was extraordinary reading the play over. How I used to toy with that Tiger Life." At its conclusion, I find myself imagining a sort of nightmare Pantomime Transformation Scene in which, at the touch of the magician's wand, instead of the workday world's turning into fairyland, the country house in a never-never Hertfordshire turns into the Old Bailey, the features of Lady Bracknell into those of Mr. Justice Wills. Still, it is a masterpiece, and on account of it Wilde will always enjoy the impersonal fame of an artist as well as the notoriety of his personal legend.

—W. H. Auden, "An Improbable Life"

Frontal knowledge of Bunbury must be renounced at the outset. Bunbury is, by definition, a character "always somewhere else at present": his person or being cannot be summoned, and knowledge of him can be sought only along the path by which his name emerges even as his body disappears. As a figure for what must not be represented, a figure thus *sans figure,* Bunbury is constituted within—not before or beyond—an irreducible oscillation of knowledge and ignorance, occultation and display. Neither liberating nor repressive in "essence," given alternately or even simultaneously to lubricious slippage and disciplinary reversal, this oscillation enables both the unspecified pleasures of serious Bunburyism and the more enforcing binarisms operating in the Auden passage above.[15] That passage is remarkable not merely for the transforming knowledge it displays but even more so for its desire to abjure that knowledge, its *volonté d'oublier:* Auden would forget Bunbury. What he most emphatically desires in these lines is the retroactive advance of a prophylactic ignorance that would undo the knowledge empowering his nearly hallucinatory perception of Wilde's play. The work of that ignorance would be to intermit the by now reflexive synapses ("whenever I see or read the play") of his historicizing, homosexualizing reading, which immediately and unwillingly collapses the "proper" aesthetic space that, Auden implies, should intervene between "going Bunburying" and going to Alfred Taylor's male brothel. This aesthetic transgression in turn excites its own fantasmatic "correction," a recourse to disciplinary procedure, when Auden imagines that "nightmare Pantomime Transformation Scene" in which "instead of the workday world's turning into fairyland," fairyland is unmasked at the Old Bailey: two years' hard labor for "gross indecency" with other males.[16] It is accession to *this* knowledge, transforming both the play and its beholder, that Auden would abjure. "I always wish I did not know what I do."

Wilde of course had devised Bunbury to inhabit the conceptual and erotic interstices of precisely this ambivalence, whose subtle instruction is not so much that knowledge be voided as that knowledge perform its work along self-blinded paths of "ignorance," nonrecognition, and misidentification. "In this light," as D. A. Miller writes, "it becomes clear that the social function of secrecy"—and Bunbury is the secret subject of an open secret—"is not to conceal knowledge so much as to conceal knowledge of the knowledge. . . . Secrecy would thus be the subjective practice in which the oppositions of private/public, inside/outside, subject/object are established, and the sanctity of their first term kept inviolate."[17] As Wilde's parodic figure for this regime of knowing and unknowing, of knowing through unknowing, Bunbury remains a being or subject always otherwise and elsewhere: he appears nowhere on stage, and wherever his name is present he is not. Appeals to Bunbury yield only repetitions of his name: "Bunbury doesn't live here. Bunbury is somewhere else at present." But if Bunbury has been thus banished from the precincts of heterosexual representation, the need to frequent his secrecy has not, as Algy explains to Jack: "Nothing will induce me to part with Bunbury, and if you ever get married, which seems to me extremely problematic, you will be very glad to know Bunbury. A man who marries without knowing Bunbury has a very tedious time of it." As these lines indicate, Bunbury operates within the heterosexual order as its hidden but irreducible supplement, its fictive and pseudonymous brother, the homosexual "excess" that it refuses to embrace but to which it continuously alludes, perhaps even aspires.

Of course the gay specificity of such allusiveness was technically unspeakable—*non nominandum inter Christianos.* Refusing to chafe under this stricture against representation, Wilde inverts it by inserting Bunbury into the text behind the ostentatious materiality of an empty signifier, a name without a being, a pure alias whose strategic equivocation between allusion and elision had already announced, a century before Foucault's formulation, "that the world of speech and desires has known evasions, struggles, plunderings, disguises, ploys."[18] Speaking strictly, *Earnest* cannot admit or acknowledge the erotic force of the gay male body, which must be staged therefore as an atopic body, a body constitutively "somewhere else at present." This accounts, at least in part, for the flickering presence-absence of the play's homosexual desire, as the materiality of the flesh is retracted into the sumptuousness of the signifier, whether in the "labial phonemics"[19] of Bunbury, all asmack with death and kisses, or in the duplicitous precincts of the play's most proper and improper name, Ernest: a name at once splayed by a pun and doubly referential, pointing with one hand to the open secret of the double life, pseudonymously enacted, and with the other to the brittle posturings of the Name of the Father, a figure whose delicate transmissibility has always required the strictest of heterosexual propaedeutics.

What then, more specifically, are the disguises and ploys of "serious Bunburyism?" Or, in Jack's more exasperated intonation: "Bunburyist? What on earth do you mean by a Bunburyist?" But before we proceed, the hermeneutical rage of a Jack must be a little undone by the interpretive insouciance of an Algy: "Now produce your explanation, and pray make it remarkable. The bore about most explanations is that they are never half so remarkable as the things they try to explain." In this spirit, some explanations. Bunbury represents or disseminates the following: (1) an actual person of no historical importance, Henry Shirley Bunbury, a hypochondriacal acquaintance of Wilde's Dublin youth, one of whose letters to Wilde is still extant;[20] (2) a remote village in Cheshire that, appropriately enough, "does not even appear on most maps";[21] (3) a tongue-on-cheek allusion to Wilde's illegal "sodomitical" practices—"not only," as Fineman puts it, "British slang for a male brothel, but . . . also a collection of signifiers that straightforwardly express their desire to bury in the bun;"[22] (4) a parody of the contemporaneous medicalization of homosexual desire ("Nor do I," says Lady Bracknell of Algy's visits to Bunbury, "in any way approve of the modern sympathy with invalids. I consider it morbid. Illness of any kind is hardly a thing to be encouraged in others. Health is the primary duty of life."); (5) a sly, even chipper, allusion to the thanatopolitics of homophobia, whose severest directives against disclosure only too axiomatically ensure that what finally gets disclosed will be, as in *Dorian Gray*, a corpse, homicide or suicide, upon whose cold or cooling flesh the now obvious text is for the first time made legible; (6) a pragmatics of gay misrepresentation, an incomparably nuanced and motile doublespeak, driven both by pleasure and, as Gide put it, "by the need of self-protection";[23] and, as we shall see before we end, (7) a pseudonym or alias for the erotic oscillation within the male subject, his fundamental waffling between Jack and Ernest.

But more crucially than any of these, before and after any of these, Bunbury insists upon his "own" difference from himself and from whatever signification, as in (1) through (7) above, he may, by caprice or compulsion, assume. From his prone, if not quite prostrate, position just offstage (to know Bunbury is "to sit by a bed of pain"), "Bunbury" performs enormous representational work, but only, as his name implies, by way of a disseminal passage, a displacing tropism whose first effect is to expel the self-identity of the signified from the neighborhood of the signifier. It is typical of Wilde's rigorously inverting wit that he should stage this expulsion as an act of ingestion, as an insistently oral practice, as a buttered and material pun on Bunbury's cryptographic name. I refer here to the "luxurious and indolent" gluttony that, by axiomatically transposing sexual and gustatory pleasures (cucumber sandwiches, muffins, breads: buns—Banbury or Bunbury—everywhere),[24] operates as a farcical screen-metaphor for otherwise unspeakable pleasures. "There can be little good in any young man who eats so much, or so often."[25] In this figural strategy the obscene becomes the scenic, as that which must not be spoken is consumed, before an audience, with incomparable relish and finesse. "Well, I can't eat muffins in an agitated manner. The butter would probably get on my cuffs. One should always eat muffins quite calmly. It is the only way to eat them." The fastidious allusion to Wilde's sexual practice here is exact—from hand to mouth: fondling "would be followed by some form of mutual masturbation or intercrural intercourse. . . . Finally, oral copulation would be practiced, with Wilde as the active agent [*sic*], though this role was occasionally reversed. It gave him inspiration, he said."[26] Thus inspired—or more literally, inspirited—by "reversed" practices and reversible tropes, Wilde deploys a polite decorum (no danger to Algy's cuffs) in order to display and displace a desire to bury in the bun. In this way, serious Bunburyism releases a polytropic sexuality so extreme, so mobile, so evanescent in speed and turn, that it traverses, Ariel-like, a fugitive path through oral, genital, anal, and aural ports until it discovers and expends itself in and as the displacements of language. It was Wilde's extraordinary gift to return this vertigo of substitution and repetition to his audience. The inspiration he derived from fellatio he then redisseminated, usually sotto voce, through the actor's mouth. "The ejaculation," says Lady Bracknell in a line that did not survive the reviser's knife, "has reached my ears more than once."[27]

Oscillating between verbal and seminal emissions, Lady Bracknell's pun manifests the equivocation fundamental to the signifying practices of serious Bunburyism: an "illicit" signification could be insinuated into the text even as it was also withdrawn under the cover of a licit one, a procedure that sometimes imparts an odd resonance— the penumbra of a not quite legible importance—to certain of *Earnest's* details. Via such strategic equivocation Wilde could introduce into *Earnest* both a parodic account of his own double life (the public thumbing of a private nose) as well as a scathing critique of the heterosexist presumption requiring, here statutorily, that such a life be both double and duplicitous. And that *Earnest* is such a text—sliding deviously between exposé and critique, saturating its reader/viewer with blinding disseminal effusions—is simply a Wilde fact whose closeting or imprisonment we must no longer forbear. In order to substantiate this claim, whose substance is in part a "subtextual" stance, I adduce in the numbered sections below a series of discrete indiscretions in which *Earnest* "goes Bunburying," in which, that is, Wilde lifts to liminality a specific subcultural knowledge of "the terrible pleasures of double life."[28] The examples to follow neither deplete the gay referentiality of Wilde's text (other instances could be adduced), nor by any means exhaust the signifying practice it pleased Wilde to call serious Bunburyism; they are merely demonstrative exempla, intended to satisfy the positivist desire for proof in the pudding. In the following enumeration, I have drawn freely from both the three-act and four-act versions of the play.[29]

1. "It is a very ungentlemanly thing to read a private cigarette case"; act 1, in both versions. In the trials of April–May 1895, Wilde would be compelled to submit again and again to such "ungentlemanly" exegesis. Cigarette cases, usually silver ones purchased in Bond Street, were a part (along with cash, other jewelry, food and drink) of Wilde's payment to the male prostitutes he frequented. As the most durable material trace of Wilde's illegal sexual practice, these cigarette cases (sometimes replete with inscriptions: "to X from O.W.") would be repeatedly introduced into evidence by the prosecution throughout the second and third trials. Consider, for instance, the following exchange between Solicitor General Frank Lockwood, prosecutor at the third trial, and the defendant:

> Did you ever give one [a cigarette case] to Charles Parker also? —Yes, but I am afraid it cost only £1.

> Silver? —Well, yes. I have a great fancy for giving cigarette cases.

> To young men? —Yes.

How many have you given? —I might have given seven or eight in 1892 or 1893.[30]

These cigarette cases are, for the following reasons, remarkably rich metonyms of Wilde's sexual practice. First, they literally inscribe the condescension implicit in Wilde's cross-class and cross-generational sexual activity. Second, they suggest Wilde's ambivalent relation to the prostitution he repeatedly enjoyed: he preferred to think of the cases as "gifts" not necessarily related to the sexual services they nonetheless purchased. Third, as evidentiary deposits purchased and distributed by a very self-conscious "first-class misdemeanant," as Jack describes Ernest, they bespeak a contradictory emotionality compounded of defiance, foolhardiness, and, it would seem, a certain desire to be caught. Fourth, they coyly and insistently point to the orality that was both Wilde's sexual preference and *Earnest's* primary trope of displaced representation. Henry Wotton, after all, had already explicated for Dorian Gray the evanescent perfection of a good smoke ("You must have a cigarette. A cigarette is the perfect type of a perfect pleasure. It is exquisite, and it leaves one unsatisfied. What more can one want?"), and Edward Shelley, one of Wilde's lovers, testified that he "had received a letter from Mr. Wilde inviting him to 'come smoke a cigarette' with him."[31] Furthermore, while reporting the events of the first (that is, the libel) trial, the London daily *Evening News* (5 April 1895) printed the following:

> The Old Bailey recoiled with loathing from the long ordeal of terrible suggestions that occupied the whole of yesterday when the cross-examination left the literary plane and penetrated the dim-lit perfumed rooms where the poet of the beautiful joined with valets and grooms in the bond of silver cigarette cases.[32]

As the affective verso to the recto of *Earnest's* gay gaming with cigarette cases, the "recoil[ing]" and "loathing" specified in these lines indicate the precarious volatility of the Victorian male bonds so deftly manipulated by Wilde on "the literary plane." A gentleman might offer his peer, or even his inferior in age or class, the benefit of a good smoke or the gratuity of a cigarette case, but only so long as the gift did not suggest a bond more intimate than "proper" gentlemanly relation or condescension. The performative success of *Earnest's* oral insouciance lies in its capacity to tease the limit of the proper without seeming to violate it seriously. Prosecutor Lockwood's "very ungentlemanly" reading of private cigarette cases reversed this rhetorical strategy by transforming the glissando of Wildean wit into that "long ordeal of terrible suggestion."

2. "I feel bound to tell you that you are not down on my list of eligible young men, although I have the same list as the dear Duchess of Bolton has. We work together, in fact"; act 1, in both versions. In these lines, Wilde ventriloquizes Lady Bracknell in order to allude, obliquely and across gender, to a then notorious transvestite/homosexual scandal, in which two men, Frederick Park (aka "Fanny") and Ernest Boulton (aka "Stella") were arrested in drag in front of the Strand Theatre and later prosecuted for "conspiracy to commit a felony"—the felony being of course sodomy. Argued before Lord Chief Justice Cockburn, the case of *Regina* v. *Boulton and Others* opened on 9 May 1871, lasted for six days, aroused immense public interest, including extensive newspaper coverage, and resulted, thanks to a paucity of evidence, in acquittal. Along with the "Cleveland Street Scandal" of 1889, the Boulton and Park case was Victorian England's most prominent homosexual "discursive event" prior to the Wilde trials of 1895. That Wilde knew of both scandals, as Lady Bracknell certainly did not, is beyond question; and no doubt it pleased Wilde immensely, and teased his imagination, that Boulton was a minor transvestite actor, appearing both on and off stage in elaborate and convincing feminine dress, so convincing in fact that a witness "named Cox, who gave evidence at the preliminary policy court proceedings but died before the trials (where his disposition was read)," was thoroughly taken in: "I kissed him, she, or it, believing at the time it was a woman."[33] But Wilde's reference to "the dear Duchess of Bolton" is also a little more than a Bunburied allusion to these "real" events; that the Duchess and Lady Bracknell "work together, in fact" suggests that propriety and impropriety, norm and transgression, are inversely conjoined in a single system whose passionate oppositions embrace, sometimes fatally, that "same list" "of eligible young men."

3. "Fathers are certainly not popular just at present. . . . At present fathers are at a terrible discount. They are like those chaps, the minor poets. They are never even quoted"; act 1 in the four-act version. Spoken by Algy, these lines refer emphatically to the escalating filial warfare between the Marquess of Queensberry and Lord Alfred Douglas. The details of this triangular narrative are too familiar to require recapitulation here, except to say that Wilde's failure to manage the situation adroitly precipitated the debacle of the trials, during which Queensberry's charge that

Wilde had been "posing as a somdomite" (*sic*) would find a decisive institutional context in which to be "quoted," at length and in detail. At the conclusion of the libel trial, the jury determined that Queensberry's charge of sodomitical "posing" had been proved and that his "Plea of Justification" elaborating this charge had been "published for the public benefit."

4.   LADY BRACKNELL. Lady Bloxham? I don't know her.

> JACK. Oh, she goes about very little. She is a lady of considerably advanced years.
>
> LADY BRACKNELL. Ah, nowadays that is no guarantee of respectability of character.

Present in both versions, this "lady considerably advanced in years" alludes (again across gender) to an "undergraduate of strange beauty," John Francis Bloxham, who, as Philip Cohen notes, "edited the one and only issue of *The Chameleon: A Bazaar of Dangerous and Smiling Chances* (December 1894) and authored 'The Priest and the Acolyte'," a story, misattributed to Wilde, blending apostasy and pederasty.[34] To this Oxford undergraduate magazine, cited repeatedly at the trials, Wilde contributed, apparently at Douglas's request, "a page of paradoxes destined originally for *The Saturday Review*" (*Letters*, 441). Douglas himself contributed what Wilde at the first trial overgenerously called two "exceedingly beautiful poems," "In Praise of Shame" and "Two Loves," both vaguely pederastic and the latter containing the line "I am the Love that dare not speak its name," which Wilde appropriated for brilliant rhetorical effect at the second trial. In a letter to Ada Leverson, Wilde alludes to "Lady Bloxham" and her literary productions (the coded allusion here to "Dorian" refers to John Gray, one of those unquoted minor poets, renowned in Wilde's circle for the beauty, especially, of his profile):

> Dear Sphinx, Your aphorisms must appear in the second number of the *Chameleon:* they are exquisite. "The Priest and the Acolyte" is not by Dorian: though you were right in discerning by internal evidence that the author has a profile. He is an undergraduate of strange beauty.
>
> The story is, to my ears, too direct: there is no nuance: it profanes a little by revelation: God and other artists are always a little obscure. Still, it has interesting qualities, and is at moments poisonous: which is something. Ever yours
>
> OSCAR
>
> (*Letters*, 379)

5. Miss Prism, speaking of dissolute Ernest just before Algy arrives, Bunburying as same: "I should fancy that he was as bad as any young man who has chambers in the Albany, or indeed even in the vicinity of Piccadilly, can possibly be. . . . I trust that unhappy young profligate will never desecrate with his presence the quiet precincts of this refined home. I would not feel safe"; act 2 in the four-act version. As both Miss Prism and the trial reports very clearly indicate, the semiotics of the double life were predicated upon the diacritical separation of spaces: on the one hand, the homosexualized space of (in Wilde's case) private "chambers in the Albany" or Savoy Hotel; on the other, the domestic and presumptively heterosexual "precincts of this quiet home" (in Wilde's case, his family residence at 16 Tite Street, Chelsea). Between those two spaces, a third and prophylactic space, a differentiating distance, is presumed to intervene; this is precisely the distance that, while permitting Miss Prism to "feel safe," also enables the oscillations of "serious Bunburyism," as when Jack/Ernest shuttlecocks between town and country. As Wilde very well understood, this fictive third space was readily traversable, so much so that its differentiating functions sometimes collapsed. At the second trail, for instance, Alfred Wood—prostitute, thief, blackmailer—testified to the events of an evening in January or February 1893:

> After dinner I went with Wilde to 166 [*sic*], Tite Street. There was nobody in the house to my knowledge. Mr. Wilde let himself in with a latchkey. We went up to a bedroom where we had hock and seltzer.
>
> Witness then stated that an act of gross indecency took place on this occasion.[35]

Here, as also in the play, where Algy is about to arrive as Ernest, Miss Prism's worst fears are realized: a "young profligate will . . . desecrate with his presence the precincts of this quiet home."

6. Canon Chasuble in response to Jack's concern that he is "a little too old now" to be rechristened as Ernest: "Oh, I am not by any means a bigoted Paedobaptist. . . . You need have no apprehensions [about immersion]. . . . Sprinkling is all that is necessary, or indeed, I think, advisable. . . . I have two similar ceremonies to perform . . . A case of twins that occurred recently in one of the outlying cottages on your estate. . . . I don't know, however, if you would care to join them at the Font. Personally I do not approve myself of the obliteration of class-distinctions";

act 2 in four-act versions; a truncated version of these lines (sans "Paedo-baptist" and "the obliteration of class-distinctions") appears in the three-act *Earnest*. The always serious Canon Chasuble repeatedly falls into oblique and unwilling licentious allusion, as in these lines, which insinuate an outrageous chain of gay metonyms: "Paedobaptist . . . sprinkling is all that is necessary . . . in one of the outlying cottages . . . if you would care to join them at the Font . . . the obliteration of class-distinctions." If "Paedobaptist" (or "sprinkler of boys") was too blatantly obscene to survive the play's revision into three acts, then the more subtly insinuated "outlying cottages" was not: only an elite audience would have known that by the late nineteenth century "cottage" had currency as a camp signifier for a trysting site, usually a public urinal. The word also had, it would seem, a more emphatically personal reference; Queensberry's "Plea of Justification" claimed that Oscar Wilde "in the year of our Lord One Thousand eight hundred and ninety-three [a year, that is, before the composition of *Earnest*] at a house called 'The Cottage' at Goring . . . did solicit and incite . . . the said . . . acts of gross indecency."[36] Once these Bunburied significations are allowed to resonate through the passage— once we recognize with Canon Chasuble that "corrupt readings seem to have crept into the text"—the references to "sprinkling" and "join[ing] them at the Font" point, directly and indirectly, to seminal experience. Similarly with the phrase "the obliteration of class-distinctions," which boisterously points to the almost pederastic, cross-class prostitution Wilde repeatedly enjoyed. Just a few lines earlier, Wilde had had the effrontery to make Jack say "I am very fond of children," a sentence definitely courting the bourgeois outrage of the thus "discounted" fathers who pursued Wilde through the court and into prison.

7. "The next time I see you I hope you will be Parker." As has been "public knowledge" (however inert) for some thirty years, the most substantial revision of *Earnest* was the deletion (demanded by George Alexander, who produced the play, and unhappily submitted to by Wilde) of an entire scene in which Algy, Bunburying as Ernest, is almost arrested for dining expenses incurred by Jack, or rather Ernest, at the Savoy Hotel, the site of both Jack-Ernest's "grossly materialistic" gluttony and some of Wilde's sexual encounters. Jack, who is delighted that Algy should suffer for extravagances that can only be correctly charged to Ernest, counsels his younger brother "that incarceration would do you a great deal of good." Algy understandably protests: "Well, I really am not going to be

imprisoned in the suburbs for having dined in the West End. It is perfectly ridiculous." Ridiculous or not, Wilde would very soon suffer the analogous imprisonment and ridicule that "fate" and the state had in store for him. But in "never-never Hertfordshire" (as Auden called it) this end is happily remitted when Jack, his "generosity [hilariously] misplaced," "pay[s] this monstrous bill for my brother."

Two aspects of this scene merit further emphasis. First, Algy's pseudo-arrest for serious overeating secures the argument that in *Earnest* "luxurious and indolent" gluttony operates as a jubilant screen-metaphor for otherwise unrepresentable pleasures. This cathexis of extravagant dining and sexual pleasure/transgression refers directly to Wilde's double life; his regular practice was to dine luxuriously with his lovers prior to sex, thereby enjoying *in camera* the same metaphor he would display on stage in *Earnest*. Often meeting his assignations in the private chambers of public restaurants (Willis's or the Solferino or elsewhere), he would dazzle them with opulence, language, and alcohol. Here is the testimony of one prostitute:

> He [Alfred Taylor, Wilde's procurer] took us to a restaurant in Rupert Street. I think it was the Solferino. We were shown upstairs to a private room, in which there was a dinner-table laid for four. After a while Wilde came in. I had never seen him before, but I had heard of him. We dined about eight o'clock. We all four sat down to dinner, Wilde sitting on my left.
>
> Was the dinner a good dinner? —Yes. The table was lighted with red-shaded candles. We had champagne with our dinner, and brandy and coffee afterwards. Wilde paid for the dinner. Subsequently Wilde said to me, "This is the boy for me—will you go to the Savoy Hotel with me?" I consented, and Wilde drove me in a cab to the hotel. He took me first into a sitting-room on the second floor, where he ordered some more drink—whisky and soda. Wilde then asked me to go into his bedroom with him.
>
> Witness here described certain acts of indecency which he alleged took place in the bedroom.[37]

The witness in this exchange is Charles Parker, a sometime valet, whose testimony against Wilde seems alternately to have been purchased and coerced; it is the name "Parker" that brings us to the last point regarding the deleted arrest scene. The scene commences with the delivery of a calling card, which Algy reads: " 'Parker and Gribsby, Solicitors.' I don't know anything about them. Who are they?" After taking and reading the card, Jack facetiously speculates: "I wonder who they can be. I expect, Ernest, they have come about some business for your friend Bunbury. Perhaps Bunbury wants to make his will, and wishes you to be executor." With these subtle intimations of Algy's forthcoming execution of Bunbury lingering in the air, Messrs. Parker and Gribsby are shown in by Merriman, the butler. But "they," it turns out, are not exactly a they but a he ("There is only one gentleman in the hall, sir," Merriman informs Jack), and the one gentleman is Gribsby "himself," come either to collect the debt or "remove" Ernest to Holloway Prison, one of those "suburb[an]" facilities through which Wilde would be funneled on his way to ignominy: "The surroundings, I admit, are middle class; but the gaol itself is fashionable and well-aired." (From the other side of the bars Wilde would not find it so.) As these threats of incarceration and death are being ventilated in the text, Jack first teases Algy for his (that is, Jack's) profligacy and then "generously" pays Ernest's debt, thereby forestalling the correction that would, Jack says, have done Algy "a great deal of good." Having thus dispatched his serious problem, Jack then luxuriates in a little trivial banter:

> JACK. You are Gribsby, aren't you? What is Parker like?
>
> GRIBSBY. I am both, sir. Gribsby when I am on unpleasant business, Parker on occasions of a less serious kind.
>
> JACK. The next time I see you I hope you will be Parker.

("After all," Wilde writes in a letter, "the only proper intoxication is conversation" [*Letters,* 749]). Unfortunately, the next time Wilde saw "Parker," Parker would be "on [the] unpleasant business" of a reverse, or disciplinary, Bunbury. Appearing in the Central Criminal Court under the guise of "Gribsby," appearing, that is, as an agent of the law, Parker would testify to "acts of gross indecency" committed with Wilde in 1893 while Gribsby, apparently, was otherwise and elsewhere engaged.

It could have come as no surprise to the creator of "Parker and Gribsby, Solicitors" that he should find himself excoriated in the Old Bailey for the same sexual practices he had been (con)celebrating just beneath the lovely pellucid "heterosexual" skin of *Earnest.* That, quite literally, his dirty linen should be "well-aired" in court (whose officers, jury, and gallery were exclusively male) he had already anticipated in this deleted arrest scene, whose self-consciously transgressive erotics I have only touchingly glossed here. Conversely and symmetrically, the extensive newspaper coverage of April–May 1895 would guarantee the dissemination of Lady Bracknell's also deleted line: a (somewhat expurgated) narrative of his "ejaculation[s]" would indeed reach respectable English "ears more than once." But there is nothing uncanny in any of this. Wilde was no mere prognosticator, foretelling the doom that was about to settle around him. He was instead a prevaricator of genius, a polymath of the pleasurable and necessary lie. As a person committed to homosexual practice, he was compelled *by law* to inhabit the oscillating and nonidentical identity structure of Jack and Ernest or "Parker and Gribsby, Solicitors." Within this structure transgression and law, homosexual delight and its arrest, are produced and reproduced as interlocked versions and inversions of each other.

Writing from this endangered position, Wilde stated with a parodist's clarity and a criminal's obscurity that the importance of being was neither x nor y, male nor female, homosexual nor heterosexual, Parker nor Gribsby, Jack nor Ernest. Being will not be disclosed by the assumption or descent of an apt and singular signifier, a proper or class name naturally congruent with the object or objects it seeks to denominate. In contrast to H.C.'s essentialist move, Wilde never heralds "a true inversion" that "respond[s] finally to a stimulus strong and prolonged enough, as a man awakens when he is loudly called." Belying such unproblematic notions of true being, Wilde insists that identity has always already been mislaid somewhere in the lane lying between such culturally "productive" binarisms as those listed above. Homosexual or heterosexual? Parker or Gribsby? Jack or Ernest? Which name should be "loudly called?" "I am both, sir." Both indeed, and therefore not quite either: this ambivalent locution emphatically does not imply recourse to the compromise formation of a (perhaps residual) bisexuality, or in Ellis's more telling contemporaneous phrase, "psychosexual hermaphroditism," for this formation is manifestly content to leave undisturbed the conveniently bifurcated gender assumptions that it only seemingly fuses. The component desires that, when added together, comprise the "bi" remain in fact quite distinct, shot with the masculine *or* feminine through and through. Wildean doubling ("I am both, sir") refers instead to a strategy of lexical or nominal traversal, of skidding within the code and between its semantic poles. In the shuttle of self-representation, being itself must slip on a name, or two. "But what own are you?" Gwen asks of Jack just as he is about to become Ernest John. "What is your Christian name, now that you have become someone else?"

∞

I love the last words of anything: the end of art is the beginning.
—Oscar Wilde

Child! You seem to me to use words without understanding
their proper meaning.
—Jack to Cecily in the four-act *Earnest*

In lieu of "serious" closure, and as if to deride even the possibility of
adequate formal solution to the fugitive mobility of Bunburying desire,
Wilde terminates his play, farcically and famously, with yet another terminological extravagance: an impudent iteration of his farce's "trivial"
but crucial pun, the earnest and eponymous homophone in which, to
borrow a locution from Barthes, "the confusion of tongues is no longer a
punishment" (*Pleasure,* 4). For *Earnest* may close only when Jack, in a sly
parody of tragic anagnorisis, "realizes for the first time in [his] life the vital Importance of Being Earnest." At this moment, as the last words of
the play swallow the first words of its title, its origin therefore finally assimilated to its terminus, Jack "realizes" himself in and as his "own" double entendre: in and as, that is, the difference between himself and the
symbolic system that seeks to determine his proper name and his true being. Jack's punning "being," such as it is, is thus located and dislocated—
located *as* dislocated—in an experience of radical *méconnaissance,* of verbal and ontological slippage, which in turn yields a terminal dividend in
his supercharged "perception of the extravagance of the signifier" (*Pleasure,* 65). Celebrating the "vital importance" of being his own pun, Jack
embraces, even as he is embraced by, the signifier's power of perverse subsumption, the delight it gives and takes as it incorporates "deviant" vectors under its nominally proper head.

Such extravagance constitutes, quite literally, both the subject and the
subjectivity of the play, their very sound and sense; the plot is so devised
that the play may end only when Jack's "being" is assimilated, however
preposterously, to his, or rather his father's, name, a requirement that enables Wilde both to acknowledge and to deride the Oedipal force of prior
inscriptions. In response to the pseudo-urgent question of Jack's identity
("Lady Bracknell, I hate to seem inquisitive, but would you kindly inform

me who I am?"), the play dutifully answers with the Name of the Father, but in doing so it also repeats its insistence upon the absurdity, and the power, of the letter; in its expiring breath *Earnest* re-sounds or sounds off Jack's other double name and so closes with a terminal openness to what Jonathan Culler calls "the call of the phoneme." Invoking the sumptuous materiality of sound and its powers of startling conjunction, the pun's "echoes tell of wild realms beyond the [semantic] code and suggest new configurations of meaning."[38] In such wild realms, as Wilde himself well knew, the pleasures of the homophone arrive just as the differentiae of the hetero dissolve into sound and same. Culler continues:

> Puns, like portmanteaux, limn for us a model of language where the word is derived rather than primary and combinations of letters suggest meanings while at the same time illustrating the instability of meanings, their as yet ungrasped or undefined relations to one another, relations which further discourse (further play of similarity and difference) can produce. When one thinks of how puns characteristically demonstrate the applicability of a single signifying sequence to two different contexts, with quite different meanings, one can see how puns both evoke prior formulations, with the meanings they have deployed, and demonstrate their instability, the mutability of meaning, the production of meaning by linguistic motivation. Puns present us with a model of language as phonemes or letters combining in various ways to evoke prior meaning and to produce effects of meaning—with a looseness, unpredictability, excessiveness, shall we say, that cannot but disrupt the model of language as nomenclature.[39]

Culler here efficiently formulates the duplicitous operations by which the pun opens in language a counterhegemonic or revisionary space, a plastic site in which received meanings ("language as nomenclature") may be perversely turned, strangely combined, or even emptied out. Because they "both evoke prior formulations, with the meanings they have deployed, and demonstrate their instability, the mutability of meaning," puns release from those prior formulations the horizon of a new possibility, a second or third meaning, or even the unhinging of meaning making itself. As a figure that itself limns the liminal, sporting on the hazy border where tongues of sound and sense intermingle, deliciously, as in a kiss, the pun characteristically broadcasts a faintly scandalous erotic power, a power of phonemic blending and semantic bending whose feinting extensions reason always does its best to reign in, as when, for instance, Samuel Johnson famously quibbles with punning Shakespeare: "A quibble is the golden apple for which he will always turn aside from his career, or stoop from his elevation. A quibble, poor and barren as it is, gave him such delight, that he was content to purchase it by the sacrifice of reason, propriety, and truth. A quibble was to him the fatal *Cleopatra* for which he lost the world, and was content to lose it."[40] Wilde's genius implicitly submits Johnson's critique to a dizzying inversion. Earnestly "sacrific[ing] reason, propriety, and truth," Wilde works his trade, transcoding golden apples into cucumber sandwiches and fatal Cleopatra into vital Ernest. (Indeed, gender transposition of the objects of male desire was Wilde's characteristic mode of gay figuration: "I do not interest myself in that British view of morals that sets Messalina above Sporus" [*Letters*, 594]).

But it was not just any gendered signifier against whose presumed integrity Wilde directed the splaying call of the phoneme. Rather, his terminal *jouissance* is aimed pointedly at the most overdetermined of such signifiers—the Name of the Father, here Ernest John Moncrieff—upon whose lips (if we may borrow a figure from the good Canon Chasuble) a whole cultural disposition is hung: the distribution of women and (as) property, the heterosexist configuration of Eros, the genealogy of the "legitimate" male subject, etc. Closing with a farcical pun on the paternal signifier, Wilde discloses, in a single double stroke, the ironic cathexis— more accurately, the sometimes murderous double binding—by which the homosexual possibility is formally terminated or "exploded" in order that a familiar heterosexualizing machinery may be installed, axiomatically and absurdly, "at last." So decisive is the descent of the father's name, so swift are its powers of compulsion and organization, that (at least seemingly) it subdues the oscillations of identity, straightens the byways of desire, and completes—*voilà!*— the marital teleology of the comic text. All three couples, "after all," are swept away ("At last!" "At last!") in the heady and "natural" rush toward presumptive conjugal bliss, a rush so heady that it peremptorily dismisses, for instance, both Cecily's exigent desire for an "Ernest" and Algy's own earlier caution against the exclusionary erotics of heterosexist integration: "Nothing will induce me to part with Bunbury, and if you [Jack] ever get married, which seems to me extremely problematic, you will be very glad to know Bunbury. A man who marries without knowing Bunbury has a very tedious time of it." Forgetting this brief but earnest dissertation on interminable Bunburyism, Algy fairly leaps toward marriage, crying simply "Cecily! At last!"—thereby fulfilling, as if by amnesia, the comic topos requiring that marital conjunction, or its proleptic image, close (for good, if not forever) the otherwise open circuits of desire.

And yet the closural efficacy of this compelling, this compulsory, heterosexual sweep, especially any gesture it might make in the direction of the "natural," is rendered instantly absurd—or, as Algy puts it, "extremely problematic"—by, first, its hypertrophic textuality, and second, by Wilde's double insistence upon the sovereignity of the signifier over the signified and upon the signifier's liability to indiscreet slippage, its power of perverse subsumption. Not only must Jack seek his "natural" or "proper" identity in an antic succession of texts (he "*rushes to bookcase and tears the books out,*" reads the stage direction), but in an earlier version this scene of frantic reading had included, besides "the Army Lists of the last forty years," an allusion to Robert Hichens's *The Green Carnation* (1894), a contemporaneous parody of the open secret of Wilde's affair with Douglas.[41] Perusing this text from her unimpeachable altitude, Lady Bracknell emits an evaluation: "This treatise, the 'Green Carnation,' as I see it is called, seems to be a book about the culture of exotics. It contains no reference to Generals in it. It seems a morbid and middle-class affair."[42] After this and other preposterous citations (Canon Chasuble, for instance, is handed a Bradshaw railway guide "of 1869, I observe"), it is of course, as in the canonical three-act version, the book with the "reference to Generals in it" that brings home the prize and so surprises Jack with his now naturally punning self.

In any case, as I have already suggested, the paternally derived and sanctioned "being" that Jack's reading hereby secures entails a literal reinscription of the same pseudo-opposition ("Jack" versus "Ernest" or "Ernest John") under which his double life had all along been conducted—except that, we should note in passing, the order of the terms has been inverted: where cognomen was, there pseudonym shall be. Thus the closural move that would repair Jack's splayed identity, even as it would also terminate the shuttle and slide of Bunburying desire, discloses again, discloses "at last," neither the deep truth of essential being nor the foundational monad of a "real" sexuality. Instead, Wilde's play of names terminates with terminological play on the terms-in-us, with a punning recognition of both the determinative force of prior inscriptions and the transvaluing power of a practice of substitution. Which is to say that it does not terminate at all, but insistently repeats and relays the irreducible oscillations, back and forth, froth and buck, of very much the same erotic binarism that would soon be definitely consolidated in the violent counterframing of homosexuality and heterosexuality (two terms that, by the way, appear nowhere in Wilde's lexicon).

But Wilde's is a crucial—a crux-making—repetition: crucial not merely because he deploys the pleasures of repetition to *make* a difference, but also because the difference he makes he then makes audible in and as the disseminal excess—itself a refined blending of slippage and spillage—with which he laves his pun, and through his pun, his audience, his readers. At once (thus twice) titular and closural, originary and terminal, Wilde's pun practices the serious erotics of repetition that Barthes, collating Sade and Freud, would later theorize so compactly: "repetition itself creates bliss . . . to repeat excessively is to enter into loss, into the zero of the signified" (*Pleasure,* 41). In *Earnest* the object of this zero targeting, the site of this obsessional emptying, is nothing less than the marriageable male subject—let us say, anachronistically, the integral and heterosexual male subject—whose strength and legitimacy are sanctioned by, and only by, the frail transmissibility of his father's empowering names. By submitting this name and this subject to the zeroing power of his preposterous homonym, thereby earnestly relieving Ernest of his earnestness, Wilde empties both name and subject of their natural content and naturalizing force; in doing so, he reopens within both an erotic space that had been prematurely closed—foreclosed, precisely, as *non nominandum.*

It should go without saying, but does not, that the erotics of punning are irreducibly ambivalent, even duplicitous. On the semantic level, puns work precisely because they presuppose and reaffirm a received difference between (at least) two objects, concepts, or meanings; "evok[ing] prior formulations, with the meanings they have deployed," as Culler puts it, puns thus operate as the semantic conservators of the hetero: they police the borders of difference. But on the phonemic level this work of differentiation is quite undone. When referred to the ear, to the waiting body of the reader/listener, the erotics of punning become homoerotic because homophonic. Somatically we experience a homogenizing action in which one sound (two sounds actually, but they are spoken and they bespeak the same) cunningly erases, or at least momentarily suspends, the semantic differential by whose contrary labor the hetero is both made to appear and made to appear natural, lucid, self-evident. Difference is repeated until difference vanishes in the ear. And when it vanishes, the result—if the pun, like Wilde's, is a worthy one—is a compensatory plosion at the mouth, the peal of laughter marking precisely the point, the vanishing point, at which good sense collapses into melting pleasure, or even bliss. This experience (loss of sense, access to pleasure) helps explain the distaste with which a homophobic critical tradition has regarded puns, an affect usually attributed to the "cheapness" of the thrills they so dearly provide. And because, as in Shakespeare and Wilde, punning tends toward repetition compulsion, with one pleasure chasing hard upon the heels of another, the economic censure under which puns operate opens onto ethical, even epistemological, grounds. For if "to repeat excessively is to enter . . . the zero of the signified," and if, as I am suggesting, punning is the rhetorical operation that best anatomizes the tremulous pleasure of such zeroing, then heterocentric culture must, in order to preserve itself, disdain the linguistic process by which the very power of the hetero—the power to differentiate among signifieds, objects, beings—is, on the phonemic level at least, so laughingly disdained.

Understanding all of this precisely, Wilde harnassed the erotic ambivalence of the pun for the affined purposes of pleasure, transvaluation, critique. "I am sending you, of course, a copy of my book," Wilde wrote to a friend in 1899 after Sebastian Melmoth had received copies of *Earnest*'s first pressings. "I hope you will find a place for me amongst your nicest books . . . I should like it to be within speaking distance of *Dorian Gray*" (*Letters*, 778). "Amongst your nicest books" but still "within speaking distance of *Dorian Gray*": the ironic phrasing here very nicely glosses the urbane duplicity by which Wilde insinuated the revisionary discourse of an "Urning"—a term of gay self-reference of which Wilde was very well aware—into his "trivial" but nonetheless titular pun on Earnest, and through this pun, into the "nicest" of his texts.[43] The intrinsic cross-switching within the pun of heterosexualizing and homosexualizing impulsions provided Wilde with the perfect instrument for negotiating an impossibly difficult discursive situation. Writing "at large" for a respectably straight (not to say heterosexist) audience whose sensibilities he could afford to tease but not openly offend, Wilde necessarily penned to a double measure. While mimicking the dramatic conventions of heterosexual triumph, he inserted within them the (legally unspeakable) traces of homosexual delight: inserted them, no less, where perhaps they would be least expected and certainly most disruptive—into the vocables of the paternal signifier, itself the guarantor of heterophallic order. The Urning would hide in "E(a)rnest," thereby punburying and Bunburying at the same time. ("Everything," Derrida says, "comes down to the ear you hear me with.")[44]

Thus, as Wilde insisted, the pun in *Earnest* is "trivial," and it is so in the technical, etymological—and punning—sense of the word. "Trivial" not only marks what is "common," "ordinary," and "of small account," but points as well to a crossroads or terminus "placed where three roads meet" (*OED*).[45] Thus ternary as well as trivial, Wilde's pun earnestly recapitulates Lady Bracknell's joke about the insertion of the origin into the terminus, with its consequent confusion of personal and familial identities. There should now be no difficulty in specifying the three semantic paths that cross and merge to such preposterous effect in "e(a)rnest": (1) a plain and proper name (ultimately disclosed as the Name of the Father) that, for obscure reasons, "produces vibrations"; (2) the esteemed high-Victorian quality of moral earnestness, of serious fidelity to truth, an attribute specifically gendered as "manly" and repeatedly derided by Wilde; 3) a pun-buried and coded allusion (and here two tongues, German and English, mingle), to a specifically homosexual thematics, to the practices and discourses of the "Urning" and of "Uranian love."

Into the highly fluid interspace of his titular pun, then, Wilde insinuated what Barthes would later theorize as a third or "obtuse" meaning: an evanescent meaning that always appears in excess of the common lexicon of symbols and that "can proceed only by appearing and disappearing," by Bunburying acts of strategic intermittence.[46] Explicating his notion of the third meaning, Barthes could just as well be writing of Wilde's articulation of his self-consciously "trivial" pun: it is "a supplement my intellection cannot quite absorb, a meaning both persistent and fugitive, apparent and evasive. . . . Analytically, there is something ridiculous about it; because it opens onto the infinity of language, it can seem limited in the eyes of analytic reason. It belongs to the family of puns, jokes, useless exertions, indifferent to moral and aesthetic categories (the trivial, the futile, the artificial, the parodic), it sides with the carnival aspects of things." At once carnivalesque and *contra naturam,* the erotics of the third meaning tend toward luxury and excess: the signifier "maintains itself in a state of perpetual erethism" even as it leans toward "an expenditure without exchange." As a kind of utopic erection atopically located, the third meaning ever approaches "but does not attain the spasm of the signified which usually causes the subject to sink voluptuously into the peace of nomination." No finality of signification, then; no sure termination of the terms-in-us; above all, no penning without punning. As I have insisted, Wilde adopted this writerly strategy for political as well as aesthetic reasons; he could only insinuate that which he otherwise could not say. Hence the felt sense among many readers that homosexuality in *Earnest* can be heard but not read. Hence as well the relevance of these last remarks from Barthes: "Ultimately the obtuse meaning can be seen as an *accent,* the very form of an emergence, of a fold (even a crease) marking the heavy layer of information and signification."

For the most part, of course, critical readings of *Earnest* remain vigilantly deaf and insensate to that "heavy layer of information and signification," although one writer at least, a viperish Mary McCarthy, has begrudgingly cocked an ear in the right direction. After complaining that "the joke of gluttony and the joke of rudeness" are too thin to sustain either the pleasure or the enlightenment of the audience ("nothing can be said by the muffin that has not already been said by the cucumber sandwich"), McCarthy directs her considerable wit at Wilde's pun:

> The thin little joke that remains, the importance of the name Ernest for matrimony, is in its visible aspects insufficiently entertaining. That the joke about the name Ernest is doubtless a private one makes it less endurable to the audience, which is pointedly left out of the fun. To the bisexual man, it was perhaps deliciously comic that a man should have one name, the tamest in English, for his wife and female relations, and another for his male friends, for trips and "lost" weekends; but Wilde was a prude—he went to law to clear his character—and the antisocial jibe dwindles on the stage to a refined and incomprehensible titter.[47]

The transparent meanness in this passage bespeaks a desperate emotional dodge, and an artful one, for what appears here as the critic's resentment at being "pointedly left out of the fun" of a "doubtless" "private joke" in fact masks her otherwise manifest relief at being so excluded: better in these matters to be left out than invited in.[48] Rather than savoring the transvaluing force of Wilde's "deliciously comic" critique of heterosexist presumption, McCarthy reduces Wilde's pun to an "antisocial jibe" referable only to the (no doubt) merely personal perversities of "the bisexual man." Like most criticism of Wilde, McCarthy's presupposes a very un-Wildean, essentialist sexuality, one of whose political effects is to withdraw the sexual from the historical field even as it also empties Wilde's play and pun of their insouciant force. The audible result of this "dwindling" operation is the "refined and incomprehensible titter" to which McCarthy then so ably condescends.

Against such facile reductionism we must continue to release the erotic and political energies of Wildean repetition, whose doubling and displacing power irreparably splits the subject of knowledge and the knowledge of subjectivity. It will no longer do to figure Wilde as master of, and therefore thrall to, the bon mot, the "mere" paradox, the "sterile" inversion, for in this reading Wilde does little more than recuperate, almost witlessly, the structural agreement that exists between dominant and mar-

ginal forms. Wilde's strength lies rather in the easy excess of his oppositions and in the blithe velocity with which he transposes their constituent
elements. Against the conceptual rigidification of sexual taxonomies (of
which of course he was well aware: "the fact that I am also a pathological
problem in the eyes of the German scientists is only interesting to German scientists: and even in their work I am tabulated, and come under
the law of averages!" [*Letters,* 695]), Wilde mobilizes the speedy poly-
semism whose effusions have reached our ears more than once. Against
the carceral ontology of inversion (*anima muliebris corpore virili inclusa*)
he unleashes a polytropic sexuality, thereby redoubling inversion (turn
and turn about) and developing in Jack or Ernest John "a subject split
twice over, doubly perverse" (*Pleasure,* 14). In these critical operations,
Wilde outstrips the mere oppositionalism of *doxa* and *paradoxa,* of white
versus black, even (proleptically) of gay versus straight, thereby managing
to achieve what Barthes almost a century later would call "subtle subversion": a signifying practice that "is not directly concerned with destruction, evades the paradigm, and seeks some *other* term: a third term, which
is not, however, a synthesizing term but an eccentric, extraordinary term"
(*Pleasure,* 55).

In *The Importance of Being Earnest,* I have been arguing, Wilde invents
just such an "eccentric, extraordinary term": a third, ternary, and trivial
term in which oppositional meanings are not synthesized or sublated so
much as they are exchanged, accelerated, derailed, terminated, cross-
switched. Wilde invents this term twice over, invents it in duplicate, so
that it may emerge only under alias, submitted to an originary masquer-
ade of two farcically overdetermined pseudonyms. The first of these is
Bunbury; the second is Ernest John. The interchangeability of these two
terms suggests the irreducible isomorphism between the technically unspeakable homoerotics of interminable Bunburyism and the structural bifurcation of the nominally heterosexual male subject, a point upon which
Algy exuberantly insists when he explains to Jack why "I was quite right
in saying you were a Bunburyist": "You have invented a very useful
younger brother called Ernest, in order that you may be able to come up
to town as often as you like. I have invented an invaluable permanent invalid called Bunbury, in order that I may be able to go down into the
country whenever I choose. Bunbury is perfectly invaluable." In the four-
act version Algy is even more concise; responding to Cecily's claim that
Uncle Jack "has got such strict principles about everything. He is not like
you," Algy disagrees: "Oh. I am bound to say that I think Jack and I are

very like each other. I really do not see much difference between us."[49] Given this invincible parallelism, and the obviously reversible erotics of "coming up" and "going down," Jack fully qualifies as "one of the most advanced Bunburyists I know," a classification that fate and fantasy ratify heartily when Jack is finally disclosed as "naturally Ernest."

And yet we recall that the heteroclosure of the plot presupposes the formal termination or expulsion of Bunbury, who is consequently "quite exploded" at play's end. But even as Bunbury is eliminated from the text, his (non)being thereby formally remanded to the closet from which at least his name had emerged, so also is he posthumously disseminated into the redoubled being of Wilde's earnest hero, in whose equivocal name Bunbury may be said to succeed his own surcease. Passing away only to be passed on, Bunbury is buried, and buried alive, within the duplicitous precincts of the presumptively "natural" male subject. With this irreducibly ambivalent movement—partly homicidal, partly carceral, partly liberatory—Wilde closes his great farce, seemingly submitting to the heterocentric conventions that his pun thereafter continues to exceed and deride. That pun, with all its gay shuttling, constitutes Wilde's bequest to a posterity that is only now learning how to receive and employ so rare a gift, one whose power of posthumous critique is conveyed in and as an excess of signification, pleasure, even bliss. In *Earnest,* this excess is never laid to rest. Apparently not every explosion, however terminal, implies a death. In Bunbury's end is Ernest John's beginning.

None of us survive culture.
    —Oscar Wilde, *Letters*

It is one of the bleaker ironies of English literary history that even as *Earnest* was brashly entertaining audiences at the St. James Theatre, where it had opened on 14 February 1895, its author was subjected to a fierce and dogged institutional chastisement, the prosecution and persecution of the famous trials of 1895. From 5 April, when Wilde was arrested for "acts of gross indecency with another male person" until late in the same month, when George Alexander was compelled by public opinion to remove *Earnest* from the boards, the two spectacles ran concurrently: the one all gay insouciance, the other pure bourgeois retribution; the one a triumph of evanescent, if not quite indeterminate, signification, the other a brutal travesty in which the author would be nailed to the specificity of his "acts." Thus juxtaposed, these two spectacles compose an almost too ready dyptich of crime and punishment, as in Auden's "nightmare Pantomime Transformation Scene in which . . . the country house in never-never Hertfordshire turns into the Old Bailey, the features of Lady Bracknell into those of Mr. Justice Wills." The very facility of these transpositions—Auden's and my own—indicates the volatile reversibility of the sexual and verbal inversions that Wilde delighted in practicing and perfecting. Predicated upon adroit manipulation of a sodomitical "pose," Wildean pleasure had always flirted with its own susceptibility to disciplinary relapse, a danger that first honed the edge of Wilde's enjoyment and later incited his disastrous prosecution of the libel charge against Queensberry. The advent of the trials marked an implacable shift to an institutional context in which the slip and slide of serious Bunburyism would be frozen by the cold face of Gradgrindian fact. This begins to define the difference between Wildean courage and the ease of a critic who may with impunity celebrate Bunbury at the cool distance of a hundred years. Wilde took chances, and Wilde paid. Not the least nor the last of his humiliations came in the second year of his imprisonment, when his wife Constance successfully petitioned to deprive him of guardianship of his sons, Cyril and Vyvyan, and to change their surnames (along with her own) to her maiden surname, Holland.[50] This irony bites. As if to chastise Wilde for trifling with the patronym in *Earnest,* the state rescinded his right to propagate the Name of the Father.

5

No Private Parts

On the Rereading of Women in Love

The wrestling had some deep meaning to them—an unfinished meaning.

—D. H. Lawrence, *Women in Love*

The imaginary now resides between the book and the lamp.

—Michel Foucault, "Fantasia of the Library"

About my first or "original" reading of *Women in Love*[1] I can remember only three things. First, that as I lay on my bed—alone, no doubt very lonely, perhaps twenty years old, and "reading as if for life"[2]—I soon enough found myself so awash in anger and frustration, even readerly despair, that I flung the book across the room, where it smacked the opposing wall with a loud report and dropped, bruised and fluttering, to the floor; and second, that after an interval whose duration I can no longer even surmise, but which must have consisted of "many uncounted, unknown minutes" (271), I traversed the same space, retrieved the book, and, cursing together both Lawrence and myself, returned to the bed where, those curses now passing into thin air, I commenced reading again. If, as I now believe, I have never "actually" (that is, physically or bodily) reenacted the melodrama of this ambivalent gesture—a gesture, not incidentally, whose angry kinesis Lawrence was happy to authorize—then this is doubtless because subsequent conspiracies of thought and fantasy have succeeded in rendering such repetition unnecessary, so much so that fantasmatically I have repeated the gesture a thousand times, just as now, under the guise of a professional obligation, I am doing so for the thousand-and-first. And if I cannot now recall—after perhaps ten or twenty actual rereadings, both in and out of school, whether as student or teacher or neither—at what point or passage in the text I had arrived when I let the book fly, then this syncope in memory perhaps does not matter very much; for how easy it would prove—has proven—to anthologize those many passages in *Women in Love* where Lawrence's hypercharged emotion, overwrought sexuality, and mystifying language (notice how I belie the imbricated tissue of the Lawrentian text as I itemize these qualities separately and serially) are sufficiently infuriating to precipitate, however passingly, the violence of such a repudiation. I only know that it could not have been at any point during the novel's last fifty pages—"pages that have," as Mark Schorer put it some forty years ago, "more power of a particular kind than any English or American novel. It is what we might call the real Russian bang."[3] It was, no doubt, this "particular" power, itself an uncanny crisscrossing of erotic, homicidal, and suicidal impulses, that (and this is the third thing I remember) banged *me* up against the bedroom wall where, transfixed and hyperventilating, I kept on reading, Lawrence's easy thrall, until the indifferent book could let me drop.

Hyperbole, no doubt. But perhaps hyperbole may be admitted as the only figure whose rhetorical proportions are distended sufficiently to represent, however self-consciously, my own experience of *Women in Love*'s traumatizing power, which not even that score of rereadings has served adequately to diminish, much less "master" or overcome. For caught up in the knotted somatism of this reader's responses—his outraged propulsion of the book and his cursing retrieval, even more his "feminine" submission to its closural *raptus*—were, as I think I see now and as anyone else surely would have seen from the start, deeply blindsided entanglements of identification and repudiation, desire and fear. A happier reading and writing ("O happy, happy love") might dispose of the dangers of such blended affects by deploying them as single adversarial binarisms (identification versus repudiation, desire versus fear, etc.) whose first order of business would be to keep these emotions safe by keeping them distinct, with the "versus" marking the bar of an insuperable division; or, not so inversely, as more complex deconstructive binarisms whose also orderly business would be their dexterous vaporization into the airy sameness of an axiomatic *différance*. But Lawrence's writing turns perversely upon the crossing of the same diacritical bar that it nonetheless also refuses to disembody or dissolve, with the consequent demand (repelling some readers, compelling others) that such irreconcilable human affects must meet, mingle, and interpenetrate—in the manner, say, of "Gladiatorial":

So the two men entwined and wrestled with each other, working nearer and nearer. Both were white and clear, but Gerald flushed smart red where he was touched, and Birkin remained white and tense. He seemed to penetrate into Gerald's more solid, more diffuse bulk, to interfuse his body through the body of the other, as if to bring it subtly into subjection, always seizing with some rapid necromantic foreknowledge every motion of the other flesh, converting and counteracting it, playing upon the limbs and trunk of Gerald like some hard wind. It was as if Birkin's whole physical intelligence interpenetrated into Gerald's body, as if his fine, sublimated energy entered into the flesh of the fuller man, like some potency, casting a fine net, a prison, through the muscles into the very depths of Gerald's physical being.

So they wrestled swiftly, rapturously, intent and mindless at last, two essential white figures ever working into a tighter, closer oneness of struggle, with a strange, octopus-like knotting and flashing of limbs in the subdued light of the room; a tense white knot of flesh gripped in silence between the walls of old brown books.(270)

"Mindless at last" "with some rapid necromantic foreknowledge" and "ever working into a tighter, closer oneness of struggle": if these phrases refer primarily and immediately to those naked male bodies "gripped in silence between the walls of old brown books"—books whose mute witness audibly situates this wrestling or "octopus-like knotting" in and as a scene of reading—then they also bespeak only too cannily the dense erotic entanglements, the impacted "physical junction," that Lawrence's writing imposes upon his readers generally and upon this particularly cathected reader especially. "Playing upon [my] limbs and trunk . . . like some hard wind," how easily Lawrence has "interfuse[d] his body through the body of th[is] other," insinuating into "every motion of the other flesh" a rhythm necessarily responsive to his own. In repeated engagements of "seiz[ure]" and release, of yielding and repulsion, of "conver[sion] and counteract[ion]," *Women in Love* and I have "wrestled swiftly, rapturously," always "working nearer and nearer"; and, as with Birkin and Gerald, this reading or wrestling has reflexively invoked a who's-on-top erotics of domination and control in which the book and I have sought "to bring [each other] subtly into subjection." Whatever effects, salutary or dysphoric, such engagements may have induced in me, *Women in Love* has easily succeeded in casting its "fine net . . . through the muscles into the very depths of [my] physical being," so much so that almost every sexual cognition or flexion I can summon, or that I have been lucky enough to have summon me, seems already to have been touched or tinged by Lawrence's turbulent infusions. This has not, I hardly need stress, always meant good times. But it has made for some heady reading: too often I have found myself "a tense white knot of flesh gripped in silence between the walls of old brown books"; and many times I have looked up blindly from the text, "hearing an immense knocking outside. What could be happening, what was it, the great hammerstrokes resounding through the house? He did not know. And then it came to him that it was his own heart beating. . . . He did not know whether he were standing or lying or falling" (271). (Subsequent recognition: falling; more subsequent still: falling in love.)

Yet it would be fatuous at this late date in the history of reading to suggest that such avid involvements as these are, or ever could be, purely or even primarily "my own," and not merely because they may claim a critical history long antedating my arrival, however bright-eyed, upon the scene. But if not mine, then whose? And to what I or me might this "mine" refer, if not to one whose most secretly enfolded being has been constituted crucially, if not entirely, through particular acts of reading, acts whose most private or even intimate aspects had no choice but to be articulated in terms of received conventions and codes, inscriptions and erasures, propulsions and reticences? Even the most rudimentary competence in reading entails the long and largely suppressed history of the reader's enabling submission to the systems of meaning, modes of production, and procedures of interpretation that make comprehension possible at all. (If reading, as the heartiest of its hawkers like to proclaim, ultimately "liberates" the mind, it does so only by disciplining it first: reading drills us in the cultural uses of regulated repetition.) On this reading no reading can ever be originary, since all reading is already rereading, with each new text impelling yet another set of a by now reflexive exercise. The very givenness of the written text, the "simple" fact that it is there to be read at all, thus indicates a truth whose homeliness is exceeded only by its transparency: reading inserts every reader into a serial proliferation (of, to mention a crucial few, signs, sounds, silences, mediations, practices, commodities, other readers and writers) whose first and final elements no reader, however scrupulous or perspicacious, can ever know. I can read today only because others have read before me, and tomorrow I will teach another how to read. Banal as this observation is doomed to seem, its implications are portentous: however isolate the scene of reading, no one ever reads alone; however unacquainted reader and text, no one ever reads *anything* for the first time.

This dynamism of repetition, while indelibly marking the cultural em-beddedness of all textual meaning and practice, necessarily impinges upon the embodiments of reading and writing. The somatics of interpre-tation may be ignored or exalted, incited or repressed, but they may not be escaped. Not only, as diverse feminisms have insisted, are individual and collective bodies, of whatever gender, construed within and as highly politicized systems of signs, but the "brute body" itself (which self, we must insist in passing, is itself a thoroughgoing abstraction) engages read-ing with an almost inconceivable immediacy: at the level of organs and functions, in the pores and along the veins.[4] I read as I breathe—in order to live. Nor is it just the (agitated or becalmed, saturated or dessicated) body of the individual reader that is at stake here, but also a whole his-tory of multiple embodiments, symbolic and material, "natural" and technological. Even, for instance, the most trite (and later contrite) of our culture's masturbatory scenarios—a boy, a book, a flashlight—hardly de-picts a practice, much less a "vice," that could by any reasonable measure be called solitary, given the interposition within this scene of a palpable surround of cultural/parental interdiction (the walls, I can attest, are whispering a "no" that sounds like "go"), of commodified representation (the book and its many incitements), and of a technology (the flashlight) sufficiently specialized to expedite the boy's eager and enlightened con-sumption of that commodity.

In the language of "Gladiatorial," this can only mean that the "whole physical intelligence" of the reader must wrestle with a knot of bodies not his own, "interfus[ing] his [elsewhere, her] body through the bod[ies] of the other[s]," and vice versa. Reading thus implicates, however invisibly, not merely the materially present body of the reader but also the ghostlier present-absent bodies within and behind texts: the bodies of characters, authors, readers; the fantasmatic bodies of class, race, and nationality; even that heavy abstraction, the "social body" at large. But any attempt to map the engagement of these surely affined but oddly incommensurate bodies onto the (highly contingent, deeply tendentious) grids of gender and sexuality will be sure to suffer resistance, slippage, even downright contradiction, especially in a culture where the pseudo-oppositions be-tween genders and sexualities actively belie the far more sinuous relations (of identification, specularity, introjection, transference, etc.) through which these seeming oppositions are tirelessly rehearsed, both by those who would consolidate them and those who would empty them out. (The routine performative exertions, for instance, of being "masculine" and staying straight can be staggering in their destructiveness and duplicity, as the violent tortuosities of *Women in Love*—and of my reading of them—should help make clear.) In any case, because different readers will assimilate themselves differently to their "own" gender and sexuality assignations and to the subject/object positionings entailed therein, the homo/hetero alignments of reading will often elude easy binary coordination, however compelling at a particular time and place the disciplinary enforcements of the binary may be. And this will be true not only between or among different readers and their readings but also, crucially, within and across individual readers and theirs. Again I stress that this readerly production of difference hardly counts as an argument for the essential indeterminacy of meaning. Quite the contrary. A reading's power and function—its utility within psychological, literary, and political fields—will almost certainly derive from its most insistent determinations and cathexes: from the way it affords, for instance, multiple or shifting or even contradictory gender identifications; or from the way it courts, despite the seeming self-evidence of one's own heterosexual "orientation," the ply and pull of homosexual desires. No reading, I am suggesting, should be so complacent as to be self-identical, so charmed by its own image as to leave itself no difference from itself. On this view, the very fragmentation of one's reading—its contradictions, dissensions, resistances, lapses—becomes something more than either the symptomatic failure to assimilate the "organic" text or the equally symptomatic triumph of a programmatic indeterminacy. It becomes instead the site of intervention or the pivot of power, the fulcrum upon which the Archimedean lever may be wedged in order to tilt the world and one's relation to it.

And so I repeat my questions. If my passionate involvements with *Women in Love* are not exactly or exclusively my own, then whose are they? Out of what skeins of knowledge and desire have they been woven, and what received compulsions and permissions do they repeat in their weave? Whose were the hands that drove me back, shall I say blindly and compulsively, to a text that I could not quite read, nor stop rereading, even as it was quite obviously reading me, as we say, like an open book? What promises of subtle instruction lay in "the beyond, the obscene beyond" (242) to which Lawrence offered, or seemed to offer, admission? More intimately still, what had Lawrence intuited (purblindly too: "a novel," he would write in the earliest phases of its composition [1913], "which I have never grasped . . . and I've no notion what its about . . . like a novel in a foreign language I don't know very well")[5] about me some forty years before my birth? What was this dark knowledge that I could recognize, if at all, only in the funhouse distortions of my own ecstatic misrecognitions? And, most urgently of all, how was this knowledge, of whatsoever constituted, related to the erotic pulsions of this big book's big bang, its terminal drive toward murder and mourning? If, as Lawrence puts it elsewhere, "death is part of the story," what then to make of Lawrence's, and my own, "desire to deal death and to take death?"[6]

But even as I put these questions, whose breathless framing exposes, even celebrates, the critical embarrassment that I have long since abandoned any hope of writing "objectively" about *Women in Love,* I know that I will withhold, for a certain duration at least, both the "merely" personal and the more broadly resonant transpersonal answers that they presume to solicit. And this for two reasons. First, to extract whatever critical advantage may derive from the temporizing erotologic made more than familiar by the repeated exercise of various behind-the-veil cultural practices, as in, for instance, confession or striptease, where the ritually stalled but nonetheless assured revelation of the "private parts" confers upon waiting its dense and urgent materiality. And second, to inscribe within this writing—rather, *as* this writing—a delay, confusion, and difficulty meant to imitate my own frustrated coming to knowledge of *Women in Love,* itself the product of an almost "scholarly" repetition compulsion variously worked out, if never exactly worked through, in bedrooms, libraries, and cafés. Hoping thereby to avoid the flattened formulations of academic thematism—say, "the homophobic interpellation within the 'heterosexual male subject' of homosexual and homicidal desires"—this writing will work, if it works at all, only to the degree that it enables what I understand to be the ethically imperative labor of transforming not just the text being read but also the writer who would hope thus to read it.

"The fundamental equivocation of *Women in Love* repels me," writes John Middleton Murry, perhaps Lawrence's acutest and certainly his most caustic (male) critic, in a reverse hagiography, *Son of Woman* (1931), whose own cognitive and erotic investments vibrate equivocally enough:

> It is not that I blame Lawrence for yielding to a longing from which in
> his inward soul he shrank away. Lawrence was Lawrence—a destiny-
> driven man, if ever there was one. If the realm of mindless sensuality of-

fered or seemed to offer the only way of escape for his tortured spirit, then he was driven to explore it. But I think he is to be condemned for painting his devil [Rupert Birkin] as an angel, for the duplicity with which he represents himself as turning away from this mindless sensuality towards a paradisal relation with the woman, yet subtly perverts this very relation (in defiance of all truth, factual or imaginative) into a form of that mindless sensuality from which it was to be an escape. Lawrence, in the essential and vital argument of *Women in Love,* behaves like a cheat.[7]

The erotic equivocation or "fundamental falsity" (*SW,* 95) that so distresses Murry here derives from Lawrence's "failure"—I would say, his refusal—to sustain the patent dichotomy upon which the action, such as it is, and the characterology, also such as it is, of *Women in Love* turn. That dichotomy, as Murry was the first to recognize and as the subsequent criticism has largely affirmed, proceeds from "the distinction between the 'love' of Rupert and Ursula on the one hand, and [that] of Gerald and Gudrun on the other": "Rupert and Ursula are represented as in the way of salvation, Gerald and Gudrun as in the way of damnation" (*SW,* 112–13). In Murry's reading this distinction is indeed fundamental, constituting both "the essential and vital argument" of the book and the scission whose decisiveness establishes two diametrically opposed (hetero)sexualities, with the Birkin/Ursula conjugation embodying (alas, illusorily) the "paradisal" ideal in terms of which the "mindless sensuality" that binds Gudrun and Gerald each to the other will be found deficient, destructive, ultimately fatal. If the oft-cited and much-hated "symbolic" complexities and indeterminacies of *Women in Love* belie so schematic a binary logic as this, Murry's proposition is nonetheless confirmed by, to cite the terminal example, the novel's strong teleological drive, its need to finish itself by finishing off not just the Gudrun/Gerald relation but also, more specifically, the character—or, more specifically still, the erotic object, so exciting from the first—of Gerald himself. In killing Gerald outright and deporting ("so to speak") Gudrun to Dresden with Loerke, the narrative critically and diacritically marks the difference between the couples according to a taxonomic principle whose conceptual simplicity and epistemological complexity anticipate the Freud of *Beyond the Pleasure Principle* (1920), a principle that organizes all human experience in terms either of an impulsion to live (Freud's *Lebenstriebe*) or an impulsion to die (his *Todestriebe*). The epistemological difficulty here lies in the fact that the latter has, from the beginning, been so deeply invaginated, or folded, into the former that the death drive will be disclosed, if at all, only insofar as it is already locked in an embrace with the life drive, the result being an epistemological tangle, another "tense white knot of flesh" in which the two component drives have become, in Murry's very worried phrase, as "indistinguishable as octopods in an aquarium tank" (*R,* 223). Freud's more sober formulation of this entanglement: "What we are concerned with are scarcely ever pure instinctual impulses but mixtures in various proportions of the two groups of instincts," a situation rendered still more perplexing because, as Freud explains, this dispersion of drive or "instinct" is topographical as well: "There can be no question of restricting one or the other of the basic instincts to one of the provinces of the mind. They must necessarily be met with everywhere." Ultimately these analytical considerations led Freud to the Lawrentian recognition that the death drive "eludes our perception . . . unless it is tinged with eroticism."

It is exactly this interfusion of vital/fatal difference that appalls Murry's judgment and triggers his hostility. Hence his lament that the crucial erotic distinction between the couples only too soon confounds its own foundations, *fond sans fond,* and forfeits its distinctness: "when we consider the principles which these opposed couples really embody, we discover that the difference between them is that Rupert and Ursula are a whole stage further on in the process of damnation" (*SW,* 113). The distinction between the couples thus collapses and falls, in a figure borrowed from the novel's own rhetoric of disintegrative sexuality, into the "dark river of dissolution," that watery site—by turns symbolic, anatomical, and topographical; by another turn, all three—in which difference itself makes, as Birkin expounds it to Ursula, both "no difference—and all the difference" (173). It is on the banks of this river, where these two modes of heterosexual interaction lose the very "hetero" that contradistinguishes them, and where difference and no difference blend in *Blutbrüderschaft,* that Murry cries foul. What had seemed a crucial ontological polarity— nothing less than "salvation" versus "damnation," an apocalyptic binarism perfectly resonant with the giant agon of Lawrence's fiction—is disclosed instead as a factitious temporal vagary: a ruse, a lie, and a "cheat." An equivocation, Murry almost says, like the fiend's ("painting his devil as an angel," etc.).

Substantiating his claim that this fundamental equivocation "subtly perverts" the novel's sexual argument, Murry locates the specimen case of this perversion in the infamous chapter "Excurse," specifically in those "crucial pages" where Ursula's touch, having traced the round of Birkin's buttocks, suddenly releases not merely typically Lawrentian "floods of ineffable darkness" "at the back and base of the loins" but also (and presumably with less intention) the fulsome waves of critical execration with which subsequent writers have so antiseptically inundated the only barely effaced anality of this scene. Not surprisingly, a postdiluvian Murry carefully positions himself *out of touch*, beyond the farthest rim of the anal caress (an "experience," he says, "which we must call *x*"), and unconvincingly pretends that he does not know what he also demonstrably knows he knows: "to us," he writes, "these crucial pages are completely and utterly unintelligible if we assume (as we must assume if we have regard for the vehemence of Mr. Lawrence's passion) that they are not the crudest sexuality" (*R*, 223). Having thus deferred not to his own palpable anxiety before the anal issue but rather to the apparently frontal dignity of Lawrentian "vehemence," Murry then proceeds by way of quasi-algebraic circumspection:

> We have given, in spite of our repulsion and our weariness, our undivided attention to Mr. Lawrence's book for the space of three days; we have striven with all our power to understand what he means by the experience *x*; we have compared it with the experience *y*, which takes place between the other pair of lovers, Gudrun and Gerald; we can see no difference between them, and we are precluded from inviting our readers to pronounce. We are sure that not one person in a thousand would decide that they were anything but the crudest kind of sexuality, wrapped up in . . . the language of Higher Thought. We feel that the solitary person may be right; but even he, we are convinced, would be quite unable to distinguish between experience *x* and experience *y*. Yet *x* leads one pair to undreamed-of happiness, and *y* conducts the other to attempted murder and suicide.
>
> This *x* and *y* are separate, if they are separate, on a plane of consciousness other than ours. To our consciousness they are indistinguishable; either they belong to the nothingness of unconscious sexuality, or they are utterly meaningless. (*R*, 224–25)

It requires no extraordinary percipience to see that this passage traverses a "fundamental equivocation" all its own, as Murry's tense analysis conscientiously abjures the very knowledge whose effects it is also in the process, however disingenuously, of deploying. Murry's first move is to lay proud claim to an oceanic ignorance whose prophylactic dictum, uttered in the form of a bewildered "masculine protest," is, quite simply, *I understand nothing of this; such things are utterly beyond me, my touch, my ken*. But the credibility of this incomprehension is rendered almost immediately suspect by the same vigor with which its claim to stupidity is prosecuted: are we seriously to believe that three full days of "undivided attention," of the unrelenting application of "all our power to understand," leave so alert and committed a reader as Murry still absolutely unenlightened as to the difference "between experience *x* and experience *y*?" Apparently not a sliver of recognition pierces the formidable barrier of Murry's cognitive shield, which fits like a tight glove both the critic's longing not to know (what, as I say, he also shows he knows he knows) and his need publicly to assume the posture and imposture of incomprehension: "This *x* and *y* are separate, if they are separate, on a plane of consciousness other than ours." Yet no sooner is this claim to cognitive blankness advanced than it is twice compromised: first by those nine-hundred-ninety-nine implied readers whose stupefaction before the anal caress ("nothing but the crudest kind of sexuality wrapped up in . . . the language of Higher Thought") nonetheless does not enervate their (however partial) acknowledgment that Lawrence is articulating a serious, if sometimes opaque discourse of the fundamental; and second in Murry's little fantasia of the prescient "solitary," that one-in-a-thousand reader whose power of Lawrentian attunement enables him, and him alone, to pass behind the veil into some "obscene beyond" (242)—the beyond in which Lawrentian contradiction and obscurity will be (in the language of light and butter) clarified, and the beyond in which the "crudest" (*sic*) of sexual gestures will be seen to have been merely a fingerpost, a pointer, a tip along the way. And yet if Murry's recourse to this "ideal reader" (let us call him Anon) amounts to a rescission of his claim to ignorance, as well as an oblique admission of an otherwise unspeakable desire to follow Ursula in her traces, this gesture remains at heart half-hearted, ever open to retraction, since Anon returns from this beyond only to ratify Murry's original claim to incomprehension. Anon returns, that is, enlightened but dumbstruck, still "unable to distinguish," in words anyway, the difference between *x* and *y*, which itself remains "to our consciousness . . . utterly meaningless."

In its transmigration among or between divergent, even incompatible subject positions (*I just don't get it . . . it's not what it looks like. . . . Anon knows but Anon can't say. . . . I still don't get it*), Murry's writing on "Excurse" enacts the same "failure"—the failure to differentiate convincingly—that had originally animated his animus; the pot, it would seem, has been calling the kettle black. Consequently, whatever prescience

Murry's criticism may claim lies less in the lucidity of its truth claims than in the hide-and-seek of its knowing and unknowing, less in the validity of its value judgments than in the highly motivated vacillation between, on the one hand, its recognitions and, on the other, its intransigent refusals thereof.[8] It lies, if we may send the errant phrase home, in Murry's own "fundamental equivocation." This in turn helps explain why Murry *is* finally so astute about *Women in Love* in at least two senses: astute to assert that equivocation informs the primary morphemes of the novel (its plot, characters, tropes, etc.), and astute to designate that equivocation as constitutive and irreducible—as, specifically, "fundamental," Murry's latinate circumlocution for the "unspeakable" darkness "at the back and base of the loins."

The embedded or muddied pun on *fundament* and anality, as obvious as it is obviously repressed in Murry's writing (1921, 1931), would not receive open critical recognition until 1961, when G. Wilson Knight delicately unpacked some indelicacies from Lawrence's notion of excursive desire. In a comparative reading of, among other texts, *Women in Love, Ulysses,* and *Lady Chatterley's Lover*—a reading that goes out of its way to count the ways in which Murry's "acute commentary has assisted my understanding"—Knight specifies the digital and phallic, not to say lingual, aspects of Lawrentian "sodomy"—a word, *not* by the way, that appears nowhere in Knight's essay, although Knight does go so far as to say that "whatever we may think of the implied teaching, Lawrence was certainly engaged on a deep problem."[9] Correctly specifying that "in *Women in Love* the implements [of this "implied teaching"] are fingers," Knight goes on to identify in Connie Chatterley a nascent desire for purgatorial sodomy, for "a phallic hunting-out" (Lawrence) at "an entrance other than the normal" (Knight). When in chapter 16 of *Lady Chatterley's Lover* Mellors's "reckless, shameless" fucking shakes Connie "to her foundations," this is because he takes her in the fundament, presumably "burning out the shames, the deepest, oldest shames, in the most secret places." In his explication (and explicitation) of this sodomitical conjunction, Knight's language recalls both Lawrence's and Murry's: "This experience Lady Chatterly now realizes that she has always unconsciously desired 'at the bottom of her soul, fundamentally'; the words are exactly chosen. The writing has compression, density, and precision."

Knight is perspicuous. Certainly "compression" and "density"—I remain skeptical about "precision"—are productive terms with which to begin retracing Lawrence's excursus into heterosexual sodomy: productive because (like their kissing cousin from the psychoanalytic lexicon, "condensation" or *Verdichtung*) these terms incorporate, without pretending to sublate or subsume, high levels of variety, contradiction, and aggregation; they indicate a mode of inclusion but not a mode of unification or resolution—the many do not become the one. As terms transported analogically from the mechanics of fluids and solids, "compression" and "density" suggest a conception of writing in which particular images (say, "the dark river of dissolution.") or image clusters (say, thinking at once of Gerald Crich and Clifford Chatterley, mud, matter, *mater*, and mining) do not so much represent single ideas or unified conceptions as they do diverse, highly cathected, and often deeply conflicted associative chains at whose points of intersection and interfusion—at whose *Blutbrüderschaft?*—these images and clusters are located. Figured in this way, such compressed images or "symbols" are best understood neither as the transparent containers of luminous signification nor as the living educts of a relentlessly monologizing Imagination, but rather as the transfer points or relay stations where vectors of meaning, desire, and power criss-cross, cross-switch, even switch off each other. Like the percussive rays of light and dark that coruscate across the surface of Willey Water as a lunatic Birkin stones the reflected face of the moon, they do not so much embody or incarnate a particular code as they record the collision and collusion of divergent codes through procedures of skewing, distortion, refraction, and denial. Not the image fixed and formulated in gemlike perfection, but the image in transit and *in extremis,* at once shattered and shattering: "He got large stones, and threw them, one after the other, at the white-burning centre of the moon, till there was nothing but a rocking of hollow noise, and a pond surged up, no moon any more, only a few broken flakes tangled and glittering broadcast in the darkness, without aim or meaning, a darkened confusion, like a black and white kaleidoscope tossed at random" (247–48). Tossed out of and into "darkened confusion," the condensed images of which I speak are compact of multiple affects and contrary significations, and they emphatically do not yield the heavily advertised consolations, at once Christological and organicist, that Coleridge dreamed to be intrinsic to the symbol: "a symbol . . . is characterized by the translucence of the special in the individual, or of the general in the special, or of the universal in the general; above all by the translucence of the eternal through and in the temporal. It always partakes of the reality which it renders intelligible; and while it enunciates the whole, abides itself as a living part in that unity of which it is the representative."[10] A vision justly famous for its powers of divine seduction, this from Coleridge, but one hardly appropriate either to Lawrence's practice of writing the symbol or to his theorizations of divergence and contradiction within what he sometimes calls "symbolic meaning" and sometimes "art-speech":

> But art-speech, art-utterance, is, and always will be, the greatest universal language of mankind, greater than any esoteric symbolism. Art-speech is also a language of pure symbols. But whereas the authorized symbol stands for a thought or an idea, some mental *concept,* the art-symbol or art-term stands for a pure experience, emotional and passional, spiritual and perceptual, all at once. The intellectual idea remains implicit, latent and nascent. Art communicates a state of being—whereas the symbol at best only communicates a whole thought, an emotional idea. Art-speech is a use of symbols which are pulsations on the blood and seizures upon the nerves, and at the same time pure precepts of the mind and pure terms of spiritual aspiration.[11]

Some examples will help elaborate my case. The passages adduced below, presented in order of their composition, resonate together with powerful affinities—though the resonance or convergence of thought, emotion, and image can hardly be called harmonic. Each passage derives from the fecund and crucial period, March 1915–July 1916, during which Lawrence was revising *The Rainbow* and seeing it first through triumphant publication and then through heartbreaking opprobrium; composing the outlandish, "philosophicalish," and "revolutionary utterance" he would ultimately entitle "The Crown" (*Letters,* 2:300); and trying to subdue the extraordinary materials (it would take six full-scale revisions, the last not completed until September 1919) that would be published first in America under the banal misnomer *Women in Love.* Each passage employs the same barely controlled constellation of grotesque images; each manifests the same deeply ambivalent sodomitical/homosexual thematics; and each derives, mediately or immediately, both from the cultural surround of escalating homophobia (the Wilde trials, remember, had transpired only twenty years before) and from Lawrence's own "actual" dreamlife, most especially from the acute nightmares he suffered in March and April 1915 after confronting (in the pyjama-clad person of John Maynard Keynes) the "too wicked and perverse" "marsh-stagnancy" of Cambridge University (*Letters,* 2:319,309). The first passage consists of two raging paragraphs extracted from an April 1915 letter to David Garnett, who was the son of Lawrence's sometime champion Edward Garnett and whom Lawrence believed to be homosexually involved with one Francis Birrell. The recto of the envelope carrying the letter bears the inscription "Absolutely Private" in Lawrence's beautiful hand. "My dear David," the letter begins,

> I can't bear to think of you, David, so wretched as you are—and your hand shaky—and everything wrong. It is foolish of you to say that it doesn't matter either way—the men loving men. It doesn't matter in the public way. But it matters so much, David, to the man himself—at any rate to us northern nations—that it is like a blow of triumphant decay, when I meet Birrell or the others. I simply can't bear it. It is so wrong, it is unbearable. It makes a form of inward corruption which truly makes me scarce able to live. Why is there this horrible sense of frowstiness, so repulsive, as if it came from deep inward dirt—a sort of sewer—deep in men like K[eynes] and B[irrell] and D[uncan] G[rant]. I never knew what it meant till I saw K., till I saw him at Cambridge. We went into his rooms at midday, and it was very sunny. He was not there, so Russell was writing a note. Then suddenly a door opened and K. was there, blinking from sleep, standing in his pyjamas. And as he stood there gradually a knowledge passed into me, which has been like a little madness to me ever since. And it was carried along with the most dreadful sense of repulsiveness—something like carrion—a vulture gives me the same feeling. I begin to feel mad as I think of it—insane.
>
> Never bring B. to see me any more. There is something nasty about him, like black-beetles. He is horrible and unclean. I feel as if I should go mad, if I think of your set, D.G. and K. and B. It makes me dream of beetles. In Cambridge I had a similar dream. Somehow, I can't bear it. It is wrong beyond all bounds of wrongness. I had felt it slightly before, in the Stracheys. But it came full upon me in K., and in D.G. And yesterday I knew it again, in B.

The subject of these paragraphs, as of this dream, is not bugs—it is buggery.[12] Or rather: the inescapable but purely arbitrary aural (and oral) affinity between these two words (there is, in fact, no etymological or genealogical connection whatsoever between them) incites Lawrence's subconscious to percolate a truly phantasmagoric pun, a pun that in turn motivates his deeply idiosyncratic, his "wicked and perverse," deployment of the beetle image. In this eerily self-reflexive missive addressed *in* his own name *to* his own name (i.e., from David to David, the name repeated six times in the letter's four paragraphs), Lawrence's image of "nasty" "black-beetles," "horrible and unclean," represents not merely the abstract possibility of male homosexual activity, the idea of "men loving men" about which of course he had had all along, via Plato and Wilde, a complacent mind knowledge; more crucially, the image embodies Lawrence's intimate and shocked coming to blood knowledge of this possibility, which he straightforwardly represents as an "unbearable" infusion (much like Birkin's fantasy of a goose's blood "entering [one's] own blood like an inoculation of corruptive fire—fire of the cold-burning mud" [89]): "And as [Keynes] stood there gradually a knowledge passed into me, which has been like a little madness to me ever since." So supercharged was this infusion with repressed desire, loathing, and anal anxiety ("a blow of triumphant decay," "a form of inward corruption," "deep inward dirt," "a sort of sewer," etc.) that it constituted, according to Lawrence's own evaluation, "one of the crises of my life," sending "me mad with misery and hostility and rage" (*Letters,* 2:321). And worse: not only did this accession to "dark knowledge" refuse to stop coming ("I had felt it slightly before. . . . But it came full upon me in [Cambridge]. . . . And yesterday I knew it again"), but it continued to traumatize the writer fantasmatically, automatically, even as he wrote against it: "I begin to feel mad as I think of it—insane."

Lawrence's dream image may be singular, but by no means is it single. His letters and other writings from this period indicate that, whether sleeping or waking, dreaming or writing, Lawrence returned with obsessive frequency to images of bugs, of "black-beetles," of dung beetles (e.g., *Women in Love*'s "ball-rolling scarab" [253]), and, in one particularly violent redaction of the nightmare, to a monstrous centaur insect, a "very large beetle" phallically endowed with the tail of a scorpion, an image to which he responded with a murderous "black fury," a desire to kill and kill again. "Black fury": as it internalizes the beetle's blackness, this phrase compactly anatomizes the compulsive processes of inversion, projection, and introjection that characterize Lawrence's use of the absolute, repellent other as a figure, however self-blinded, for the self one would prefer to deny—for, that is, "David . . . the man himself." In any event, Lawrence in his dream sees the bug and moves, at first incompetently, to destroy it: "They [those Cambridge boys again] made me dream in the night of a beetle that bites like a scorpion. But I killed it—a very large beetle. I scotched it—and it ran off—but I came upon it again and killed it. It is this horror of little swarming selves that I can't stand: Birrells, and D. Grants, and Keynses" (*Letters,* 2:319). If Lawrence's dream insect here, like Kafka's elsewhere, is both morphologically impossible and entomologically inaccurate (scorpions of course do not bite their prey, they sting with their tails), it is nonetheless grotesquely evocative as fantasy: the mouth/tail or orifice/penetrator confusion expresses with hallucinatory accuracy the semantic lability of "sodomy," the elastic and "absolutely confused category" that historically had subsumed, among other variations, both oral and anal modes of conjunction, often without modernity's fastidious concern for the anatomical sex of the persons thus conjoined.

But we have yet to comprehend adequately either the extent of Lawrence's deployment of this imagery or the ferocity of his disgust when confronted, either physically or imaginatively, by "these 'friends,' these beetles." In this regard let us put a fundamental recognition in place: Lawrence's repulsion is directly proportional to the ardor of his cathexis; he stands riveted by the same thought/image he feels compelled to repudiate. However psychologically untenable such a position may seem, it nonetheless quickened Lawrence's textual pulse (never slack anyway), the result being not merely a spasmodic overpopulation of bugs and beetles in the prose of this period, but also a striking proliferation of like or related images, some of them rivaling the "black-beetle" for sheer repulsiveness. The basic structure shared by each of these images may be easily diagrammed: a rigid exoskeletal form encloses, and thereby occludes, a pulpy and putrescent interior, itself quite formless. Or again, a "dry and scaly and brittle" shell envelopes a seething "viscous mass" that itself cannot be seen or touched or smelled until the surrounding rind has been cracked by—what else?—the deft hammerstrokes of Lawrence's writing (*DP,* 473). In its schematic version the image rarely varies—fixed form on the outside, all seethe and amorphousness within; but in its local avatars the image is "humanwarious" indeed, sometimes impossibly abstract, other times unbearably concrete. In the following sequence, which pretends neither to exhaustiveness nor to rigorous logical coordination, I have listed some examples, some "black-beetle" cognates, each example already a figure for its brothers, all threatening to fall or fold indistinguishably one into the other, composing thereby a decomposing mass "full of corruption" (*DP,* 276, 277). If the images to follow seem to "run brittly hither and thither," mounting reflexively one upon the other "like some extreme instrumental insects" (*DP,* 473), then the cause lies not merely with myself, compiler of these images, but with Lawrence too, who after all dreamed them up and wrote them out. Our indiscriminate series, then, may begin: (*a*) the whited sepulchre, or "state of the animated sepulchre," its bright, firm architecture belying the organic mass decaying within (*DP*, 229); (*b*) the moribund cabbage, "hide-bound" with "enveloping green leaves outside, the heap round the hole," "rotten within" from the "threshing, threshing, threshing" of its interior bud (*DP*, 273–76); (*c*) modern European (especially English) individuals, who remain "a wincing mass of self-consciousness and corruption, within [their] plausible rind" (*DP*, 276); (*d*) "the envelope of the achieved self," or "shell of utter nullity," "wherein the flux of corruption boils hotly and in supreme gratification" (*DP*, 472, 474); (*e*) modern cognition generally, or "the static entity of our conception," for "the glassy envelope of the established concept is a foul nullity" (*DP*, 294); (*f*) the "collective activity" of the First World War, in which "we thresh destruction further and further, till our whole civilization is like a great rind full of corruption, of breaking down, a mere shell threatened with collapse upon itself" (*DP*, 277); (*g*) contemporary intellectuals like Russell and Keynes, "our most advanced minds," who "have reduced their own instinctive, sensuous sel[ves] to a viscous mass" and whose "minds triumph, dry and scaly and brittle," (*DP*, 473); (*h*) the self-and-other-annihilating protagonist of Poe's "mechanical" fiction, whose "cruelty-lust is directed almost as much against himself as against his victim. He is destroying, reducing, breaking down that of himself which is within the envelope" (*DP*, 284); (*i*) many characters in Dostoevsky, master of "the theme of reduction through sensation after sensation, consciousness after consciousness, until nullity is reached," the individual having become "an amorphous heap of elements" (*DP*, 282); (*j*) the "soldier who violently rapes a woman in the war" thus "destroying, reducing, breaking down that of himself which is within the ["glassy"] envelope. . . . And [notice please that this is an afterthought] he reduces, destroys the woman also" (*DP*, 472); (*k*) Gudrun "walking swiftly down the main road of Beldover" and "feeling like a beetle toiling in the dust . . . filled with repulsion" (11); (*l*) the mirrored interior of the Cafe Pompadour (in "the real world," the Cafe Royal), where "one seemed to enter a vague dim world of shadowy drinkers humming within an atmosphere of blue tobacco smoke," where "the red plush of the seats [seemed] to give substance within the bubble of pleasure," and where lisping, black-eyed Pussum says to Gerald (who will soon mount her) "I'm not afwaid of anything essept black-beetles" (62, 69); (*m*) the first of *Women in Love*'s racist "fetishes," or "strange and disturbing" "negro statues," which depicts "a woman sitting naked in a strange posture [i.e., the posture of childbirth], and looking tortured, her abdomen stuck out," an image that propels Birkin into rapt discourse, half paean, half lamentation: "it is an awful pitch of culture, of a definite sort. . . . Pure culture in sensation, culture in the physical consciousness, mindless, utterly sensual. It is so sensual as to be final, supreme" (74–79); (*n*) "gall apples" or "apples of Sodom," outside "very nice and rosy" but whose "insides are full of bitter, corrupt ash" (126); (*o*) "your healthy young men and women" who, like the apples of Sodom that represent them, "won't fall off the tree when they're ripe" and therefore become "balls of bitter dust" (126); (*p*) the uncentered and terrified being of Gerald Crich who, as his father lies dying, feels "day by day . . . more and more like a bubble filled with darkness (322); (*q*) more specifically still, Gerald's about-to-burst eyes, "blue and keen as ever, and as firm in their sockets. Yet he is not sure that they were not blue false bubbles that would burst in a moment and leave clear annihilation" (232); (*r*) the second of *Women in Love*'s "African fetishes," this one in some ways the inverse of the first, "a statuette about two feet high, a tall slim figure," "a woman with her hair dressed high, like a melon-shaped dome. . . . [Birkin] remembered her: her astonishingly cultured elegance, her diminished beetle face, the astonishing long elegant body, on short, ugly legs, with such protruberant buttocks" (253); (*s*) the Egyptian dung beetle that Birkin remembers as he meditates upon this fetish's buttocks/face: "This was why her face looked like a beetle's: this was why the Egyptians worshipped the ball-rolling scarab: because of the principle of knowledge in dissolution and corruption" (253); (*t*) the "pit-head surrounding the bottomless pit," a figure surely familiar to the coal-miner's son and creator of Gerald Crich (*DP*, 274); (*u*) "the cunning hyaena with his cringing, stricken loins" "preserving a glassy, fixed form about a voracious seethe of corruption" (*DP*, 297, 295); (*v*) the equally repellent "baboon, almost a man," who "arrested himself and became obscene, a grey, hoary rind closed upon an activity of strong corruption" (*DP*, 295); (*w*) "the louse, in its little glassy envelope, bring[ing] everything into the corrupting pot of its little belly" (*DP*, 295); (*x*) a tubercular man's fantasy or "knowledge of the gas clouds that may lacerate and reduce the lungs to a heavy mass" (*DP*, 475); (*y*) the intestinal being of industrial man, an envelope of pulsing "self-consciousness," in whom "the threshing has continued . . . till our entrails are threshed rotten. . . . Fools, vile fools! Why cannot we acknowledge and admit the pulse and thresh of corruption within us" (*DP*, 276); and, perhaps most luridly of all, (*z*) a putrescent and undelivered "foetus shut up in the walls of an unrelaxed womb," the "womb of the established past" where "the horror of corruption [has] begun already within the unborn, already dissolution and corruption set in before birth" (*DP*, 278, 279).

From *a* to *z*: what else is there to say, except that compared with this the notorious catalogs of Whitman are as nothing? And yet of course there is something to say, if only because Lawrence has said too much, or has said so much so perversely. The obvious point, and the crucial one, regards the writer's volatile transferential relation to the materials he must employ in order to repel: the very qualities intrinsic to the figures that incite his loathing also characterize and dominate his articulation of those figures. With his own imagination immersed in the "seethe" and "Flux of Corruption," Lawrence can only expectorate—as prose—the very stuff he refuses to swallow (383). The manic proliferation and sheer repetitiveness of these "instrumental insects" and their cognates (a "brittle" shell or "null envelope" under every rock and phrase); the "obscene" collapse of all divisions and distinctions into writhing indifferentiation, "the black river of corruption" "reducing reducing reducing the unequal mass to amorphousness" (172; *DP*, 473–74); the frenzied "hither and thither" motion of "these 'friends,' these beetles," these "little swarming selves," these "automatic" "little monsters" mounting one upon the other until we "pile ourselves over with dead null monstrosities of obsolete form" (*DP*, 473, 295): are these not the very qualities that, once transposed from the image objects of Lawrence's revulsion, infuse his own writing? Does not Lawrence enact what he also denounces? And in doing so does not his writing itself become, as in his own critique of Poe, "a keen, fierce, terrible reducing agent" in which sepulchres, cabbages, rinds, hyaenas, eyeballs, mines, lice, pregnant women of color, half-dressed economists, and "nasty" "black-beetles" lose all difference and become (like the bright affront of the baboon's ass) inflamed visions and versions of each other (*DP*, 284)? And, as I continue to insist, visions and versions of sodomy and buggery—of, that is, certain "repulsively attractive" or "bestial" or "degrading" acts of sexual conjunction whose modalities are by no means necessarily limited to the anal, but whose overwrought figuration, especially given Lawrence's excrementitious delirium, generally is (412–13). Consider, again from "The Crown," this retrograde and highly condensed passage in which Lawrence recoils from the erotic proclivities of "men of finer sensibility and finer development"; the passage swarms with the by now overfamiliar Lawrentian phantasmata:

> In physical contact he ["the sensitive man"] seeks another outlet. He loves men, really. This is the inevitable part of the activity of reduction, of the flux of dissolution, analysis, disintegration, this homosexuality.
>
> It is only coarse, insensitive men who can obtain the prime gratification of reduction in physical connection with a woman. A sensitive man is too

subtle, he cannot come like a perverse animal, straight to the reduction of the self in the sex. Many many processes intervene. There are all the complexities of the mind and the consciousness to reduce first. . . .

The sensitive man, caught within the flux of reduction, seeking a woman, knows the destruction of some basic self in him, while the complexity and unity of his consciousness remains intact above the reduction. Which gives him jangled horror. He is too conscious, too complete. Instead of obtaining the gratification of reduction, he has got only a wound in his unified soul, a sort of maiming. He is horrified at his own mangled, maimed condition, of which he is painfully aware in his complete consciousness. So that a woman becomes repulsive to him, in the thought of connection with her. It is too gross, almost horrible.

What he loves is a man who is to a certain degree less developed than himself. Then he can proceed to reduce himself to his level. It may be he wishes to reduce himself back to the level and simplicity, the undevelopment, of a boy. It may be he wishes to reduce himself only to the level of a lower type of man. In which case he will love boy or man, as it may be. His ideal, his basic desire, will be to get back to a state which he has long surpassed. And the getting back, the reduction, is a sort of progress to infinite nullity, to the beginnings. So that his progress has some sort of satisfaction.

He is given up to the flux of reduction, his mouth is upon the mouth of corruption. This is the reason of homosexuality, and of connection with animals. (*DP*, 472–73)

Virulent ranting this, terrible in its conviction and predictably replete with half-assimilated historical detritus: homophobia, gynephobia, fear of atavism, the allure of degeneration, even a vestigial sodomitical linkage between homosexuality and bestiality. If Lawrence had written only in this (heavily pumping) vein, there would be little reason left to read him. Fortunately there is more and better elsewhere (even elsewhere in "The Crown"), and this because Lawrence wrote in order to exceed himself, and expressly so. His famous-because-catchy maxim—"Never trust the artist. Trust the tale. The function of a critic is to save the tale from the artist who created it"—bespeaks his strategy of productive excess.

Hence the critical utility of this diatribe from "The Crown," beneath which courses very much the same bifurcated erotic trajectory for male sexuality that Lawrence explores (old theme in Lawrence criticism) with greater deftness and vacillation in his fiction, most compellingly in *Women in Love,* where, if we may admit a momentary Lawrentian reduction, the man of "finer sensibility" and the "coarse, insensitive" man are known, respectively, as Rupert Birkin and Gerald Crich. Very much the walking (and especially talking) incarnation of the "sensitive man," Birkin indeed "is horrified at his own mangled, maimed condition" when he contemplates the depleted horizons of heterosexual desire ("The possibilities of love exhaust themselves," Gerald reminds Birkin just before they embrace in "Gladiatorial" [271]), and surely in Gerald Birkin finds himself loving "a man who is a certain degree less developed than himself," "a lower type of man" in whom (listen to the late-Victorian inflection of Lawrence's homophobia jangling through here) Birkin "can proceed to reduce himself" "to a state which he has long surpassed"; so obviously does Gerald embody, again beyond the brittle formulations of "The Crown," the cruder male "who can obtain the prime gratification of reduction in physical connection with a woman" and whose primary erotic "relation with woman is [until Gudrun and Loerke turn the tables] the activity of rape and gross destructivity." The isomorphism that obtains here between *Women in Love* and "The Crown," an isomorphism governing masculine (i.e., male homosexual) desire in relation to a typology of male being and character, cannot, I think, be reasonably refuted; the *prima facie* textual symmetries are simply too compelling to be dismissed. These texts *do* speak each other's language. But the importance and irrefutability of this fact must be counterposed to, and compounded by, what can only be called the difference within this sameness, a difference whose manifold truth (and fiction) effects distinguish the turbulent greatness of *Women in Love* from the turgid mediocrity of most of "The Crown" and a good deal of Lawrence's subsequent fiction.[13] The remainder of this chapter will explore the devious narrative operations by which this difference in sameness, this homo-differential, is diverted into the bifold trajectory of *hetero*sexual desire for which *Women in Love* is famous. As I have already argued, whatever "plot" the novel may claim derives from this four-term, double-coupled difference whose "duplicity," in Murry's cranky phrasing, "subtly perverts" the book's "essential and vital argument" (*SW,* 116).

A brief historical reprise: I have argued at length in Chapter 1 that the metaphor of inversion—the turning inside out or upside down of desire in relation to gender—constituted the dominant, if not sole, explanatory paradigm by which late-nineteenth-century and early-twentieth-century

Euro-American culture structured its understanding of both the ontology and the etiology of "homosexuality." In the paradigmatic instance of the male homosexual or "invert," this explanatory figure would be reduced to a suspiciously convenient formulation: *anima muliebris virili corpore inclusa,* a female soul/spirit/psyche lodged or encased in a male body. The historical instantiation of this model of same-sex desire entailed the fluctuant and (ultimately only) partial supersession of the precedent model, "sodomy," whose taxonomic mission was less to define the relation between being and desire than it was to classify and order the relation between bodies and acts. Above all, and in clear contradistinction to the inversion paradigm, the sodomy model did not presuppose, either theoretically or practically, an essential "heterosexual" linkage between an already gendered desire rooted in the depths of the subject (*anima muliebris*) and the objects of that desire's gratification; thus the "unnaturality" of sodomy did not lie in the twisted or cross-gendered composition of the subject's desire, but rather in the "mistaken" way in which the subject chose to lay his, or her, body down.

The cultural deployment of the inversion model was hardly a linear development. Sodomy did not concede overnight, nor was inversion irrevocably installed by the vertical imposition of power. As divergent but copresent sexual taxonomies, sodomy and inversion jostled one another, cheek to jowl, for both discursive space and institutional validation, with the latter model achieving taxonomic dominance largely because of its close filiation with the ascendent discourses and institutions of modernity: medicine, psychiatry, psychology, and psychoanalysis. A more than vestigial sodomy is, after all, still with us, especially in statutory law, where the human body remains directly subject to the intervention of the state. Furthermore, the discursive and institutional "implantation" of the inversion model was complicated, but also subtly facilitated, by two modifications that might at first seem to have vitiated or impaired the efficacy of inversion as a model of same-sex desire. First, the language of "homosexuality," whose origins are roughly contemporaneous with those of "inversion," would overtake and largely displace the vocabulary (but not the metaphorics) of inversion, whose currency in any event proved more durable in England than elsewhere in Europe or in America, no doubt in part because Havelock Ellis, having entitled his influential volume *Sexual Inversion,* promoted the term successfully there. But this supplanting of one lexicon by another did not vitiate the figural power of inversion, whose fundamental trope—the notion of a twist or torsion in the alignment between (the gender of) the subject's desire and (the sex of) his or her body—would continue to operate, pseudonymously but effectively, within the discourse of homosexuality. And second, the obviously rudimentary articulations of the inversion metaphor, especially etiological formulations like the quasibiological *anima muliebris virili corpore inclusa,* would yield over time to more sophisticated psychological, and especially psychoanalytical, permutations, part of whose revisionary effect was to bestow upon inversion the benefit of an afterlife it otherwise could not have enjoyed. Even Freud, who in 1905 disqualified the idea of a "natural" or intrinsic sexuality and severed all but the most arbitrary linkages between "sexual instinct" and "sexual object," nevertheless continued to deploy both the erotics of inversion and the essentialist gender assumptions behind those erotics.

All of this impinges immediately upon Lawrence's writing, which wrestles to a fatal draw with exactly these serpentine contradictions regarding homosexual cathexis. Freud was driven to theoretical incoherence, Lawrence to "fundamental equivocation" and narrative violence. For these are the contradictions that inflect the sexual argument of *Women in Love* and constitute the novel's interpretive crux: it is from *this* "tense white knot of flesh" that the narrative unwinds itself so gorgeously, so heterosexually, and finally so murderously. In the published version of the novel, the homotextual problematic surfaces as such in "Man to Man," the talky chapter that sets up the grunting athleticism, some seventy pages later, of "Gladiatorial." Having suffered another of his episodic fits of gynephobic revulsion ("It filled him with almost insane fury, this calm assumption of the Magna Mater, that all was hers, because she had borne him. Man was hers because she had borne him . . . she now claimed him again, soul and body, sex, meaning, and all. He had a horror of the Magna Mater, she was detestable" [200]), Birkin unloads upon Gerald a pounding lecture about "the slopes of degeneration—mystic, universal degeneration" (204). Gerald, who is just bright enough to play dumb on the subject, remaining in this way the "dark horse to the end," looks "at Birkin with subtle eyes of knowledge. But he would never openly admit what he felt. He knew more than Birkin, in one direction— much more" (205–6). And then, as if by the solar effect of Gerald's gaze, "the problem" dawns on Birkin:

> Quite other things were going through Birkin's mind. Suddenly he saw himself confronted with another problem—the problem of love and eternal conjunction between two men. Of course this was necessary—it had

been a necessity inside himself all his life—to love a man purely and fully. Of course he had been loving Gerald all along, and all along denying it.

He lay in the bed and wondered, whilst his friend sat beside him, lost in brooding. Each man was gone in his own thoughts.

"You know how the old German knights used to swear a Blutbrüder-schaft," he said to Gerald, with quite a new happy activity in his eyes.

"Make a little wound in their arms, and rub each other's blood into the cut?" said Gerald.

"Yes—and swear to be true to each other, of one blood, all their lives.—That is what we ought to do. No wounds, that is obsolete.— But we ought to swear to love each other, you and I, implicitly and perfectly, finally, without any possibility of going back on it.

Birkin's musing here may begin in Platonic abstraction—"the problem of love and eternal conjunction between two men"—but it moves expeditiously enough to the barely effaced, and appropriately Germanic, sexual fantasy of *Blutbrüderschaft,* the fantasy, obviously, of opening the body and sharing its fluids, implying in turn the subjacent transposition of blood and semen.[14] And if Birkin is rather quick to subtract his own body from the proposition he is in the process of making ("No wounds, that is obsolete," he demurs once Gerald-the-literalist has diagrammed, in red crayon, the scene of conjunction), then this subtraction itself presupposes the extension, literally the transfusion, of the body into language—into, that is, the logos of what we now pathetically call "male bonding" (a phrase that, in my ears at least, continues to ring of the hardware store). No "strange conjunction" (*148*), just promises of same: instead of "rub[bing] each other's blood into the cut," Birkin instructs Gerald, "we ought to swear to love each other, you and I . . . finally, without any possibility of going back on it." In this retrofantasy, language is first saturated, as if blood could be bled back into words, and then frozen, as if language could hold forever the full charge and discharge of Eros. Words "of one blood."

The projectile force of this Lawrentian desire impels fantasy well beyond the conversation of Birkin and Gerald. In a letter of August 1916 to Amy Lowell, who had just given him a typewriter, Lawrence implicates first the media of novel writing itself, and then the body of his wife:

> I am busy typing out a new novel, to be called *Women in Love.* Every day I bless you for the gift of the type-writer. It runs so glibly, and has at last become a true confrere. I take so unkindly to any sort of machinery. But now I and the type writer have sworn a Blutbrüderschaft.

We go down and bathe—not the typewriter, but Freida and I. Today there were great rollers coming from the west. It is so frightening, when one is naked among the rocks, to see the high water rising to a threatening wall, the pale green fire shooting along, then bursting into a furious and wild incandescence of foam. But it is great fun. It is so lovely to recognize the non-human elements: to hear the rain like a song, to feel the wind going by one, to be thrown against the rocks by the wonderful water. I cannot bear to see or to know humanity any more. (*Letters*, 3:645)

It is worth more than a laugh, that tumbling confusion between Freida and the typewriter. Lawrence's comic sequence may seem benign enough, but consider the phantasmagoria. The simple typing of *Women in Love* (a task, by the way, that Lawrence soon abandoned) begins as a "glib" exercise in interfluent masculine erotics, the neuter machine having been gendered as a "true confrere" who needn't balk at an easy *Blutbrüderschaft;* perhaps the writer's imagination was piqued by the saturation of the typewriter's ribbon with ink. However indisputably solid such a machine may be as a physical object, it is, like all physical objects for Lawrence, absolutely susceptible to symbolic appropriation—unstable as water, and light as air. Notice, for instance that in the course of the eight sentences I have just quoted from the letter, the mutability of the machine is adumbrated orthographically; the word *typewriter* "itself" is spelled in three ways: "type writer," "type-writer," and "typewriter"; Lawrence may have been averse "to any sort of machinery," but the nuts and bolts of language were putty in his hands. And no sooner does the fluid bonding of man and machine achieve its happy apotheosis in *Blutbrüderschaft* than the paragraph breaks, as the whole passage is dipped, with barely a pause, "into the great rollers coming from the west." Thus immersed, the typewriter dissolves and emerges by a kind of transsexual magic as . . . none other than Freida herself, the Magna Mater incarnate, and "naked" to boot. Luckily for everyone involved, the reader too, this vision is immediately eclipsed by apocalytic seas of serendipitous ejaculation, as the strong water "burst[s] into a furious wild incandescence of foam."[15]

I am not being facetious. The fantasmatics of desire and gender that frolic "naked among the rocks" in Lawrence's letter repeat those that operate, in a very different emotional tenor, throughout *Women in Love*. A recognizable sequence unfolds in both texts, roughly as follows. An irrepressible but nonetheless repressed desire for "eternal conjunction between two men" incites a barely effaced fantasy of sharing bodily fluids, a fantasy that, were it permitted to lip the rim of the genital, we could unproblematically designate as "sodomitical"; the term, with all its anatomical dubiety, would apply precisely. But this fantasy about human bodies is prematurely disembodied. Or rather, it has been arrested in the body of the signifier, literally in the pseudochivalric blah blah of *Blutbrüderschaft*, which displaces the act sufficiently ("No wounds," etc., those having become "obsolete") to shield the implicated males from the untenable anagnorisis of homosexual self-recognition. (Without the "wounds" one may always retreat, via a technical honesty anyway, to the high ground of masculine protest, which in turn predictably generates so much violence between, among, and within men: *I, whoever I may be, am not one of "these 'friends,' these beetles"; if need be, I will "scotch" them, especially if they are in me.*) But the sequestration of desire in an airy discourse of eternal devotion (promises, promises) hardly solves what Birkin correctly thinks of as "the problem," which remains so acute, and acutely tempting, that some other "solution"—narrative, figural, characterological—must be attempted, if only to redistribute the considerable tensions generated by the conflict between desire and interdiction. In both the novel and the letter Lawrence resorts to the same rhetorical narrative solution; he deploys a metathesis of gender—less technically, an inversion—in which submerged homosexual desire, or a typewriter, resurfaces in (sometimes extra-urgent) heterosexual guise: Freida in the foam, buck naked; Gudrun, fully clothed, spasming to rhythms identical to those driving Birkin's desire for Gerald—or, in the chilled Latin of the sexological formula, *anima muliebris virili corpore inclusa.* In each case the gender dynamics are the same: where man was, there woman shall be; *cherchez la femme; la donna é mobile.* Such is the fraudulent substitution subtending all articulations of the inversion metaphor, which thus refuses to countenance the masculinity of male homosexual desire, a refusal shared, we should note, by Lawrence's title *Women in Love,* which silently ingests, all the better to occlude, the open secret of the novel's secret subject: men in love.

The gender metathesis embedded within the inversion figure entails a specific violence: the elimination of at least one male, either by murder or "castration." In the sexological formulation, that castration requires no messy instrumentation, neither scalpel nor gelding spoon, since the masculine subject has been handily dispatched via theoretical feminization (no *animus virili* to disturb the complacency of the equation); and in Lawrence's comic letter of 1916 his "true confrere," that mute but pliable typewriter, leaps (or is it pushed?) from the paragraph break into the sea, never to type again: Freida Victrix. Only in *Women in Love* does Lawrence adequately calculate the destructiveness of this process, and there only equivocally. In sacrificing the character whose radiant maleness so exacerbates Birkin's nagging "problem," Lawrence unleashes, with a little help from Gudrun and Loerke, the implacable death drive that crouches within the inversion trope. From the beginning of the narrative, and in direct proportion to the miner's son's energy and desirability, this push "for the smash of extinction at the bottom" targets Gerald's person and Gerald's body with a sniper's patient calculation (*DP*, 280). All the claptrap early on in the novel about Gerald having slain his brother, and therefore presumably deserving the violence that befalls him, provides at best an improbable justification for the itch in the sniper's finger, which derives rather from the narrative's "profound but hidden lust" (33) to murder and to be murdered, a reciprocating *Todestriebe* that anticipates Freud's own by several years. It is the gratification of this complex lust that charges the closure of *Women in Love* with its irresistible momentum, thereby providing "the real Russian bang" (the sniper having yielded to his itch) that Schorer so admired. To Gudrun's ominous question in "Diver"—"where does his *go* go?" (48)—the novel answers emphatically, unswervingly, "To the Alps—to die." "Death by perfect cold" (254).

And so Gerald is put on ice; more accurately, put on display *as* ice, "bluish, corruptible ice," his once-resplendent body now an "inert mass," "cold, mute, material" (480). With this "frozen carcase of a dead male" (477) the novel coolly repudiates the possibility that Birkin's desire might ever warm to adequate human gratification, and it is enough to provoke in Birkin a double, or bifurcated, recollection, one hot and one cold. Memory: "Birkin remembered how once Gerald had clutched his hand, with a warm, momentous grip of final love. For one second—then let go again, let go forever. If he had kept true to that clasp, death would not have mattered" (480). Counter-memory: "Birkin looked at the pale fingers, the inert mass. He remembered a dead stallion he had seen: a dead mass of maleness, repugnant" (480). (The whole of *Women in Love*'s murderous homosexual teleology is condensed in this juxtaposition of Birkin's memories: from "warm, momentous grip" to cold, "pale fingers . . . inert . . . repugnant"; from the "gleaming beauty [of] maleness" [14] to "a dead mass of maleness, repugnant.") But before that stallion's impressive energies are subdued by the narrative's deep freeze—the blond stallion, I mean, who drives Gudrun to "strange transport" (15) in "Coal-Dust" when he stupendously dominates the red Arab mare, his "strong, indomitable thighs" "clenching the palpitating body of the mare into pure control; a sort of soft white magnetic domination from the loins and thighs and calves, enclosing and encompassing the mare heavily into unutterable subordination" (113)—before that stallion is subdued by cold, the author requires first that things heat up and then that they melt down. (This is, after all, a *Lawrence* novel.) This thermal process precipitates the crisis in reading that so disturbed Murry's poise; for once these couples begin heating up, they also begin melting into each other, couple into couple, thereby compromising (thereby eroticizing) the only distinction upon which the dualistic heterosexual argument of the text has even the ghost of a chance of establishing itself. The line inscribing this difference dissolves in the heat of sex, despite the continuing narrative imperative that the sense of difference—a difference that *makes* sense—be sustained. This is to say that both couples obsessively "lapse" (crucial Lawrentian process) not just into each other, but also into *Women in Love*'s swampy language of "flux" and "dissolution," a tendency about which critics have just as obsessively complained. In one of the best essays ever written on the novel, Leo Bersani, far kinder to Lawrence than most, puts the critical frustration with just the right touch of loving parody: "When the connection is made between two life currents or two death currents, minds 'go,' people 'lapse out' and 'swoon,' they have 'transports' and 'keen paroxysms,' and the 'veil' of 'ultimate consciousness' is 'torn.' Nothing is more disorienting in *Women in Love* than the use of such expressions as descriptive narrative accompaniments to the most banal action or the most controlled, unremarkable dialogue."[16]

Ever since Murry's original complaint about *x* collapsing indiscriminately into *y*, critical anxiety (more rarely: critical excitation) over trip-wire lapsing and knee-jerk swooning has proceeded largely from sheer cognitive frustration: with both couples lapsing apace, the language of the novel works perversely to block or intermit the fundamental binarism that organizes its plot. If the erotic path represented by Birkin and Ursula leads, by whatever obscure turns, to life and (equivocal) marriage, and that represented by Gudrun and Gerald leads to death and destruction, then the difference between the couples *must* signify; literally it is vital, the difference between life and death. But it is also virtually illegible, beyond clear specification except in its ultimate effects, and repeatedly undermined both by the writing's most vigorous energies and by the insistent obscurity of particular sex acts that are after all never very particularly performed (whether by the copulars or their author, who can tell?). Bersani reads this indifference to difference as Lawrence's major strategy in his war against "the anecdotes of personality," against conventional notions of a unitary self, however complicated or vexed, whose coherence and intelligibility are grounded in a traceable personal history (example: Paul Morel). In *Women in Love*, Bersani argues, Lawrence attempts "to destroy the superstructure of personality in order to redefine human beings in terms of their primary impulses to live or to die" (*A*, 168). As with Freud's *Beyond the Pleasure Principle*, a text Bersani also invokes, this is a dualism whose vengeance overrides the vicissitudes of character or person: "Now the impulse to live and the impulse to die are not exactly attributes of personality; rather, they are attempts to enlarge on or to obliterate the very field in which the anecdotes of personality are possible. Personality must therefore be read as a system of signs or of choices which can be deciphered back to a primary choice of life or death" (*A*, 164). Unimpeachable as far as it goes (farther in this regard than anyone else has yet gone), this argument recalls Lawrence's own account of his intention at the time of writing; in an oft-cited letter to Edward Garnett, father of the "Dear David" whose impending gayness would drive the novelist to fantasies of "inward corruption" and "triumphant decay," Lawrence puts his purpose with characteristic vehemence:

> You musn't look in my novel for the old stable ego of the character. There is another ego, according to whose action the individual is unrecognisable, and passes through, as it were, allotropic states which it needs a deeper sense than any we've been used to exercise, to discover are states of the same radically-unchanged element. (Like as diamond and coal are the same pure single element of carbon. The ordinary novel would trace the history of the diamond—but I say "diamond, what! This is carbon." And my diamond might be coal or soot, and my theme is carbon.)
>
> You must not say my novel is shaky—It is not perfect, because I am not expert in what I want to do. But it is the real thing, say what you like. And I shall get my reception, if not now, then before long. Again I say, don't look for the development of the novel to follow the lines of certain characters: the characters fall into the form of some other rhythmic form, like when one draws a fiddle-bow across a fine tray delicately sanded, the sand takes lines unknown. (*Letters*, 2:183–84)

"You musn't look," etc. Suppose we resist this authorial directive long enough to focus attention upon the middle ground that intervenes between "the old stable ego of the character," a mere derivative or epiphenomenon according to this letter of 1914, and its ontological foundation or bedrock, that "same radically-unchanged element" toward which

Lawrence would turn his reader's blinking gaze, much in the manner of the magician who captivates his audience with the loud business in his left hand while he works the real trick silently in his right. What do we find there, wherever *there* is, in this middle distance, the intervenient space between diamond and carbon? What we find is Lawrence's deliberately perverse inscription, not exactly what he says he has put there, but rather a version of it: strange "allotropic states" that indeed render individual characters "unrecognizable" and that require "a deeper sense than any we've been used to exercise, to discover are states," *not* of a "pure single element" (the plain truth of carbon), but rather of a relentless narrative impulsion, a death/sex drive everywhere in the process of gender transference. *Allotropic* is instructive in this regard. Semantically, it means "having different properties, though unchanged in substance" or essence (*OED*); such a definition firmly roots the different in the same, thereby exposing transformation as a secondary process whose dazzling operations nonetheless leave the base element or essence "radically-unchanged": diamonds are but carbon in evening dress.[17] Etymologically, *allotropic* indicates a turning or twisting (from the Greek *tropos,* to turn) toward or through the different (the Greek *allos,* or other); as such, it suggests a perversion (from the Latin *vertere,* to turn) that stops just short of the foundation, leaving its *homo* intact. This compound term thus describes with formidable economy the perverse itinerary that controls this novel's admitted but admittedly blocked homosexual desire: its desire of the homo for the *homo:* of the man for the man who stands not merely as himself but also as the representative, even the guarantor, of the same, of the same man, of the man, that is, whose self-sameness must not be overthrown or degraded by the "feminine" cast of his desire. Viciously and ironically, this itinerary ultimately requires that homosexual desire seek its release in the Absolute Other (death, here "by perfect cold"), which after all reduces everything to the same cold mute material, that "inert mass" of "repugnant" dead matter. But the directness of this trajectory is interrupted by a violent detour whose feminine contours I have already suggested: masculine desire must "pass through, as it were" the allotropy of Lawrence's All-But-Absolute Other, the *anima muliebris* that haunts his texts: woman, mother, *mater,* matter, here doubly and duplicitously incarnated in Gudrun and Ursula. Through *mater,* then, toward matter: toward the "cold, mute Matter" (480) that Gerald finally becomes at novel's end. Fully feminized by death, Gerald's "dead mass of maleness" becomes "repugnant" to Birkin's eye, so much so that Birkin must immediately re-

member Gerald, contrary to the evidence of his senses and his own previous description, as warm, even warming: "That dead face was beautiful,
no one could call it cold, mute, material. No one could remember it without gaining faith in the mystery, without the soul's warming with new,
deep life-trust" (480).

The teleological ferocity of this itinerary—death for some men, hostility toward women, unappeasable homosexual longing in the men who
survive—must not be underestimated, especially in a culture whose every-
day scenarios continue to play it out with an efficient reflexivity usually
called "natural." Nor can we afford to ignore the serpentine entanglement
here between homophobia and misogyny, since the desperation of this
itinerary responds to a perceived "feminine" threat. In Lawrence's fiction
at this time, as in the never quite perverse enough logic of inversion, the
ever-imperilled male (the male, that is, who must work ceaselessly to erect
and sustain an always impossible masculine subjectivity) is open to invasion on two fronts, front and back: from the woman without (her name
is legion), and from the woman within (the legion having been condensed
into the subject's own name, say "Dear David"). Not the least of *Women
in Love*'s extraordinary power derives from the blinded lucidity with
which the novel both enacts and exposes this oppressive dynamic, which
operates simultaneously as a (seemingly essential) truth of (in)human psychology and as a (manifestly artificial) mode of representation. This homophobic appropriation of the feminine (a process by no means re-
ducible to the aberrations of a merely personal psychology) helps to
explain, if not to justify, *Women in Love*'s obsessive thematization of gynephobia and the sometimes flat functionalism of Lawrence's female
characters, here and elsewhere. (Ursula, for instance, too often seems neither the subject nor object of "authentic" desires so much as the formally
imposed mouthpiece of the opposition: the woman required by the narrative to kick sand in Birkin's face.) Lawrence understood, if never quite
thoroughly enough, his appropriation of the feminine and was not em-
barrassed by it: "I don't care so much about what the woman *feels*—according to the usage of the word," he writes just before launching into
"allotropic states." "That presumes an *ego* to feel with. I only care about
what the woman *is*—what she *is*—inhumanly, physiologically, materially—according to the use of the word: but for me, what she *is* as a phenomenon (or as representing some greater, inhuman will), instead of
what she feels according to the human conception" (*Letters,* 2:183; italics
original). And so woman is deployed—"used"—according to the writer's

rhetorical need to represent that "greater, inhuman will," "according to the use of the word . . . for me." Women I have known have questioned the beneficence and legitimacy of this "greater" will, discerning in it, after all the metaphysical huffing and puffing, a formula of sufficient brutality: cunt for cock's sake.

Or, in my argument, cunt in cock's *place*. This modification of the feminist recognition may be put more "professionally": given the logic of gender substitution governing homoerotic displacement in *Women in Love,* female genitalia (never of course offered in the pink) will come to represent something other than the specificity of woman's desire and pleasure, a subject about which Lawrence seemed to believe he knew everything; the vagina and its amazing surround will come to represent, even in its textual ablation, a particular mode of castration anxiety, specifically that which advenes upon a certain male subject when he realizes, or even as he works assiduously not to realize, that his desire may be situated beyond the phallus, or beside it, or astride it, or even no longer in terms of it. ("Life has all kinds of things," Birkin tells Gerald during their not quite postcoital chat after all the sweating in "Gladiatorial." "There isn't only one road" [276].) Suppose this male discovers (with what widening shock he may never be able quite to say) that his pleasure is no longer seated firmly in his cock, or that the focus of his desire is, or has become, the "contour and movement" of men in the street.

> All the time, he recognised that, although he was always drawn to women, feeling more at home with a woman than with a man, yet it was for men that he felt the hot, flushing, roused attraction which a man is supposed to feel for the other sex. Although nearly all his living interchange went on with one woman or another, although he was always terribly intimate with at least one woman, and practically never intimate with a man, yet the male physique had a fascination for him, and for the female physique he felt only a fondness, a sort of sacred love, as for a sister.
>
> In the street, it was the men who roused him by their flesh and their manly, vigorous movement, quite apart from all individual character, whilst he studied the women as sisters, knowing their meaning and their intents. It was the men's physique which held the passion and the mystery to him. The women he seemed to be kin to, he looked for the soul in them. The soul of a woman and the physique of a man, these were the two things he watched for, in the street. (501–2)

The person doing the breathless watching here is the Ur-Birkin of *Women in Love*'s infamous prologue (appendix 2 in the Cambridge edition), written in the spring of 1916 as the novel's opening chapter and rejected some months later as Lawrence wrestled once again to subdue his unruly leviathan. Much that is direct and clear-sighted here would become diffused and deflected in the version finally published in 1920. Birkin's urgent genital response ("hot, flushing, roused") to the provocation of male flesh, "quite apart from all individual character," would suffer inflation into the quasimetaphysical problematics of "eternal conjunction between two men"; his "terribly intimate" feminine identification, that affinity with the "meaning and intents" of "the women he seemed to be kin to," would be transposed into, among other things, his peaky misogyny and lackluster desire for women generally and Ursula particularly; and Lawrence's recognition that Birkin's homosexual desire is shadowed by an inverse subjective correlative, a deeply internalized homophobia whose considerable energies drive the novel in its final form to furious closure, would lose the perspicacity that it has here: "This was the one and only secret he kept to himself, this secret of his passionate and sudden, spasmodic affinity for men he saw. He kept this secret even from himself. He knew what he felt, but he always kept the knowledge at bay. His a priori were: 'I *should not* feel like this,' and 'It is the ultimate mark of my deficiency, that I feel like this' " (505; italics original). This analysis of Birkin's emotional and psychological duplicity is impressively clear. In order to keep a secret from oneself, one must first possess the very knowledge ("He knew what he felt") that one will then proceed, with a disingenuousness born of genuine desperation, to disown; too dangerous to be allowed to curl around hearth or heart, such knowledge must be kept "at bay" by the effort of a continuous pressure; only in this way may such knowledge be sustained just beyond the horizon of a consciousness too frightened to embrace it openly and too lucid to foreclose it entirely. And as Lawrence also clearly understood, the subjective operations of this duplicity are objectively mandated; that is, they derive from, and continue to incarnate in the form of human feeling, certain culturally specific a prioris.

Among these a prioris are the obvious, such as those that misidentify gay desire as "the ultimate mark of my deficiency," and the not so obvious, such as those that indicate the path of gendered signification through which such a misidentification must wind its tortuous way. When, for instance, Birkin's eye scans the street for objects of identification and desire, it proceeds by way of the same binarism that informs the metaphorics of inversion: "The soul of a woman [*anima muliebris*] and the physique of a man [*corpore virili*], these were the two things he watched for in the street." The almost technical specificity of Lawrence's phrasing here suggests both the broad cultural diffusion of inversion as an explanatory paradigm and Lawrence's own familiarity with particular textual versions of it.[18] But Birkin's erotic gaze is differentiated from the sexological formula by its mode of articulation; the formula proceeds by conjunction or compaction, the gaze by dislocation and dispersion. The two components that the diagnosticians of sexology had so conveniently conjugated (a female soul *enclosed* in a male body) are disjoined, bifurcated again, in the dissociated field of Birkin's watching: a soul here and a body there. *Here* I identify, *there* I want. Obviously, this splitting does not occasion the "liberation" of homosexual desire, its happy effusion into the drift of the gaze. On the contrary, it dictates a subtler reinscription, under much more complex narrative conditions, of an erotics of inversion within the figure constituted by the novel itself.

Or rather, by the novel as it was about to become. As Lawrence retreated from so direct a vis-à-vis with homosexual desire (a retreat, we should note, just some months subsequent to his visit to Cambridge and the ensuing dreams of black beetles), his narrative would adopt and elaborate the gender trajectory he had already begun to map in his acute analysis of Birkin's gaze. In *Women in Love* as finally published, the desires that the prologue so emphatically lodges within Birkin's "own innate being" (504) have been transported, across gender, into "the soul of a woman" whose body also "just happens" to be female. The result for the narrative is an enabling distortion that may be expressed in another convenient formula, this one my own: *where Birkin's desire had been, there Gudrun's body shall be;* and what this distortion enables is a "fundamental equivocation" much like the one toward which Murry himself had so equivocally gestured. Birkin can sustain the technical nicety of a "true" heterosexuality even as he grapples, however wordily and incompetently, with the problematics of "eternal conjunction" between men, while Gudrun and Gerald can explore, via the gender transposition that Gudrun now literally embodies, the murky sex that Birkin and Gerald can't quite wrestle themselves into. The subjacent anatomical fantasy operating here, never of course articulated in the text, should be obvious. Gudrun and her (implied) vagina, both repeatedly associated with mud and the Flux of Dissolution, come to substitute for the male subject's bodily orifices and for the possibility that he might (or worse: might want to) be penetrated, most specifically at the anus, a site so overburdened with desire, pleasure, loathing, and anxiety (just to mention the obvious few) that it must be blocked from direct representation even as it also promises, for exactly the same reasons, to release an overwhelming millenial satisfaction: "floods of ineffable darkness and ineffable riches" far "deeper than the phallic source" (314). As Bersani suggests apropos of *Lady Chatterley's Lover,* such great expectations are a lot to ask from an asshole, "except as a consequence of fantasies which, to begin with, attribute extraordinarily intense affective and moral value to anal pleasure. That is, the explicit value conferred on anal sex [or, as here, its digital complement] makes no sense except as the sign of a more complicated fascination with anality" (*A,* 172). In *Women in Love* that "more complicated fascination" infuses, if not everything, then just about everything else, most especially the book's fundamental heterosexuality, that heavy and funless sexuality that is by no means focused exclusively upon the fundament.

But if not there, then where? If, as Jonathan Dollimore writes, "Lawrence finds ecstasy not in heterosexuality *per se* but [in] its radical perversion,"[19] then where shall that perversion root its representations when, at the level of what may be said or shown, the specific loci of the perverse have been, by law or convention or "taste," already foreclosed? How else, in Lawrence, than by a displacement into frontal violence, a violence that traverses the bestial? Interdiction, whether specific or general, whether internalized within the subject as the murmurings of nature or externally codified in the muscular body of the law, does not produce silence and blankness, or not merely these, but also representation elsewhere and otherwise, representation responsive to the subtle but profound violence of metamorphosis. In "Rabbit," after having instructed her charge, Winifred Crich, Gerald's younger sister, to sketch the family pet, Gudrun reaches into the rabbit hutch to remove "the great, lusty" beast and is astounded to discover that, instead of a rabbit, a "thunderstorm . . . had sprung to being in her hand" (240):

> They unlocked the door of the hutch. Gudrun thrust in her arm and seized the great, lusty rabbit as it crouched still, she grasped its long ears. It set its four feet flat, and thrust back. There was a long scraping sound as it was hauled forward, and in another instant it was in mid-air, lunging wildly, its body flying like a spring coiled and released, as it lashed out, suspended from the ears . . .
>
> . . . Her heart was arrested with fury at the mindlessness and the bestial stupidity of this struggle, her wrists were badly scored by the claws of the beast, a heavy cruelty welled up in her.
>
> Gerald came round as she was trying to capture the flying rabbit under her arm. He saw, with subtle recognition, her sullen passion of cruelty.
>
> "You should let one of the men do that for you," he said, hurrying up.

"Oh he's so horrid!" cried Winifred, almost frantic.

He held out his nervous, sinewy hand and took the rabbit by the ears, from Gudrun. . . .

The long, demon-like beast lashed out again, spread on the air as if it were flying, looking something like a dragon, then closing up again, inconceivably powerful and explosive. The man's body, strung to its efforts, vibrated strongly. Then a sudden sharp, white-edged wrath came up in him. Swift as lightning he drew back and brought his free hand down like a hawk on the neck of the rabbit. Simultaneously, there came the unearthly, abhorrent scream of a rabbit in the fear of death. It made one immense writhe, tore his wrists and his sleeves in a final convulsion, all its belly flashed white in a whirlwind of paws, and then he had slung it round and had it under his arm, fast. It cowered and skulked. His face was gleaming with a smile. . . .

Gudrun looked at Gerald with strange, darkened eyes, strained with underworld knowledge, almost supplicating, like those of a creature which is at his mercy, yet which is his ultimate victor. He did not know what to say to her. He felt the mutual hellish recognition. And he felt he ought to say something, to cover it. He had the power of lightning in his nerves, she seemed like a soft recipient of his magical, hideous white fire. He was unconfident, he had qualms of fear. . . .

She lifted her arm and showed a deep red score down the silken white flesh.

"What a devil!" he exclaimed. But it was as if he had had knowledge of her in the long red rent of her forearm, so silken and soft. He did not want to touch her. He would have to make himself touch her, deliberately. The long, shallow red rip seemed torn across his own brain, tearing the surface of his ultimate consciousness, letting through the forever unconscious, unthinkable red ether of the beyond, the obscene beyond. (240–42)

The genius of this passage (which I have truncated mercilessly), and of the great chapter from which it comes, derives from characteristic Lawrentian strengths: from the way in which the writing catches the sheer animality of the rabbit in its homely facticity and in the extremity of its motion; from the way in which that animality, while being thus materially rendered, is nonetheless also seamlessly insinuated into a complex and contradictory symbolic web whose impalpable filaments ultimately flutter into the "red ether of the beyond, the obscene beyond," an abstraction that in turn is immediately reincarnated, folded back into "the long red rent of [Gudrun's] forearm, so silken and soft"; from the way in which the physical action (trying to pick up a rabbit) and its associated dialogue collate and condense the erotic violence that had begun in "Coal-Dust" when Gudrun identified with the red Arab mare being dominated by Gerald and that ends with Gerald's perplexed submission, in "Snowed-Up," to a dominatrix whose power he has always felt with an electrifying *frisson* but never once understood, much less mastered; and, finally, from the way in which the entire chapter, as part of the narrative ensemble, mediates between the chapter that immediately precedes it ("The Industrial Magnate," in which Gerald's need to dominate matter receives a highly abstract analysis) and the chapter that immediately follows ("Moony," in which Birkin's sexual desperation ignites a parallel scene of "strange conjunction" [148], as Ursula watches her lover, in still another whirring of limbs, stone the reflected face of the moon in Willey Water). All of this is incomparably done, in Lawrence's casual, offhand manner.

But in "Rabbit" the strangest inflection of all is the homoerotic (but hardly gay) one—an inflection doomed from the beginning to seem "forced," the compulsory imposition of an obsessive criticism, since in this chapter Birkin is, of course, nowhere to be found, off somewhere, no doubt, being sick or disgusted or bitching at the stars. In any event, *not here*. Yet what is this scene if not the graphic and spectacular realization, in the wrong body, of Birkin's desire for *Blutbrüderschaft* with Gerald? And what is the narrative function of the rabbit (named Bismark!) if not to overwhelm, in a flurry of tremendous kicks, the very civility that mandates the obsolescence and "obscenity" of ritual mutilation, as when men "make a little wound in their arms, and rub each other's blood into the cut"? "No wounds, that is obsolete," Birkin reassures Gerald as they consider the exchange that *they* will never share, but the rabbit's violence hardly acknowledges such polite considerations—the wounds it inflicts are immediate, multiple, and profuse. Both Gerald and Gudrun are "badly scored," appropriately enough, at the wrists, although Gudrun appears to be redundantly cut, both at the wrists and along the (whole?) length of her forearm; indeed, Lawrence's odd use of a preposition suggests that, upon display, Gudrun's arm, or perhaps her whole being, metamorphoses into a wound, a slit, a gash: "She lifted her arm and showed [Gerald] a deep red score down the silken white flesh . . . it was as if he had had knowledge of her in the long red rent of the forearm." The criticism has largely agreed to see a gynephobic and hallucinatory genitality here, a reading obviously encouraged by the heavily thumbed Biblicism of the phrasing "he had had knowledge of her." And although Gerald and Gudrun do not literally "rub each other's blood into the cut," as Gerald says to Birkin, this omission would hardly seem to count, since precisely this ritual is being enacted at the level of the gaze, where the lovers look alternately into each other's eyes and into each other's wounds; Gerald even wants to enumerate the cuts— "How many scratches have you?" (242)—as if to say, *let me count the ways.* The gaze exchanged between Gudrun and Gerald seals a "mutual hellish recognition" that, even as it bypasses words of love, nonetheless perversely fulfills Birkin's desire "to swear to love each other, you and I, implicitly and perfectly, finally, without any possibility of going back on it" (206–7): "Glancing up at him, into his eyes [Gudrun] revealed again the mocking, white-cruel recognition. There was a league between them, abhorrent to them both. They were implicated with each other in abhorrent mysteries" (242). And again, a page later: "There was a queer, faint, obscene smile over his face. She looked at him and saw him, and knew that he was initiate as she was initiate" (243). Joint initiation, mutual implication, abhorrent league: this diction confirms the recognition that the transposition of *Blut-brüderschaft* into demonic heterosexuality is being ritually completed, here "with shocking nonchalance" (243). And all thanks to a rabbit.[20]

One final point, worth underscoring because the chapter closes by repeating its violence, closes, that is, by reopening its wounds, slash after slash, upon Gerald's person specifically. New wounds open as old wounds are eyed. (In the exchange in gazes in which Gudrun is the transparent master, Gerald merely participates, and a bit blindly.) For as Gerald looks, so is he cut, both inside and out: "the long, shallow red rip ["of" Gudrun's arm] seemed torn across his own brain, tearing the surface of his ultimate consciousness." And once more: "He felt again as if she had hit him across the face—or rather, as if she had torn him across the breast, dully, finally" (243). The sheer redundancy of these descriptions obsessively inscribes an oddly gendered violence: if, as seems inescapable, the display of Gudrun's "deep red score" represents, in a single cut, both the female genitalia and the terror that a man may feel in his own fascination with that cut, then this is a vaginality that Gerald must share, as his own and in his own body; for what Gerald "recognizes," however dumbly, in the mirror of Gudrun's slash is nothing other than his own desire to be violated, to be torn, and thereby to abdicate the power that is indissociable from his sense of masculine being and performance—from, we might say, the performance of being masculine. ("You should let one of the men do that for you," he tells Gudrun just before he takes the rabbit and assumes his wounds.) Furthermore, Gerald receives this recognition not merely as a proleptic anxiety ("I see that this might happen to me"), but as a species of *déjà vu:* even before he watches, after all, Gerald is already bleeding from analogous wounds, and as he watches he is cut again and again. Caught thus in an overwhelming ocular "league" with Gudrun, even the novel's incarnation of male beauty and virile power suffers a mocking feminization, "castrated" by a woman whose gaze bespeaks the desire of a man formally absented from the exchange. Gerald, who thus finds himself many leagues beyond his natural depth, is perhaps wise to experience all of this so "dully" and "finally." In any event, however darkling his recognitions, Gerald "turned aside" (243).

A double slap: Loerke is a faggot and Loerke is a Jew. Hardly accidental or unmotivated, Lawrence's malicious superposing of "perversions"—of differences whose perceived extremity or otherness derives from the imperiled subject's need to sustain, against whatever increasing odds, the seeming centrality of his own subject-position—bespeaks the urgency of the narrative demand that Loerke's menace be convincing; hence one "deviation" is projected upon another. (That the psycho-logic of this superposition is, minimally, racist and heterosexist should go without saying but must nevertheless be remarked, if only parenthetically here.) Nor can there be any doubt: Lawrence *means* Loerke to repel on both counts; for the language employed, whether by Birkin or the anonymous narrative voice, to describe Loerke, that "lop-eared rabbit," that "troll" (422), works overtime to secure the reader's revulsion: "a small, dark-skinned man with full eyes, an odd creature, like a child, and like a troll, quick, detached" (405); Gudrun "could see in his brown, gnome's eyes, that black look of organic misery, which lay behind all his small buffoonery" (422); "His figure interested her—the figure of a boy, almost a street arab. He made no attempt to conceal it" (422); "He lives like a rat, in the river of corruption, just where it falls over into the bottomless pit. . . . I expect he is a Jew—or part Jewish" (428); "He is a little gnawing negation, gnawing at the roots of life" (428); "and he's the wizard rat that swims ahead . . . he ebbs with the stream, the sewer stream" (428). Shrunken, misshapen, malproportioned, a blackened rodent awash in excrement and gnawing at the roots of life: Loerke's reduced body collocates, in a facile and highly concentrated form, a paranoid multiplicity of perversions— sexual, aesthetic, ethical, religious. That multiplicity finds its objective correlative not in sexual acts *per se,* since at no point does the novel (whatever its shadowy intimations) directly represent Loerke as engaged in any of these, but rather in self-conscious acts of verbal exchange, "in an endless sequence of quips and jests and polyglot fancies" (468), in the Wildean conversation that Loerke offers Gudrun, full as it is "of odd, fantastic expressions, of double meanings, of evasions, of suggestive vagueness" (453). (Loerke's erotic motto, on the other hand, reads like simplicity itself: "Women and love, there is no greater tedium" [458].) The language thus shared between Loerke and Gudrun represents not a discourse of the body exactly, nor of the genitals, but rather of "the nerves":

> The whole game was one of subtle inter-suggestivity, and they wanted to keep it on the plane of suggestion. From their verbal and physical *nuances* they got the highest satisfaction in the nerves, from a queer interchange of half-suggested ideas, looks, expressions and gestures, which were quite intolerable, though incomprehensible, to Gerald. He had no terms in which to think of their commerce, his terms were much too gross. (448; italics original)

If perversity has always been a figure of speech, then here speech becomes a figure *for* perversity. The propensity of this "queer interchange" to turn back upon itself in pursuit of thrills both cheap and dear indicates a crisis in the novel's representation of sexual desire generally and homosexual desire particularly. To some degree this crisis is a simple function of interdiction; after the debacle that followed publication of *The Rainbow,* Lawrence would deploy language—here, specifically, "conversation"—as a modality of sexual activity, its displaced representative, in part because he was inhibited, both externally and internally, from a more explicit articulation of bodies and body parts. "Sex in the head" would have to do. Hence the predictable reticence regarding the specifics of homosexual connection, as when Lawrence writes that Loerke and his "love-companion" Leitner, a blond and bland Gerald clone, "had travelled and lived together in the last degree of intimacy" (422). Never quite embodied in sexual action, the particulars of this "last degree" must be inferred (if they are to be conceptualized at all) from, as it were, the dark backward of language: from phrases like "sewer stream," "wizard rat," "river of corruption," "falls over into the bottomless pit," etc., etc.—phrases whose incipient anality is easy to see, hard to touch, and harder still to prove. In this way specific sexual practices partake of an obviousness that is immediately remanded to the crepuscular realm of "suggestive vagueness" and "subtle inter-suggestivity"; they are remanded, that is, to the "shadow kingdom" of connotation, where referentiality hangs by the slenderest of ropes (always ready to be cut) and where "what must be read" in language cannot definitively be distinguished from "what need not be read into it." The very real (but always deniable) knowledge effects thus produced are emitted from a dubiety that, "being constitutive, can never be resolved."[21] Under just such a discursive regime, Loerke shadows forth a paranoid fantasy of anal sexuality; "an odd little boy-man" (468) representing "the rock-bottom of all life" (427), he is sodomy's dark distillate standing in the snow, wearing "a Westphalian cap" and a "simple loden suit, with knee breeches" (422). And so, by extrapolating the curve of the obvious, we may come to understand that what Loerke offers Gudrun, as the uncomprehending Gerald could never do, are the hieratic services of a well-practiced Back Door Man: "He, Loerke, could penetrate into depths far out of Gerald's knowledge, Gerald was left behind like a postulant in the ante-room of this temple of mysteries, this woman. But he, Loerke, could he not penetrate into the inner darkness, find the spirit of the woman in its inner recesses, and wrestle with it there, the central serpent that is coiled at the core of life" (451). Poor industrialist, master neither of *mater* nor matter, just "grinding dutifully at the old mills" (463), Gerald is simply "left behind" *at* the behind, stuck "like a postulant in the ante-room," unable to post up and take that last step into "the obscene beyond."

But of course this won't quite do. Or rather, it will do only if we scrupulously restore to the narrative field the fundamental contradictions, "deeper than the phallic source" (314), that the preceding paragraph rather too glibly effaces as it elides Lawrence's elisions by propelling the "merely" connotative into the glaring legibility of anal denotation. This critical excess is ours; we have seen and said too much: who is so obtuse as not to feel Lawrence's corpse flushing now with rage? But if there are no patent assholes in *Women in Love* (Birkin excepted of course), neither is there any anal dearth; it is not merely that the text abounds with "floods of ineffable darkness" and "river[s] of corruption" and "bottomless pit[s]," but rather that these figures of speech both bind the characters each to each and establish, however tenuously, the indistinct boundaries of the novel's intelligibility. The implication for the reader here cannot be escaped: Lawrence compels us to rim the text in order to coax its yield of knowledge, power, and pleasure; either this, or suffer an intolerable contraction into cognitive darkness. Refusing this banishment of sense, what then do we find at *Women in Love*'s margins of intelligibility if not the operations of contradiction and displacement?

Three of these will be central to our analysis of the text's closure. First, as obvious as it is that Loerke and Leitner enter *Women in Love* as the narrative's Manifest Homosexuals, and thus embody the "explicit" textual irruption of the physical possibility of gay sex, so should it be equally clear that this is *a homosexuality immediately to be superseded.* A single gesture efficiently admits *and* expels homosexual praxis, for no sooner do Loerke and Leitner make their bows of introduction than it becomes "evident that the two men . . . had now reached the stage of loathing. Leitner hated Loerke with an injured, writhing, impotent hatred, and Loerke treated Leitner with a fine-quivering contempt and sarcasm. Soon the two would have to part" (422). And second, the homophobic logic subtending this passage (its first axiom: that the future of sex between men can hold only "loathing," "impotent hatred," and mandatory separation) effectively guarantees that the perversity inheriting the site and function of a thus-evacuated homosexuality will perforce be a "heterosexuality" at once "obscene" and "beyond." Obscene because its refinement into "unthinkable subtleties of sensation" (452) propels it past the reach of direct sexual representation, and beyond because its irreducibly surrogative function ensures that it can be articulated only in terms of the homosexual desire it works both to adulterate and "explain." As with the erotic epiphany in "Rabbit," this is a sexuality whose hetero is crossed with a bestial thrill: for Gudrun "there *were* no new worlds, there were no more *men,* there were only creatures, little, ultimate *creatures* like Loerke. . . . There was only the inner, individual darkness, sensation within the ego, the obscene religious mystery of ultimate reduction . . . of diabolic reducing down" (452; italics original). That these "mystic frictional activities" consist primarily in involuted conversation and some heady tobogganing suggests the difficulty Lawrence encountered in sexually embodying the last phases of "ultimate reduction." Finally, although it is Loerke's personal pleasure and narrative responsibility to sheath in Gudrun "the fine, insinuating blade" of wit that this "final craftsman" alone may wield, and thereby to superannuate the thickness of a Gerald who in any case cannot comprehend, much less perform, "the last series of subtleties" that Gudrun demands (452), still it is not quite correct to say that this "sexuality," whatever its specific modalities, supplants Gerald absolutely. He is not entirely "left behind." And this because it is Gerald who receives the violent "bliss" of the narrative's ultimate sexual act, that "great downward stroke" of Gudrun's fist, which brings all of this perversity to "satisfaction" and this novel to its banging close (471).

This last equivocation must not be evaded: only as sexual agent is Gerald superseded. As Gudrun's pathic he still has important duties to perform. But what other "being," beyond or before such agency, may Gerald claim, this man who is all get-up-and-go and going nowhere but to sleep in a lap of snow? What possible relations to sexual "passivity" may Gerald entertain or enjoy, except the "death by cold" that the novel is about to confer upon him with the rigor of destiny? The very death that thereby negatively affirms the fraudulent equation between masculine self-identity and the obdurate "will to subjugate [the] Matter" and the *Mater* that, whether searching them out or not, he will always find both within and without himself—even, as the novel puts it, in "his own ends" (223). Hence Gerald's imperative to search and destroy: "The subjugation itself was the point, the fight was the be-all, the fruits of victory were mere results" (223). Not that Gerald hasn't longed for a different relation to passivity. Early on in their affair, before its escalation into murky sex and transparent violence, Gudrun and Gerald experience mutual satisfaction as they float one evening in a canoe on Willey Water. His right hand bandaged thanks to the fortuitous narrative intervention of "some machinery," (163), Gerald cannot man the oar that would, no doubt "naturally," fall to his hand; with the paddling therefore entrusted to Gudrun, Gerald uncharacteristically relaxes:

> He was listening to the faint near sounds, the dropping of water-drops from the oar-blades, the slight drumming of the lanterns behind him, as they rubbed against one another, the occasional rustling of Gudrun's full skirt, an alien land noise. His mind was almost submerged, he was almost transfused, lapsed out for the first time in his life, into the things about him. For he always kept such a keen attentiveness, concentrated and unyielding in himself. Now he had let go, imperceptibly he was melting into oneness with the whole. It was like pure, perfect sleep, his first great sleep of life. He had been so insistent, so guarded, all his life. But here was sleep, and peace, and perfect lapsing out.
> "Shall I row to the landing-stage?" asked Gudrun wistfully.
> "Anywhere," he answered. "Let it drift." (178)

This "perfect lapsing out" is the closest Gerald will ever come to a non-purposive erotic "drift," the kind to which Barthes would later lend the prestige of his name and the facility of his style. As Gerald abandons the "keen attentiveness" and "guarded" concentrat[ion]" whose joint duty it is to patrol the borders of a masculinity otherwise susceptible to flux and lapse, he begins to merge, "for the first time in his life, into the things about him."

But as if in anticipation of such dissolution at the margins of his being, Gerald has already assumed a managerial obligation, the impossibility of whose execution should at least have forestalled such a lapse in character; just before the boats are launched he tells Gudrun and Ursula: "Don't, for *my* sake, have an accident—because I'm responsible for the water" (163). The mortifying rigor imposed by such a responsibility freezes Gerald's attempt at "letting go." To his lovely and woozy "Let it drift," the novel responds with a direct countermand, a loud shout, a call for immediate action: "Then as if the night had smashed, suddenly there was a great shout, a confusion of shouting warring on the water, then the horrid noise of paddles reversed and churned violently" (178). The foreshadowed accident is now fully under way. Gerald soon realizes that his sister Diana has fallen, fatally it turns out, into Willey Water, across whose darkened surface a prophetic alarm sounds in the form of a truncated name: "Di—Di—Di—Di—Oh Di—Oh Di—Oh Di!" (179). Instantly, as in a reflex, Gerald reverts to the vigorous agency, the purposive athleticism, that is his only mode of being and being masculine, and for the abandonment of which he is now being punished. ("Wasn't this *bound* to happen?" Gudrun says, "with heavy, hateful irony" [179; italics original].) Thus compelled to act, to discharge his responsibility for (and in) the water, Gerald dives repeatedly into the reservoir to save his sister, only to discover the futility of his best effort. His agency—all agency—is annulled: "There's room under that water for thousands . . . a whole universe under there; and as cold as hell, you're as helpless as if your head was cut off" (184).

"As if." This watery decapitation will be propelled from the conditional to the indicative some three hundred pages later, when Gudrun lets fall her "great downward stroke, over the face and on to the breast of Gerald" (471), and specifically in a frozen environment where "that water" has indeed become "cold as hell." But not before Gerald comes to realize, in his own balked and intermittent way, that he *wants* this release, that this surcease has been all along the occluded objective of his stopless success: "There's something final about this. And Gudrun seems like the end, to me. . . . It blasts your soul's eye . . . and leaves you sightless. Yet you *want* to be sightless, you *want* to be blasted, you don't want it any different . . . it tears you like a silk, and every stroke and bit cuts hot—ha, that perfection, when you blast yourself, you blast yourself!—And then . . . you're shrivelled as if struck by electricity' " (439–40; italics original). Decapitation, blinding, blasting, cutting, shrivelling: the law of castration here parades its metonyms "with a queer histrionic movement" (440), a movement disclosing, as when one inverts a glove to examine its lining, the *Todestriebe,* or drive to cease, that impels Gerald's "infinitely repeated motion" (228). Gerald's self-recognition, flickering as it is, thus effectively condenses (1) a compulsive (not to mention compulsory) heterosexuality; (2) a heated gynephobia bordering on the idolatrous; (3) the "feminine" masochism secreted beneath the rippling cuts of a hypertrophic masculinity, the business of whose overbusy agency is to render that agent "sightless" and befuddled in his relation to (4) the death drive that is for all purposes indistinguishable from a desire for castration, a desire not simply to find the stop of death, but also to be released by death (no other remedy being likely or practicable) from the impossible responsibility of bearing the phallus aloft. Hence when Gudrun's blow finally descends after many pages of *tête-à-tête* between herself and Loerke, it comes not so much as the ultimate in heterosexual declensions, the definitive Salomean cut that brings Gerald's closeted passivity to its alpine consummation; it arrives as well as an action Gerald must emulate as he enters the last phase of a terminal process whose "satisfaction" will require his full participation. (Every mother's son knows: you must "blast yourself, blast yourself" to find that last "hot" stroke of "perfection.") Of course Gerald's immediate response to being struck is romantic reciprocation—that is, to strike back. Converting pain into power, passivity into action, he takes "the throat of Gudrun between his hands, that were hard and indomitably powerful. . . . And this he crushed, this he could crush. . . . The pure zest of satisfaction filled his soul" (471). But this reflex is little more than the last pulsation of Gerald's murderous sexual agency, and he botches his own consummation ("I didn't want it, really" [472]), although the attempted strangulation offers Gudrun rush enough to bring her off with impressive alacrity: "struggling was her reciprocal lustful passion in this embrace, the more violent it became, the greater the frenzy of delight, till the zenith was reached, the crisis, the struggle was overborne, her movement become softer, appeased" (472). At precisely this moment, in the interstitial pause between Gudrun's having finished and Gudrun's being finished off, Loerke intervenes masterfully with a rhetorical coup ("*Mon-*

sieur! Quand vous aurez fini—"; 472) whose inhuman composure disarms Gerald's violence and induces him to release Gudrun before her little death graduates to a big one. And so Gerald lets go: "A revulsion of contempt and disgust came over Gerald's soul. The disgust went to the very bottom of him, a nausea. . . . A weakness ran over his body, a terrible relaxing, a thaw, a decay of strength. Without knowing, he had let go his grip, and Gudrun had fallen to her knees" (472).

Gerald now turns and walks away, "sheering off unconsciously from any further contact" (472). Once again, this time for the last time, he drifts: "A fearful weakness possessed him, his joints were turned to water. He drifted, as on a wind, veered, and went drifting away" (472). A no doubt formidable muscular effort is yet required to take Gerald "higher, always higher" toward the mountain summit and "the hollow basin of snow" where his activity will find its cool caesura; but these are little more than the incipiently posthumous reflexes of an automaton, the movements no longer of the imposing "industrial magnate" who had dominated "thousands of blackened" miners "all moving subject to his will" (222), but rather those of a man-machine awaiting, in the only modality left to it, the absolute depletion of an energy it does not know how to refuse (473, 474). Thus Gerald moves toward his death "unconscious and weak, not thinking of anything, so long as he could keep in action" (472). And "keep in action" he mechanically does, despite "a wind that almost overpower[s] him with a sleep-heavy iciness," until he is driven at last to hallucination: "Somebody was going to murder him. He had a great dread of being murdered. But it was a dread which stood outside him, like his own ghost. . . . He could feel the blow descending, he knew he was murdered. Vaguely wandering forward, his hands lifted as if to feel what would happen. . ." (473). The imaginary blow whose descent Gerald gently reaches up to receive partakes of the same trajectory as the many "downward stroke[s]," whether brachial or pelvic, that the novel has busied itself in suggesting; most obviously, it repeats as fantasy the "fatal" stroke of Gudrun's most recent delivery. As fantasmatic emulation, then, Gerald's dream blow simultaneously introjects Gudrun's violence as a violence he must visit upon himself and projects that violence outward in a repudiation of individual agency, since it is the nobody of an externalized "somebody" (say, given the shortage of plausible candidates, "his own ghost") who is about to blast Gerald into eternity. With this disembodied gesture, Gudrun and Gerald finally join hands in a loving liaison whose immediate result is the absolute elision of Gerald's being. "Death by perfect cold" indeed, but whether by murder or suicide it is no longer possible to tell.

I have denied it all along, but now it is time to come clean: *Women in Love* ends not with a bang, but a whimper. Birkin's whimper, Lawrence's, my own: "I didn't want it to be like this. . . . He should have loved me" (479–80). One sees immediately that this formulation conveniently projects the failure of love upon the lost object of desire, now banished by death, thereby exculpating the speaking subject who, after all, had abandoned his friend at the height of the latter's erotic crisis with his demon lover. (Had Birkin stayed with Gerald in the Alps, would the "great downward stroke" ever have fallen?) The formal title Lawrence gives to this whimper is "Exeunt," the brief concluding chapter in which Birkin and Ursula return to the Alps to retrieve what love has left of Gerald—"the frozen corpse of a dead male" (477). Immediately putting this corpse to use, "Exeunt" performs, against the novel's impending closure, what by now should be the familiar labor of extension and deferral: it inscribes mourning as the afterlife of the interminable homosexual longing that outlives whatever "finish" (more bitterly: whatever dead end) may be offered by a heterosexuality whose promises of satisfaction, however hard the sell or obsessive the pursuit, nonetheless always leave something to be desired. For if Gudrun, Loerke, and Gerald ("A pretty little sample of the eternal triangle" is Gudrun's curt dismissal [477]) have effectively eliminated Gerald as either sexual agent or viable sexual object, they have hardly diminished his capacity to generate desire; instead they have provided the formal centerpiece—in effect, the ice sculpture—for the dialogic tableaux that conclude the novel by rehearsing its (now postmortem) fantasy of "eternal conjunction between two men." Thus, for instance, it is entirely appropriate that Birkin's self-exculpating lament should be addressed to (a none too pleased) Ursula across the mute expanse coldly occupied by "the frozen dead body that had been Gerald," as if to suggest that only the interposed "carcase of a dead male" could adequately incarnate not just the erotic distance separating husband and wife, but also the very condition or prerequisite for the terminal heterosexuality that inherits *Women in Love's* decimated erotic field: the prerequisite that the homosexual desire to which the novel resolutely refuses any gay chance whatsoever must be assimilated instead as melancholic equivocation (477). And, of course, it is exactly this equivocation that informs the novel's famous last words—the domestic dispute, I mean, in which Birkin and Ursula openly contest the sufficiency of heterosexual connection and the correlative necessity of "another kind of love":

> Gudrun went to Dresden. She wrote no particulars of herself. Ursula stayed at the Mill with Birkin for a week or two. They were both very quiet.
>
> "Did you need Gerald?" she asked one evening.
>
> "Yes," he said.
>
> "Aren't I enough for you?" she asked.
>
> "No," he said. "You are enough for me, as far as woman is concerned. You are all women to me. But I wanted a man friend, as eternal as you and I are eternal."
>
> "Why aren't I enough?" she said. "You are enough for me. I don't want anybody else but you. Why isn't it the same with you?"
>
> "Having you, I can live all my life without anybody else, any other sheer intimacy. But to make it complete, really happy, I wanted eternal union with a man too: another kind of love," he said.
>
> "I don't believe it," she said. "It's an obstinacy, a theory, a perversity."
>
> "Well—" he said.
>
> "You can't have two kinds of love. Why should you!"
>
> "It seems as if I can't," he said. "Yet I wanted it."
>
> "You can't have it, because it's false, impossible," she said.
>
> "I don't believe that," he answered. (481)

As "closure" this fails miserably, if by that swaybacked term we mean to indicate the substantial resolution—or at least the polite suspension, for the purpose of saying goodbye—of the conflicts that have generated the narrative's interest and power. Not only is there no resolution here, Lawrence makes no plausible attempt to produce it; with its last words *Women in Love* straightforwardly abjures the closural consolations traditionally afforded by heterosexual marriage, at least to characters in fiction. Hence even a passing analysis of this scene must minimally acknowledge the perdurance, beyond closure, of: (1) Birkin's intransigent sense of heterosexual insufficiency, of a gap or aporia that cross-gender sexuality can neither bridge nor fill ("But to be complete, really happy, I wanted . . ."); (2) a correlative drive for homosexual fulfillment, here figured as a supplementarity whose specific modalities are still (some five hundred pages later) obscurely situated somewhere between an idealized "eternal union" and an eroticized "sheer intimacy"; (3) an opposed and equally intransigent refusal of this same desire, a position embodied here by an offended Ursula, who peremptorily dismisses her husband's longing as "an obstinacy, a theory, a perversity," the last term suggesting, as the editors of the Cambridge edition bashfully acknowledge, Ursula's familiarity with certain "technical" (e.g., sexological, psychoanalytic) material; and thus (4) an insuperable dissension whose narrative function is not to reconcile or sublate items 1 through 3 but to sustain, now in an elegiac register, the conflict of which they have been all along the constituent elements.

Women in Love thus expires upon the posthumous instantiation of a disgruntled heterosexuality whose terminal oscillations ("You can't have it" / "I don't believe that") dialogically rehearse the catastrophic homosexual loss that both founds this heterosexuality and confounds its powers of satisfaction and completion. Once upon a time I thought this a brave and admirable ending, characteristically Lawrentian in its transgression of narrative convention, both to the degree that it belies the tirelessly rehearsed pieties of marital finality and to the degree that it insists upon the vital intransigence of an only momentarily defeated homosexual desire. I am no longer so confident or so easy, and not least because I think I can now see what I needed not to see before: that Lawrence's novel works, with a sometimes psychotic intensity, to produce this loss, this corpse, this murder as its narrative telos, the single definitive event toward which this whole creation moves; that the mechanism of this production is a gender inversion whose fatal work is to transpose Birkin's homosexual longing for Gerald onto a "demonic" heterosexuality that likewise finds its most compelling object in a dumb blonde just dying to be blasted; and that my first, enthralled submission to this big bang bespoke not merely the purblind and mobile nature of a particular reader's identifications but also his own appalling openness to what Lawrence in "The Crown" calls the "desire to deal death and to take death" (*DP*, 476). Caught in the surge and flux of multiple identifications, I did not merely (like Birkin) want Gerald's superlative maleness, all thrust and drive—I also wanted (like Gudrun) to kill him for the extraordinary imposition his desirability entailed. *My* homosexual desire (which of course I did not see at all) was thus fundamentally linked to a murderous impulse, itself no doubt the subjective correlative of a deeply insinuated homophobia to which I was equally blind. (Remember here Lawrence's dream insect: "I scotched it—and it ran off—but I came upon it again and killed it.") And out of the ferocious conjugation of these desires, one homosexual and one homicidal, a third torsion unfolded itself, as if some iron law of necessity would compel me to complete, in and as my own "blasted" being, another "pretty little sample of the eternal triangle." Not content (or even able) simply to desire Gerald, I also identified with him, and most especially with his extravagant *Todestriebe,* his urgent impulsion toward extinction. In the fantasia of my reading and rereading, Gerald's bewildered death sentence had become my own: "You *want* to be sightless, you *want* to be blasted, you don't want it any different." Whatever "I" I may have had when I entered the text was now thoroughly dispersed among conflicting desires. Hence, once pinned to the wall by the novel's last pages, I could assume all subject-positions and enact the entire drama "myself": I did not merely receive Gudrun's "great downward stroke" of annihilation— *I delivered it too,* no doubt with a homicidal relish indistinguishable from suicidal relief. And once done with the killing and the dying, with Gerald cold and Gudrun gone, I could invoke my reader's exemption and (like Birkin) exit the text intact, saved (more accurately, made safe) by the freshness of a grief that occluded, even as it inherited, my guilt: "I didn't want it to be like this. . . He should have loved me."

This unhappy story (the novel's and my own) both explicates and repeats the chilling cathexis between homosexual desire and death that has compelled so much attention in the present study. I must insist in closing that this is a cathexis grounded nowhere in "nature" (itself, after all, one of the more tendentious categories of culture) but everywhere in a complex historical figuration whose brutal production schedule continues to supply a fresh yield of corpses, day after day, with no end in sight. The dead have been many too many, but apparently not enough to satisfy a culture grown too facile both in its consumption of corpses and in its criminal prosecution of a post-mortem pedagogy. Not the least of the daily lessons still being inscribed upon bodies, both living and dead, is the disciplinary constitution of a desiring male subject whose heterosexual security demands the continual performance of his "fundamental equivocation": first the solicitation of this subject's homosexual desire, then his repudiation of its possibilities in the real. I take Birkin at novel's end as a figure of this regime—if not its most docile subject, then nonetheless one of its representative men: one of many who have been instructed to exorcise their homosexual desire through the murderous exercise of an interminable grief itself virtually indistinguishable from erotic longing. "I didn't want it to be like this. . . . He should have loved me." I admit in the end that I still find these simple, plangent lines extremely moving. But I also know that this very plangency confirms that the desire these sentences recall now speaks only to the dead—speaks, that is, *in memoriam.* And I know, too, that the subject speaking them must hereafter wake each day to a fresh mourning, bereft of his friend but not exactly alone: haunted, rather, by the ghost of a murder he cannot shake.

Notes

1. Bram Stoker, *Dracula* (1896; New York, 1979), 51–52. All subsequent references to Stoker's novel are cited parenthetically in the text.

2. The simple truth of this factually correct statement is belied only by the fact that, as a reasonably perspicuous member of the culture into which I was inserted at birth, I had been thoroughly saturated in the semiotics of vampirism long before I read *Dracula* "for the first time." How could it have been otherwise? In the age of mechanical and (now) electronic reproduction, vampires and their images are as widely diffused as the blood on which they are supposed to feed: in the movies, on the television (where at least one partially sanitized avatar teaches entranced children how to count), between the covers of comic books and "adult magazines," and even (on special occasions) in our mouths, assuming, as I do, that many of us have tried out those waxen vampire dentures that help Halloween maintain the sweetness of its annual bite. None of this, of course, presupposes a specialist's (or a fetishist's) devotion to his topic; research proves unnecessary when a particular image system (here, that of vampirism) has been virtually imposed upon any subject even half possessed of an open eye or a cocked ear. I am thus gratified, if not exactly happy, to affirm that my first reading of *Dracula* was, without any bad faith on my part, anything but a first reading, installed as it was from the beginning in a series of repetitions and replications whose indiscriminate proliferation had already influenced my particular cathexis.

3. Sigmund Freud, "From the History of an Infantile Neurosis," in *The Standard Edition of the Complete Psychological Works*, trans. James Strachey, 24 vols. (London, 1955–1974), 17:50–51.

4. John Addington Symonds, *A Problem in Modern Ethics: An Inquiry into the Phenomenon of Sexual Inversion, Addressed Especially to Medical Psychologists and Jurists* (1891; London, 1896), 3.

5. D. A. Miller, *The Novel and the Police* (Berkeley, 1988), vii; italics original.

6. Roland Barthes, *The Fashion System*, trans. Matthew Ward and Richard Howard (Berkeley, 1990), 49.

7. Roland Barthes, *Roland Barthes by Roland Barthes*, trans. Richard Howard (New York, 1977), 138, 114.

8. Ibid., 114.

9. Just ask Springsteen: *you can look but you better not touch.* Or rather more accurately: *you can look* and *touch, but only if what you touch is already your own.* How else, one might plausibly wonder, to explain why so much straight porn (at least of the variety currently available at both mom-and-pop video outlets and peep-show emporiums) focuses so relentlessly upon the disseminal glories of the "money shot" (the tightly framed close-up of the ejaculating penis), almost always to the detriment of the nubile fellatrix who, still on her knees, has not much left to do but help demonstrate the cinematic truth that, indeed, the proof is in the pudding? Given the see-Spot-cum inflection of most straight porn, it becomes hard to escape the conclusion that the genre's *pièce de resistance* is not, as we might naively have suspected, the infinitely compliant female body open at every door, but rather the impatient young buck who, pausing momentarily at the doorjamb to scrape his antlers, stands and delivers before trotting off to the next scene.

CHAPTER I

1. John Addington Symonds, *The Memoirs of John Addington Symonds*, ed. Phyllis Grosskurth (London, 1984), 182.

2. Michel Foucault, *The History of Sexuality*, vol. 1, *An Introduction*, trans. Robert Hurley (New York, 1978), 20.

3. Michel Foucault, *The Use of Pleasure*, vol. 2 of *The History of Sexuality*, trans. Robert Hurley (New York, 1985), 3.

4. In Wilde's *The Importance of Being Earnest*, Lady Bracknell responds to the scandal of Jack's origins as follows: "Until yesterday I had no idea that there were any families or persons whose origin was a Terminus." The relations between origins, termini, and sexuality in Wilde's writings are explored at length in Chapter 4.

5. Foucault, *Use*, 4.

6. Foucault, *History*, 149: "While it is true that the analytics of sexuality and the symbolics of blood were grounded at first in two very distinct regimes of

power, in actual fact the passage from the one to the other did not come about (any more than did these powers themselves) without overlappings, interactions, and echoes."

7. John Addington Symonds, *The Letters of John Addington Symonds*, 3 vols., ed. H. M. Shueller and R. L. Peters (Detroit, 1969), 3:642.

8. Symonds, *Memoirs*, 183, 281.

9. Ibid., 63.

10. Ibid., 183.

11. Arnold I. Davidson, "Sex and the Emergence of Sexuality," *Critical Inquiry* 14, no. 1 (1987): 10.

12. Jeffrey Weeks, *Sex, Politics, and Society: The Regulation of Sexuality since 1800* (London, 1981), 20–21.

13. Foucault, *History*, 101.

14. Lord Alfred Douglas, "Two Loves," reprinted in Brian Reade, *Sexual Heretics: Male Homosexuality in English Literature from 1850 to 1900* (New York, 1971), 361–62.

15. This sentence is taken from the "Sodomia" section of Lodovico Maria Sinistrari, *De Delictis, et Poenis* (Venice, 1700). The anonymous English translation I have used is *Peccatum Mutum Alias Sodomy*, from "Le Ballet de [*sic*] Muses" Collection (Paris, 1958), 29. The title of this chapter is derived from this translation.

16. William Blackstone, *Commentaries on the Laws of England*, vol. 4, *Of Public Wrongs* (Oxford, 1769), 215; I have used the University of Chicago facsimile edition (Chicago, 1979); Edward Hyde East, *A Treatise of the Pleas of the Crown*, (Philadelphia, 1806), 480.

17. Pierre Klossowski, "The Philosopher-Villain," in *Sade My Neighbor*, trans. Alphonso Lingis (Evanston, Ill., 1991), 32.

18. Jane Gallop, *Intersections: A Reading of Sade With Bataille, Blanchot, and Klossowski* (Lincoln, Neb., 1981), 80.

19. Ibid., 80.

20. Ibid., 78.

21. Ed Cohen, "Legislating the Norm: From Sodomy to Gross Indecency," *South Atlantic Quarterly* 88, no. 1 (1989): 181–217.

22. Edward Coke, *The Third Part of the Institutes of the Laws of England* (1644; London, 1809), 58–59.

23. For more on the relation of lesbianism to sodomy see Judith Brown, *Immodest Acts* (Oxford, 1986), 3–20.

24. Jonathan Goldberg, *Sodometries: Renaissance Texts, Modern Sexualities* (Stanford, Ca., 1992), 18. Goldberg's study was published after the composition and revision of the present chapter, and I have made no attempt to integrate my argument with Goldberg's. I am, however, happy to agree with Goldberg that the disciplinary efficiency of the category "sodomy" derived in part from its semantic plasticity, not to say its vacuousness.

25. My account of the Audley trial is derived from *A Complete Collection of State-Trials and Proceedings for High-Treason and Other Crimes and Misdemeanors from the Reign of King Richard II to the End of the Reign of King George I*, 2 vols. (London, 1730), 1:366–73.

26. In 1828, an omnibus bill entitled "Offenses Against the Person Act." (9 George 4, c. 31) was passed by Parliament. Intended to reorganize and simplify the criminal code, this bill rescinded the requirement "to prove the actual emissions of seed in order to constitute carnal knowledge," which hereafter "shall be deemed complete upon the proof of penetration only." See *Hansard Parliamentary Debates*, new series, vol. 19 (1828), 350–60. Cohen discusses the historical importance of this bill in "Legislating the Norm"; his analysis has helped me here.

27. *Select Trials at the Session House in the Old Bailey* (London, 1742). I have used the Garland reprint, ed. Randolph Trumbach (New York, 1986).

28. Weeks, *Sex, Politics, and Society*, 102.

29. Ibid., 104.

30. Havelock Ellis and John Addington Symonds, *Sexual Inversion* (London, 1897), 1; italics added. Here I have used the Arno Press reprint (New York, 1975) of the first edition.

31. John Boswell, *Christianity, Social Tolerance, and Homosexuality* (Chicago, 1980), 318.

32. St. Thomas Aquinas, *Summa theologicae*, vol. 43, *Temperance* (Cambridge, 1967), 2a2ae.154,11. All further citations to Aquinas are to this volume.

33. Ibid., 2a2ae.153,2.

34. Augustine, quoted in Stephen Greenblatt, *Renaissance Self-Fashioning* (Chicago, 1980), 242.

35. Aquinas, 2a2ae.153,3,2,4.

36. Ibid., 2a2ae.153,5.

37. Ibid.

38. Louis Crompton, "Jeremy Bentham's Essay on 'Paederasty': An Introduction," *Journal of Homosexuality* 3, no. 4 (1978): 383.

39. Blackstone, *Commentaries*, 215.

40. Jeremy Bentham, "Offences Against One's Self: Paederasty," ed. Louis Crompton, *Journal of Homosexuality* 3, no. 4 and 4, no. 1 (1978), 391. All further citations to Bentham, noted or otherwise, are to this essay.

41. Ibid., 390.

42. Ibid., 391.

43. Coke, *Third Institute*, 58.

44. For the best account of noneffeminated male homosexuality in classical Greek culture, see Foucault, *Use*, 78–93. For instance:

> The dividing line between a virile man and an effeminate man did not coincide with our opposition between hetero- and homosexuality; nor

was it confined to the opposition between active and passive homosexuality. It marked the difference in people's attitudes toward the pleasures; and the traditional signs of effeminacy—idleness, indolence, refusal to engage in the somewhat rough activities of sports, a fondness for perfumes and adornments, softness (*malakia*)—were not necessarily associated with the individual who in the nineteenth century would be called an "invert," but with the one who yielded to the pleasures that enticed him: he was under the power of his own appetites and those of others.

45. I say "(only) potentiated" because Bentham's essay, unpublished until 1978, had no revisionary effect at all.

46. The word *preposterous,* which appears repeatedly in eighteenth century sodomitical contexts, entails an anal implication. Derived, like *posterior,* from the Latin *poster* (coming after) and from the prefix *prae* (before), *preposterous* refers to that which is inverted or unnatural in order or position; more graphically, it may mean "ass forwards." Bentham, for instance, refers to "paederasty" as the "preposterous propensity." See Edward Ward, *The Secret History of London Clubs* (London, 1709), 299, where Ward presents a mock genealogy of the sodomite:

Sure the curs'd Father of this Race,
That does both sexes thus disgrace,
Must be a Monster, Mad, or Drunk,
Who, bedding some preposterous Punk,
Mistook the downy seat of Love,
And got them in the Sink above;
So that, at first, a T—d and they
Were born the very self same Way.

Here "preposterous Punk" is a female prostitute who offers her anus ("the Sink above"), instead of her vagina ("the downy Seat of Love"). I am thankful to Kent Gerard for directing me to this text.

47. See Alan Bray, *Homosexuality in Renaissance England* (London, 1982), especially 81–144; and Randolph Trumbach, "London's Sodomites: Homosexual Behavior and Western Culture in the 19th Century," *Journal of Social History* 11, no. 1 (1977): 1–33.

48. Bray, *Homosexuality,* 88.

49. Weeks, *Sex, Politics, and Society,* 108.

50. All quotations regarding *Rex* v. *Wiseman* refer to John Fortescue Aland, *Reports of Select Cases in all the Courts of Westminster* (London, 1748), 91–97. The same text is more readily available in *The English Reports,* vol. 112 (London, 1909), 774–76.

51. William Eden, *Principles of Penal Law* (London, 1771), 268.

52. In addition to the work of Bray and Trumbach cited above, see G. S. Rousseau, "The Pursuit of Homosexuality in the Eighteenth Century: 'Utterly Confused Category' and/or Rich Repository," *Eighteenth-Century Life* 9, no. 3 (1985): 133–68. For a historiographical survey see Trumbach, "Sodomitical Subcultures, Sodomitical Roles, and the Gender Revolution of the Eighteenth Century: The Recent Historiography" in the same issue of *Eighteenth-Century Life*, 109–21.

53. *Hell Upon Earth: or, the Town in an Uproar*, (London, 1729), 41–43. I have used the Garland Press reprint, ed. Randolph Trumbach (New York, 1985).

54. Bray, *Homosexuality*, 92.

55. Cohen, "Legislating the Norm," 187–27.

56. Foucault, *History*, 65.

57. Arnold Davidson, "How to Do the History of Psychoanalysis: A Reading of Freud's *Three Essays on the Theory of Sexuality*," *Critical Inquiry* 13, no. 2 (1987): 258.

58. Ellis and Symonds, *Sexual Inversion*, 1.

59. Davidson, "How to Do the History of Psychoanalysis," 259, 260.

60. Richard von Krafft-Ebing, *Psychopathia Sexualis*, trans. Harry Wedock (New York, 1965), 29. Davidson also quotes the first passage and the one from Moll below.

61. Ibid., 52.

62. Albert Moll, *Perversions of the Sex Instinct: A Study of Sexual Perversion*, trans. Maurice Popkin (Newark, 1931), 171.

63. Davidson, "How to Do the History of Psychoanalysis," 264.

64. Symonds, *Modern Ethics*, 12.

65. Edward Carpenter, *Love's Coming of Age: A Series of Papers on the Relations of the Sexes* (London, 1911), 136. Earlier editions appeared in England in 1896 and 1906; the latter is the first edition to contain the chapter "The Intermediate Sex," from which the quoted passage is taken.

66. Foucault, *History*, 43.

67. Krafft-Ebing, *Psychopathia Sexualis*, 108.

68. Symonds, *Modern Ethics*, 84.

69. Ellis and Symonds, *Sexual Inversion*, 27.

70. Symonds, *Modern Ethics*, 90, 100.

71. Symonds, *Letters*, 3:799.

72. I take the phrase "heterosexual paradigm" from George Chauncey, Jr., "From Sexual Inversion to Homosexuality: Medicine and the Changing Conceptualizations of Female Deviance," *Salmagundi* 58–59 (1982): 114–46. The phrase "microstructural heterosexual attitudes" comes from Gayatri Chakravorty Spivak, *In Other Worlds: Essays in Cultural Politics* (New York, 1987), 87.

73. Joel Fineman, "Psychoanalysis, Bisexuality, and the Difference Before the Sexes," in *Psychosexual Imperatives*, ed. Marie Coleman Nelson and Jean Iken-

berry (New York, 1979), 109. The undifferentiated fetus would be inscribed with a similar ideological duplicity. Fineman's synopsis of nineteenth-century developments in embryology, especially Wittlich's and Waldeyer's studies of the fetal vicissitudes of the genital apparatus, will help us here:

> When it was discovered in the middle of the nineteenth century that the urogenital systems of the two sexes derive from a common embryonic origin, the elegant hypothesis of human bisexuality seemed once and for all to have been established as biological fact. . . . Thereafter, the programmed separation of a primal, androgynous blob into two categorically opposed sexual entities was to be the model for both a vaguely imagined, residually bisexual archetype and, at the same time, for a teleologically defined division of gender by kind. . . . By jumping from the demonstrable "androgyny" of the fetal sex organs to an assumed bisexuality in the developed cerebellum, it seemed to such influential theoreticians as Krafft-Ebing, Havelock Ellis, and Magnus Hirschfeld that one could clearly and precisely define the difference between men and women by referring to relative proportions in them of fixed, gender-specific, neurological elements. (109–10)

Here Fineman's metaphor of "jumping" precisely identifies the analogical leap that transposes an interpretation of the physiology of fetal development into a normativizing psychological register. The as-yet-undetermined fetal genital apparatus would be readily implanted with an available fiction; it would be construed in terms of the oppositionally structured gender code already in force when the embryological discoveries were made. Nature cheerfully repeated culture's script: a presumptive fetal "androgyny" could be employed to explain gender and sexual disorder while leaving the conventional gender code quite intact. Fineman explains:

> On the one hand, bisexuality confuses the notion of the categories of gender, suggesting that the sexes are a kind of mixture of each other, each one containing at least a little bit of each other. On the other hand, the concept presupposes a fixed opposition between the sexes, at least theoretically, so that the categorical poles—male, female—remain distinct even in the compromise they accomplish. (112–13)

To Fineman's analysis of the duplicitous reinscription of gender difference within the notion of "bisexuality" we need only to add a brief lexical note. In the 1897 edition of *Sexual Inversion*, before Ellis had recourse to the word "bisexuality" (used in later editions), he employed instead the phrase "psychosexual hermaphroditism," a descriptive label that emphatically betrays its ideological grounding in oppositional notion of gender. Indeed, Ellis went so far as to suppose a kind of infra-individual biological warfare: "Putting the matter in a purely speculative shape, it may be said that at conception the organism is provided with about 50 percent of male germs and about 50 percent of female germs, and that as development proceeds either the male or the female germs assume the upper hand, killing out those of the other sex, until in the maturely developed individual only a few aborted germs of the opposite sex are left" (132–33). This sentence—with its concomitant imagery of domination, warfare, murder, and abortion—describes normal heterosexual development. In the case of "the homosexual person" or "the psychosexual hermaphrodite," however, "the process has not proceeded normally" and we therefore "have a person who is organically twisted into a shape that is more fitted for the exercise of the inverted than of the normal sexual impulse, or else equally fitted for both" (133).

74. Carl Westphal, "Die Conträre Sexuelempfindung," *Archiv für Psychiatrie und Nervenkrankheiten* (1870): 73–108.

75. Arrigio Tamassia, "Sull'inversione dell'instinto sensuale," *Revista Speriment di Treniatria* (1878): 97–117. J. M. Charcot and P. Magnan, *"Inversion du sens genital," Archives de Neurologie* 3, no. 7 (1882): 53–60.

76. Ellis and Symonds, *Sexual Inversion*, 30.

77. Krafft-Ebing, *Psychopathia Sexualis*, 83.

78. Sigmund Freud, *Three Essays on the Theory of Sexuality*, in *The Standard Edition*, 7:147–48.

79. Davidson, "How to Do the History of Psychoanalysis," 265.

80. Ibid., 274, 275.

81. Sigmund Freud, "Female Sexuality," in *The Standard Edition*, 21:230. Hereafter page numbers will be cited within the body of the chapter.

82. Sarah Kofman, *The Enigma of Woman*, trans. Catherine Porter (Ithaca, 1985), 123.

83. Spivak, *In Other Worlds*, 151.

84. Kofman, *The Enigma of Woman*, 205.

85. Luce Irigaray, *This Sex Which Is Not One*, trans. Catherine Porter (Ithaca, 1985), 194–96.

86. Freud, *Three Essays*, 7:144–45. This passage appears in a footnote added by Freud in 1910.

CHAPTER 2

1. Havelock Ellis, *Sexual Inversion*, 3rd ed. (Philadelphia, 1931), 328. See note 38 below.

2. Ibid., 341.

3. Ibid., 341.

4. Symonds, *Memoirs*, 194, 189, 190.

5. Ellis and Symonds, *Sexual Inversion*, 60–61.

6. Symonds, *Memoirs*, 189.

7. Ellis, *Sexual Inversion*, 339.

8. Edward Carpenter, *Iölaus: An Anthology of Friendship* (1917; reprint, New York, 1982), 181. My use of the notion of "homosociality" is derived from Eve Kosofsky Sedgwick's *Between Men: English Literature and Male Homosocial Desire* (New York, 1985). Following Sedgwick I understand "male homosociality" to denote an entire spectrum of male bonds, only some of which are sexual; and I understand this spectrum or continuum to be historically marked by a phobic disruption that would severely disjoin the homosocial from the directly homosexual. It might be said of the intensity of *In Memoriam*'s elegiac desire that it problematically overrides or elides the disjunction that conventionally intervenes, so phobically, between what is social and what is sexual.

9. Alfred, Lord Tennyson, *In Memoriam*, lyric 64; I have used the Norton Critical Edition, ed. Robert H. Ross (New York, 1973). Subsequent citations of *In Memoriam* refer to this edition and appear in parentheses.

10. Carol T. Christ, *Victorian and Modern Poetics* (Chicago, 1984), 117.

11. This contemporary review is most readily accessible in John Dixon Hunt, ed., *In Memoriam: A Casebook* (London, 1970), 100–12.

12. Charles Kingsley's unsigned review of *In Memoriam* first appeared in *Fraser's Magazine* (September 1850), 245–55; it is most readily available in *Tennyson: The Critical Heritage*, John D. Jump, ed. (London, 1967), 172–85. Christopher Ricks's remarks may be found in his *Tennyson* (New York, 1972), 215.

13. Ricks, *Tennyson*, 215.

14. Harold Bloom, "Tennyson, Hallam, and Romantic Tradition" in *Ringers in the Tower* (Chicago, 1971), 149–50.

15. Ricks, *Tennyson*, 215.

16. Quoted in Ricks, *Tennyson*, 218.

17. I take the phrase "the desire and pursuit of the whole" from Benjamin Jowett's translation of Plato's *Symposium*, where it is employed by Aristophanes to explicate a problematically sexual desire whose recuperative energy seeks to restore a lost ontological wholeness. David M. Halperin, in "One Hundred Years of Homosexuality," *Diacritics* 16 no. 2 (1986): 34–45, explains:

According to Aristophanes, human beings were originally round, eight-limbed creatures, with two faces and two sets of genitals—both front and back—and three sexes (male, female, and androgyne). These ancestors of ours were powerful and ambitious; to put them in their place, Zeus had them cut in two, their skin stretched over the exposed flesh and tied at the navel and their heads rotated so as to keep that physical reminder of their daring and its consequences constantly before their eyes. The severed halves of each former individual, once reunited, clung to one another so desperately and concerned themselves so little with their survival as separate entities that they began to perish for lack of sustenance; those who outlived their mates sought out persons belonging to the same gender as their lost complements and repeated their embraces in a foredoomed attempt to recover their original unity. Zeus at length took pity on them, moved their genitals to the side their bodies now faced, and invented sex, so that the bereaved creatures might at least put a terminus to their longing and devote their attention to other, more important matters.

From this narrative Aristophanes extracts, as Halperin says, "a genetic explanation of the observable differences among human beings with respect to sexual object-choice," an explanation that clearly establishes a formal isomorphism between female-female, male-male, and male-female desire. As Aristophanes says, "the reason is that human nature was originally one and we were whole, and the desire and pursuit of the whole is called love." *The Dialogues of Plato*, ed. and trans. Benjamin Juwett, *3* vols. (Oxford, 1875), 2:43–44). For an excellent analysis of the relation between the Aristophanic myth and modern notions of homosexuality, see Halperin.

18. The cross-lingual pun "hom(m)osexual" comes from Luce Irigaray, *This Sex Which Is Not One*, where it is used to designate the androcentric assumptions grounding Western notions of same-sex desire. See especially "Commodities among Themselves," 192–98.

19. Ricks, *Tennyson*, 218.

20. Gerhard Joseph, *Tennysonian Love* (Minneapolis, 1969), 68.

21. T. S. Eliot, "In Memoriam," from *Essays Ancient and Modern* (London, 1936), 186–203. This essay is also available in Hunt, ed., *A Casebook*, 129–37.

22. Although the first lyrics in memory of Hallam were composed as early as 1833, the prologue was not composed until 1849, as Tennyson arranged and assembled the individual elegies into the long poem we know as *In Memoriam*.

23. Bloom, "Tennyson," 154.

24. John D. Rosenberg, "The Two Kingdoms of *In Memoriam*," *Journal of English and Germanic Philology* 58 (1959), 228–40; reprinted in Ross, ed., *In Memoriam*, 206–19.

25. Symonds, *Memoirs*, 209–10.

26. Ibid., 119–20.

27. Ibid., 94.

28. Other Victorian texts, specifically two canonical American ones, offer comic and comically displaced versions of Tennyson's fellowship of hand; if the examples I am about to cite are already familiar, they nonetheless merit our brief recognition. The first of these examples, chapter 94 of *Moby Dick*, coyly entitled "A Squeeze of the Hand," literally expresses—that is, presses out or fluidly extrudes—its almost homosexual homosociality by way of the exuberant topos of

"spermatic" immersion. As part of the Pequod's systematic capitalist transfiguration of natural object into commodity, of whale into product, of sperm oil into money, the members of the crew are compelled by "business" and "unctuous duty" into the blissful hiatus of a good squeeze. After "the baling of the Heidelburgh Tun, or Case," the sperm thus removed

> had cooled and crystallized to such a degree that when, with several others, I sat down before a large Constantine's bath of it, I found it strangely concreted into lumps, here and there rolling in the liquid part. It was our business to squeeze the lumps back into fluid.

The immediate effect of the "carefully manipulated" sperm is a subjective sense of benign metamorphosis ("After having my hands in it for only a few minutes, my fingers felt like eels and began, as it were, to serpentine and spiralize") which in turn mediates a fluid masculine intersubjectivity:

> I squeezed that sperm till I myself almost melted into it; I squeezed that sperm till a strange sort of insanity came over me; and I found myself unwittingly squeezing my colaborer's hands in it, mistaking the hands for the gentle globules. Such an abounding, affectionate, friendly, loving feeling did this avocation beget; that at last I was continually squeezing their hands and looking up into their eyes sentimentally. . . . Come; let us squeeze hands all around; nay, let us squeeze ourselves into each other; let us squeeze ourselves universally into the very milk and sperm of kindness.

If the rhetorical densities and fluidities of this passage are so manifold and interfluent as to preclude comprehensive analysis here, we are nonetheless constrained to remark the figural duplicity by which the self-evident homoerotics of such a vision of intermasculine community are rendered visible by an occulting that is at once ocular (Ishmael cannot see the squeeze he loves to feel) and auricular (the homosexual valence of this passage is, as it were, pun-buried in a comic homophone—in, that is, the handy wordplay on, in, of "sperm"). We should also note, if only again in passing, Ishmael's claim that the opulent tactility exercised here releases or "discharges"—his verb not mine—a specific renovatory effect, a direct counterfluence to the brutalizing and suicidal homosocial pact, or "indissoluble league," explicit in the crew's promise to man the harpoon of Ahab's vengeance. "In that inexpressible sperm," says Ishmael in recalling the moment on the quarterdeck, "I forgot all about our horrible oath" and "I washed my hands and heart of it."

When Melville has Ishmael dream that he might squeeze himself and his fellows "into the very milk and sperm of kindness," he is deploying a particular cultural fantasy about the body's dark hydraulics: a fantasy of what Thomas Laqueur calls "the fungibility of [bodily] fluids" in "Orgasm, Generation, and the Politics of Reproductive Biology," *Representations* 14 (Spring 1986): 1–41, a belief that the body's base fluid, blood, may under particular conditions of heat and pressure be "concocted" or expressed into other bodily fluids—milk and semen most particularly. And when that cultural fantasy is conjoined with its masculist writerly analogue (most familiar in its Freudian version) that a telling half pun obtains between pen and penis, and between semen and semantics, then there are large implications for the hands of the writer and the reader, specific implications for the craft of writing and for the semiotics of reading. "I find it hard to write of these things," Symonds writes in the erotic diary entry I have already quoted, "yet I wish to dwell on them and to recall them, pen in hand."

If Symonds is comically *un*selfconscious here, if the trope works him rather than he the trope, then this was never the case with Symonds's "Master," Whitman, who very self-consciously exploited this analogy to considerable cultural effect. The assault that Whitman launched on literary culture derived in fair part from his refusal to subdue this trope, from a specific refusal to idealize the difference between textual production and bodily discharge: "bathing [his] songs in sex," he then presses the reader with the texts, that are for him indistinguishable from the "limitless jets" of his "slow rude muscle." ("Enfants D'Adam," poems 12, 3, 4). Obviously, this strategy was calculated to disrupt idealizations of reading by putting a problematic text directly into the hands of the reader, who must hereafter equivocate over just what it is that he or she is holding now. The (homo)erotics of this readerly dilemma are specifically thematized in the third poem of the "Calamus" sequence:

> Whoever you are holding me now in hand,
> Without one thing all will be useless,
> I give you fair warning, before you attempt me further
> I am not what you supposed, but far different.

If the quotidian dynamics of reading require a certain tactility—if, after all, we must hold the books we read and touch the texts we also see—then it is also implicitly the case that these dynamics open within the primarily ocular trope of reading another aperture for the writer's promiscuous address. The reader reading thus touches, retouches, the writer's touch, even touches back, and in doing so finds himself (the implied reader of "Calamus" is, I would argue, male) implicated in the comic Melvillian topos we have just explicated: finds himself squeezing hands squeezing sperm, and staring sentimentally into the eyes of the poet. Here, from stanza 5 of "Calamus" 3, is another, or rather the same, trope of reading:

> Or, if you will, thrusting me beneath your clothing,
> Where I may feel the throbs of your heart, or rest upon your hip,

Carry me when you go forth over land or sea;
For thus, merely touching you, is enough—is best,
And thus, touching you, would I silently sleep and be carried eternally.

By way of a fatal trajectory characteristic of Whitman, the palpable "thrusting" of these lines touches or taps into a desire for death's cradling, as if the writer could die into the reader, thereafter to be "carried eternally." Whitman very capably exercised the ambivalence that the metonymy of hands conveys: if he liked to finger pulses, he also said "my tap is death" ("Sleep-Chasings"). In "Calamus" 3 this ambivalence, partly self-protective, is figured by the reversal of touch that closes the poem, closes it by leaving its grasp open:

But these leaves conning, you con at peril
For these leaves, and me, you will not understand—

. . . .

Even while you should think you had unquestionably caught me, behold!
Already you see I have escaped from you.

And then the poem's last line:

Therefore release me, and depart on your way.

Whitman's writing exuberantly exercises the same hands that shake and haunt Tennyson in *In Memoriam*, but pivotal differences in tact intervene to separate their discourses on tactility: Whitman specifies what Tennyson prefers to diffuse, just as he incarnates what Tennyson instead drives into the recesses of the incarnation. But these are differences that serve to texturize the therefore palpable sameness that otherwise we would not be able to feel. Herman Melville, *Moby Dick* (New York, 1972). Walt Whitman, *Leaves of Grass*, facsimile edition of the 1860 text (Ithaca, 1961).

29. Rosenberg, "The Two Kingdoms," 214.

30. In broad terms of Christocentric desire the strong parallel to Tennyson is Hopkins, who finds in Christ both "beauty's self and beauty's giver" and whose sermons on the body and the blood of Christ—"of our noble lover, our prince, our champion"—describe a theology of desire with unembarrassed sensuality:

I leave it to you, brethren, then to picture him, in whom fullness of the godhead dwelt bodily, in his bearing how majestic, how strong and yet how lovely and lissome in his limbs, in his look how earnest grave but kind. In his Passion all this strength was spent, this lissomeness crippled, this beauty wrecked, this majesty beaten down. But now it is more than all restored, and for myself I make no secret I look forward with eager desire to seeing the matchless beauty of Christ's body in the heavenly light. (*Sermons*, 34–38.)

Hopkins's eager desire for "the matchless beauty of Christ's body" can be borne only because it is contrapuntally and agonistically matched with, or wedded to, Hopkins's own matchless passion for substitute satisfaction and submission to his "mastering me/God." In the complex and beautiful way that J. Hillis Miller has explicated in *The Disappearance of God*, the world for Hopkins is so radically inscribed with the grandeur of God that phenomenal things are literally—that is, as letters—the dispersed fragments of the originary integral word:

> All things therefore are charged with love, are charged with God, and if we know how to touch them give off sparks and take fire, yield drops and flow, ring and tell of him. (*Sermons*, 175)

Right perception—luminous, fluid, harmonic—is sacramental reading.

And what the perceiver reads when reading is right are the literal traces of Christ's blood—his "lessons" "written upon lovely limbs / In bloody letters." The figural mechanism that so charges Hopkins's world is, very explicitly, the saving "discharge" of Christ's "dense" and "driven Passion" ("The Wreck of the Deutschland," stanza 7). By way of a powerful temporal inversion, Hopkins deploys a historical event, the crucifixion, as the only trope adequate to represent the otherwise inaccessible, ahistorical moment of the "great sacrifice" of God's own selving—of, that is, the fracturing or "cleaving" of Christ out of God that Hopkins calls "the Incarnation proper." For Hopkins this originary fracture creates flesh, invents time, enables redemption, and sets desire to its reparational yearning. But because this moment is ontologically prior to the divisiveness it is in the process of creating, it can only be figured belatedly and retrospectively by a reversal of origin and terminus. Thus Hopkins interpolates Jesus' last moment where Christ's first one should be; the sensations of the crucifixion bespeak the incarnation:

> The first intention then of God outside himself or, as they say, *ab extra*, outwards, the first outstress of God's power was Christ; and we must believe the next was the Blessed Virgin. . . . It is as if the blissful agony or stress of selving in God forced out drops of sweat and blood, which drops were the world. (*Sermons*, 197)

Here Christ's originary self-expression must take as its expressive figure the terminal moment of "the piercing of Christ's side," when "the sacred body and sacred heart seemed waiting for an opportunity of discharging themselves." (*Sermons*, 255). This tropological inversion is predictably double. It is epistemologically negative in the deconstructive sense that the presumptively originary origin must submit to the belatedness of historical figuration. Thus the Christocentric origin is already blocked or decentered by the writhing body of Christ himself. But it is phenomenologically positive in the sense that the world and the things in it are spectacularly reified as the sacramental distillations of Christ's saving effluence; thus "bathe[d] in his fall-gold mercies," "this world then is the word, expression, news of God" ("The Wreck of the Deutschland," stanza 23; *Sermons*, 129). Exactly this extreme incarnationism, with its celebratory corollary that "Christ plays in ten thousand places / lovely in limbs, and lovely in eyes not his" (poem 57, "As kingfishers catch fire"), enables Hopkins to sustain himself on the supplemental satisfactions that intervene between the patient time of writing and the eager time when the poet will be restored "to the dearest him that lives alas! away)" (poem 67, "I wake and feel the fell of dark"). In the parallel cases of Hopkins and Tennyson, that distanced and dearest him—that "first, fast, last friend" (poem 40, "The Lantern Out of Doors")—is an ambivalent figure or compound ghost, a copula who conjoins both Christ and that other "He that died": in the case of Tennyson, Hallam obviously; in the less renowned case of Hopkins, the boy-poet Digby Mackworth Dolben. *The Poems of Gerard Manley Hopkins*, 4th ed., ed. W. H. Gardener and N. H. MacKenzie, (Oxford, 1970); and *Sermons and Devotional Writings*, ed. Christopher Devlin (London, 1959).

31. Eliot, "In Memoriam," 133.

32. Sigmund Freud, "Mourning and Melancholia," in *The Standard Edition*, 14:244–45.

33. Ricks, *Tennyson*, 216.

34. Irigaray, *This Sex Which Is Not One*, 193.

35. Tennyson, quoted in Hallam, Lord Tennyson, *Alfred, Lord Tennyson: A Memoir*, 2 vols. (London, 1897), 1:300.

36. Rosenberg, "The Two Kingdoms," 216.

37. Coventry Patmore, *The Unknown Eros* (London, 1878), 8–12. In the streamlined analysis offered here, I have somewhat simplified Patmore's rather more elusive sexual representation in order to foreground the poem's homosexual/pedophilic valences. Not surprisingly, Patmore embeds such valences within a rhetoric that is idealizing, interrogative, sometimes downright obscure. There is, furthermore, some shifty gender identification that permits the "Unknown Eros" to be figured sometimes as male ("bashful love, in his own way and hour") and sometimes, though less emphatically, as female. Of course anything like a complete account of Patmore's poem and volume would have to negotiate these differences.

38. R.S. is "History IX" in the third American edition (1931) of Ellis's *Sexual Inversion*, 111–15. Readers interested in this citation should note that different editions of *Sexual Inversion* have differently numbered case histories; revising his text for each edition, Ellis both added and deleted individual case histories. The Ellis-Symonds English edition of 1897 does not contain R.S.'s history.

39. Patmore, "The Child's Purchase," *Unknown Eros*, 208–9.

CHAPTER 3

1. Joseph Sheridan Le Fanu, *Carmilla*, in *The Best Ghost Stories of J. S. Le Fanu* (New York, 1964), 337. This novella of lesbian vampirism, which appeared first in Le Fanu's *In A Glass Darkly* (1872), predates *Dracula* by twenty-five years.

2. Franco Moretti, *Signs Taken for Wonders* (Thetford, 1983), 100.

3. Bram Stoker, *Dracula* (New York, 1979), 51. All further references to *Dracula* appear within the chapter in parentheses.

4. The paradigmatic instance of this triple rhythm is Mary Shelley's *Frankenstein*, a text that creates—bit by bit, and stitch by stitch—its resident demon, then equips that demon with a powerful Miltonic voice with which to petition both its creator and the novel's readers, and finally drives its monster to polar isolation and suicide. Stevenson's *Dr. Jekyll and Mr. Hyde* repeats the pattern: Henry Jekyll's chemical invitation to Hyde corresponds to the gesture of admission; the serial alternation of contrary personalities constitutes the ambivalent play of the prolonged middle; and Jekyll's suicide, which expels both the monster and himself, corresponds to the gesture of expulsion.

5. Readers of Tzvetan Todorov's *The Fantastic* (Ithaca, 1975) will recognize that my argument about the Gothic text's extended middle derives in part from his idea that the essential condition of fantastic fiction is a duration characterized by readerly suspension of certainty.

6. John Ruskin, *Sesame and Lilies* (New York, 1974), 59–60.

7. This group of crusaders includes Van Helsing himself, Dr. John Seward, Arthur Holmwood, Quincey Morris, and later Jonathan Harker; the title Crew of Light is mine, but I have taken my cue from Stoker: Lucy, *lux*, light.

8. Renfield, whose "zoophagy" precedes Dracula's arrival in England and who is never vamped by Dracula, is no exception to this rule.

9. Sedgwick, *Between Men*, 99.

10. Ibid., 21. The anthropologically derived paradigm of "triangular desire," according to which women are reified as counters of exchange within an essentially hom(m)osexual circuit, has been brilliantly deployed by feminists for certain revisionary purposes. The ground-breaking feminist/lesbian articulation is Gayle Rubin's "The Traffic in Women: Notes Toward a Political Economy of Sex" in *Toward an Anthropology of Women*, ed. Rayna Reiter (New York, 1975), 157–210. Sedgwick modified and redeployed this paradigm to tremendous critical effect in *Between Men*. A post-Lacanian psychoanalytic version of the same idea can be found in Irigaray's *This Sex Which Is Not One*, especially the chapter "Commodities Among Themselves," 192–97.

11. Symonds, 2:169.

12. Havelock Ellis, quoted in Jeffrey Weeks, *Coming Out* (London, 1977), 92.

13. D. A. Miller, "*Cage aux folles*: Sensation and Gender in Wilkie Collins's *The Woman in White*," *Representations* 14 (Spring 1986): 112; also available in *The Novel and The Police*, 155.

14. This bifurcation of woman is one of the text's most evident features, as critics of *Dracula* have been quick to notice. See Phyllis Roth, "Suddenly Sexual Women in Bram Stoker's *Dracula*," *Literature and Psychology* 27 (1977): 117, and her full-length study *Bram Stoker* (Boston, 1982). Roth, in an argument that emphasizes the pre-Oedipal element in *Dracula*, makes a similar point: "one recognizes that Lucy and Mina are essentially the same figure: the Mother. Dracula is, in fact, the same story told twice with different outcomes." The most extensive thematic analysis of this split in Stoker's representation of women is Carol A. Senf's "*Dracula*: Stoker's Response to the New Woman," *Victorian Studies* 26 (1982): 33–39, which sees this split as Stoker's "ambivalent reaction to a topical phenomenon—the New Woman."

15. Maurice Richardson, "The Psychoanalysis of Ghost Stories," *The Twentieth Century* 166 (1959): 427–28.

16. In this instance, at least, Van Helsing has an excuse for his ungrammatical usage; in Dutch, Van Helsing's native tongue, the noun *bijbel* (Bible) is masculine.

17. John Stuart Mill, *The Subjection of Women*, in *Essays on Sex Equality*, ed. Alice Rossi (Chicago, 1970), 148.

18. Ibid., 187.

19. Susan Hardy Aiken, "Scripture and Poetic Discourse in *The Subjection of Women*," *PMLA* 98 (1983): 354.

20. Nina Auerbach, *Woman and the Demon: The Life of a Victorian Myth* (Cambridge, Mass., 1982), 11.

21. Roth, "Suddenly Sexual Women," 116.

22. George Chauncey, Jr., "From Sexual Inversion to Homosexuality: Medicine and the Changing Conceptualization of Female Deviance," *Salmagundi* 58–59 (1982): 132.

23. The symbolic interchangeability of blood and semen in vampirism was identified as early as 1931 by Ernest Jones in *On the Nightmare* (London, 1931), 119: "in the unconscious mind blood is commonly an equivalent for semen."

24. Auerbach, *Woman and the Demon*, 22.

25. Sedgwick, *Between Men*, 1.

26. Stoker's configuration of hypnotism and anaesthesia is not idiosyncratic. Ellis, for instance, writing at exactly this time, conjoins hypnosis and anaesthesia as almost identical phenomena and subsumes them under a single taxonomic category: "We may use the term 'hypnotic phenomena' as a convenient expression to include not merely the condition of artificially-produced sleep, or hypnotism in the narrow sense of the term, but all those groups of psychic phenomena which

are characterized by a decreased control of the higher nervous centres, and increased activity of the lower centres." The quality that determines membership in this "convenient" taxonomy is, to put matters baldly, a pelvis pumped up by the "increased activity of the lower centres." Ellis, in an earlier footnote, explains the antithetical relationship between the "higher" and "lower" centers: "The persons best adapted to propagate the race are those with the large pelves, and as the pelvis is the seat of the great centres of sexual emotion the development of the pelvis and its nervous and vascular supply involves the greater heightening of the sexual emotions. At the same time the greater activity of the cerebral centres enables them to subordinate and utilise to their own ends the increasingly active sexual emotions, so that reproduction is checked and the balance to some extent restored." The pelvic superiority of women, necessitated by an evolutionary imperative (better babies with bigger heads require broader pelves), implies a corresponding danger—an engorged and hypersensitive sexuality that must be actively "checked" by the "activity of the cerebral centres" so that "balance" may be "to some extent restored."

Hypnotism and anaesthesia threaten exactly this delicate balance, and especially so in women because "the lower centres in women are more rebellious to control than those of men, and more readily brought into action." Anaesthesiology, it would seem, is not without its attendant dangers: "Thus, chloroform, ether, nitrous oxide, cocaine, and possibly other anaesthetics, possess the property of exciting the sexual emotions. Women are especially liable to these erotic hallucinations during anaesthesia, and it has sometimes been almost impossible to convince them that their subjective sensations have had no objective cause. Those who have to administer anaesthetics are well aware of the risks they may thus incur." Ellis's besieged physician, like Stoker's master-monster and his monster-master, stands here as a male whose empowerment anxiously reflects a prior endangerment. What if this woman's lower centers should take the opportunity—to use another of Ellis's phrases—"of indulging in an orgy"? Dracula's kiss, Van Helsing's needle and stake, and Ellis's "higher centres" all seek to modify, constrain, and control the articulation of feminine desire. (But, it might be counterargued, Dracula comes precisely to excite such an orgy, not to constrain one. Yes, but with an important qualification: Dracula's kiss, because it authorizes only repetitions of itself, clearly articulates the destiny of feminine desire; Lucy will only do what Dracula has done before.) Havelock Ellis, *Man and Woman*, 4th ed. (New York, 1904), 299, 73, 316, 313 respectively. The first edition appeared in England in 1895.

27. Sedgwick, *Between Men*, 76.

28. Havelock Ellis, *Erotic Symbolism*, vol. 5 of *Studies in the Psychology of Sex*, 6 vols. (Philadelphia, 1906), 142.

29. Ibid., 140.

30. Roth plausibly reads Lucy's countenance at this moment as "a thank you note" for the corrective penetration; "Suddenly Sexual Women," 116.

31. C. F. Bentley, "The Monster in the Bedroom: Sexual Symbolism in Bram Stoker's *Dracula,*" *Literature and Psychology* 22 (1972): 30.

32. While revising this chapter, I benefited from the opportunity to read William Veeder's "Tales That Culture Tells Itself: *Dracula* and the Mothers," an essay, still in draft, in which Veeder offers a powerful pre-Oedipal and anti-Oedipal reading of the novel. I cite Veeder several times in this chapter, but without further footnoting; Veeder's essay is not yet published. I quote with permission of the author.

33. Daniel Paul Schreber, *Memoirs of My Nervous Illness*, trans. Ida Macalpine and Richard A. Hunter (1903; Cambridge, Mass., 1988), 63. All quotations from Schreber's *Memoirs* are from the Harvard English edition and will be cited parenthetically in the text as *M*.

34. Sigmund Freud, "Psycho-Analytic Notes on an Autobiographical Account of a Case of Paranoia (*Dementia Paranoides*)," in *The Standard Edition*, 12:3–82; all further references to this case study (hereafter designated as PN) will appear in parentheses within the body of the chapter.

35. I take this phrase from Jane Gallop, *The Daughter's Seduction* (Cornell, 1982), 57, where it is used to describe an intertextual encounter between Freud and Irigaray: "Yet Irigaray's encounter with Freud is not a psychoanalysis. Freud is not there to associate."

36. Here I am quoting from James Strachey's editor's note to Freud's "Psycho-Analytic Notes," 6.

37. Guy Hocquenghem, *Homosexual Desire*, trans. Daniella Dangoor (London, 1978), 105–6.

38. Sedgwick, *Between Men*, 91.

39. For a compelling account of the conceptual contradiction inhering in Freud's use of the notion of "perversion," see Davidson's "How to Do the History of Psychoanalysis," 252–77.

40. Sedgwick, *Between Men*, 113–14.

CHAPTER 4

1. Ellis, *Sexual Inversion* (1931), 175. H. C.'s narrative offers further evidence of the power of Wilde's fictions to determine the real. One evening H. C. is escorted by a fellow reader of *Psychopathia Sexualis* to "several of the cafes where inverts are accustomed to foregather." At one of these "trysting places," he meets a youth who answers some of his "book-begotten queries": "The boy-prostitutes gracing these halls, he apprised us, bore fanciful names, some of well-known actresses, others of heroes in fiction, his own being Dorian Gray. Rivals, he complained,

had assumed the same appellation, but he was the original Dorian; the others were jealous imposters" (177).

2. Michel Foucault, "Nietzsche, Genealogy, History," in *The Foucault Reader*, ed. Paul Rabinow (New York, 1984), 83.

3. Ellis, *Sexual Inversion* (1931), 175–76.

4. Ibid., 179.

5. Joel Fineman, "The Significance of Literature: *The Importance of Being Earnest*," *October* 15 (1980): 79. My thinking about Wilde remains indebted to the brilliant but gnomic analysis in Fineman's essay.

6. Jacques Derrida, *Of Grammatology*, trans. Gayatri Chakravorty Spivak (Baltimore, 1976), 61.

7. The pseudo-opposition between "trivial" and "serious," with which I play repeatedly in this chapter, is Wilde's own; the subtitle of *Earnest* is "A Trivial Comedy for Serious People." That Wilde intended a pseudobinarism subject to parodic reversal is made emphatically clear by the subtitle of an earlier draft: "A Serious Play for Trivial People."

8. Oscar Wilde, "The Critic as Artist" in *Intentions* (London, 1891); reprinted in *The Artist as Critic: Critical Writings of Oscar Wilde*, ed. Richard Ellmann (Chicago, 1969), 399.

9. André Gide, *Oscar Wilde: A Study*, trans. Stuart Mason [Christopher Millard] (Oxford, 1905), 30.

10. Oscar Wilde, "The Decay of Lying" in *Intentions*; reprinted in Ellmann, ed., *The Artist as Critic*, 305.

11. Oscar Wilde, *The Letters of Oscar Wilde*, ed. Rupert Hart-Davis (New York, 1962), 185. Hereafter cited parenthetically in the text as *Letters*.

12. Ed Cohen, "Writing Gone Wilde: Homoerotic Desire in the Closet of Representation," *PMLA* 102, no. 5 (October 1987): 801–13. During the writing and revising of this essay, I benefited enormously from Cohen's generous conversation regarding Wilde, the trials of 1895, and the history of homosexuality.

13. Jonathan Dollimore, "Different Desires: Subjectivity and Transgression in Wilde and Gide," *Textual Practice* 1, no. 1 (1987): 56; reprinted in *Genders* 2 (Summer 1988): 24–41.

14. Fineman, "Significance," 79.

15. The epigraph, from W. H. Auden, "An Improbable Life," in *Forewords and Afterwords* (New York, 1973), 323, is from a review of Hart-Davis's edition of Wilde's letters and appeared originally in the *New Yorker* (March 9, 1963); it is also available in *Oscar Wilde: A Collection of Critical Essays*, ed. Richard Ellmann (Englewood Cliffs, N.J., 1969), 116–37.

16. Wilde was not, as is often assumed, convicted of sodomy; rather he was prosecuted and convicted under section 11 of the Criminal Law Amendment Act of 1885, which criminalized "acts of gross indecency" committed between males,

whether in public or private. For an analysis of the conceptual shifts entailed by this legislation, see Ed Cohen, "Legislating the Norm," 181–217.

17. Miller, *The Novel and the Police*, 207. Miller's landmark essay "Secret Subjects, Open Secrets," from which I quote here, has informed my thinking throughout these pages.

18. Foucault, "Nietzsche, Genealogy, History," 76.

19. Fineman, "Significance," 83.

20. For more on Henry Shirley Bunbury, see William Green, "Oscar Wilde and the Bunburys," *Modern Drama* 21, no. 1, (1978): 67–80. I disagree with Green emphatically on the importance and function of Bunbury, to wit: "Even allowing for the possibility that the term may have existed in the form of a private joke, Wilde had ample opportunity to avoid using it in the play if he suspected it had any homosexual connotations which might have drawn attention to him. . . . Wilde could have substituted another name for Bunbury."

21. Ibid., 71.

22. Fineman, "Significance," 89. The English colloquialism for buttocks is of course not *bun* but *bum,* but the frail consonantal difference distinguishing the two terms always remains liable to elision, especially in performance, whether in a slip of the actor's tongue or in the labyrinth of the auditor's ear. *Bun,* as I argue above, points immediately to Algy's serious overeating and mediately to Wilde's sexual practice, which, his biographers agree, was primarily oral.

23. André Gide, *The Journals of André Gide,* trans. Justin O'Brien, 4 vols. (New York, 1948), 2:410.

24. The *OED* citation for *Banbury* reads: "A town in Oxfordshire, England, formerly noted for the number and zeal of its Puritan inhabitants, still for its cakes." See also the Mother Goose nursery rhyme "Ride a cock-horse to Banbury Cross." The phonemic and imagistic affinities between *Bunbury* and *Banbury* proved too much for at least one of the typists working from Wilde's handwritten manuscripts. In a typescript of the play dated "19 Sep. 94" by Mrs. Marshall's Type Writing Office, *Bunbury* repeatedly appears as *Banbury.* Wilde, whose careless, looping handwriting no doubt encouraged the error, patiently restored the *u*'s.

25. This line, spoken by Miss Prism about Ernest (whom, of course, she has not met), does not appear in the canonical three-act *Earnest* with which most readers are familiar; it is to be found, rather, in the various manuscript and typescript drafts of the so-called "original" four-act version. There is, I believe, no single text qualified to make "legitimate" claim to definitive status, a belief that requires at least a brief explanation of the textual confusions surrounding *Earnest.* When in 1898, *après le deluge,* M. Melmoth sought to publish Mr. Wilde's farce, his only recourse to "the play itself" was to a truncated or castrated copytext, George Alexander's prompt copy, which had provided the basis for the short-lived 1895 production. Since Wilde's own drafts and copies of *Earnest* had been

auctioned off in the bankruptcy proceedings following his imprisonment, "Alexander's manuscript," as Wilde called it, was for all purposes the only extant text upon which to base the published version of 1899. The problem with Alexander's typescript is that it contained substantial cuts, some authorial and some not, including, most famously, the excision of an entire scene in which Algy is almost arrested for Ernest's outstanding debts; this cut was essential to the structural reorganization of four acts into three. That Alexander's emendations were significant there can be no doubt; upon seeing the play on opening night, Wilde (whom Alexander had dismissed from rehearsals) is reported to have remarked: "My dear Aleck, it was charming, quite charming. And, do you know, from time to time I was reminded of a play I once wrote myself, called THE IMPORTANCE OF BEING EARNEST." Quoted in A. E. W. Mason, *Sir George Alexander and the St. James Theatre* (New York, 1969), 79. Not until the 1950s would the various working manuscripts and typescripts of the "original" four-act versions begin to surface, so that, by way of a temporal inversion that Wilde surely would have delectated, *Earnest* is a work whose lost origins *post*date its publication by some fifty years.

With due respect, then, for such vertiginous reversals, and for the problematics in authorization they imply, I refer throughout this essay to both the canonical three-act version and the antecedent four-act versions without worrying the issue of textual authority. If this runs counter to sober scholarly method, so much the better, since it acknowledges the elusive present-absence of "the text itself," which like Bunbury is always "somewhere else at present." Unless otherwise specified all references here to the four-act version are to *The Importance of Being Earnest: A Trivial Comedy for Serious People in Four Acts As Originally Written by Oscar Wilde*, ed. Sarah Augusta Dickson, 2 vols. (New York, 1955); hereafter this text will be cited as Dickson. Miss Prism's line as quoted above can be found in Dickson, 1:77. See also *The Definitive Four-Act Version of The Importance of Being Earnest*, ed. Ruth Berggren (New York: 1987), 23–41.

26. H. Montgomery Hyde, *Oscar Wilde* (New York, 1975), 187.

27. Dickson, 1:146. This line occurs during a wonderful bit of stage business in which, while Jack and Lady Brancaster (as she is called in the four-act versions) are discussing "the painful circumstances of [Jack's] origin," Algy and Cecily are hiding "Behind [a] screen . . . whispering and laughing." As the good lady speaks, Algy's attempts to silence or "hush" Cecily interrupt her discourse; annoyed by these intrusions into her speech, Lady Brancaster complains: "It is clear that there is someone who says "Hush" concealed in this apartment. The ejaculation has reached my ears more than once. It is not at any time a very refined expression, and its use, when I am talking, is extremely vulgar, and indeed insolent. I suspect it to have proceeded from the lips of someone who is of more than usually low origin." In this brilliant and, sadly, excised tableau, Wilde compactly stages the sociopolitical operations of Bunburying representation, in which a dis-

course of social rectitude is interrupted or saturated by an "ejaculation" that can be heard but not seen. As the screen behind which Cecily and Algy are sporting very nicely materializes the strategy of visual occlusion, so does the transposition of "hush" and "ejaculation" make audible, as laughter, the Bunburying operations by which a silent or secret erotics may be mouthed but not quite bespoken. We should note in passing, too, that Wilde here anticipates the more than audible ejaculation with which Roland Barthes closes *The Pleasure of the Text* (New York, 1975): cinema, Barthes writes, "succeed[s] in shifting the signified a great distance and in throwing, so to speak, the anonymous body of the actor into my ear: it granulates, it crackles, it caresses, it grates, it cuts, it comes: that is bliss" (67). Barthes's text will hereafter be cited parenthetically in the text as *Pleasure*.

28. Oscar Wilde, *The Picture of Dorian Gray* (Oxford, 1981), 79.

29. See note 25 above.

30. *Oscar Wilde: Three Times Tried*, 2 vols. (Paris, n.d.) 389. This privately printed text, which appears to be a pirated edition of another book also issued anonymously under the same title by the Ferrestone Press (London, 1912), claims to be the most "complete and accurate account of this long and complicated case. Special care, it will be seen, has been devoted to the elucidation of abstruse legal points. . . . The evidence of witnesses, together with the prolonged cross-examination of Wilde in each of the three trials, is given as fully as possible, with due regard to discretion." I cite this text by page number only, since the two volumes are consecutively paginated.

31. *Three Times Tried*, 355.

32. I encountered this passage while reading Ed Cohen's doctoral dissertation "Talk on the Wilde Side: Toward a Genealogy of the Discourse on Male Sexuality" (Stanford, 1988), to which I remain indebted. I quote with permission of the author.

33. H. Montgomery Hyde, *The Love That Dared Not Speak Its Name* (Boston, 1970), 95.

34. Philip K. Cohen, *The Moral Vision of Oscar Wilde* (Rutherford, N.J., 1979), 217.

35. *Three Times Tried*, 203.

36. Queensberry's "Plea of Justification" is reprinted as appendix A in H. Montgomery Hyde, *The Trials of Oscar Wilde* (New York, 1962), 323–27. The 1843 Criminal Libel Act, the statute under which Wilde sued Queensberry for accusing him of "posing as a somdomite [*sic*]," permitted the defendant (Queensberry) to place before the court a document, or "Plea of Justification," supporting the allegation for which the libel suit was being prosecuted.

37. *Three Times Tried*, 191.

38. Jonathan Culler, "The Call of the Phoneme" in *On Puns: The Foundation of Letters*, ed. Jonathan Culler (New York, 1988), 3.

39. Ibid., 14.

40. Samuel Johnson, "Preface to Shakespeare," in *Poetry and Prose*, ed. Mona Wilson (London, 1970), 500; quoted in Culler, 6–7.

41. Hichens's travesty of the Wilde-Douglas affair was originally published anonymously (London, 1894); for Wilde's bemused response to *The Green Carnation*, see *Letters*, 373.

42. Dickson, facsimile typescript of act 4, 2:34; also Berggren, p. 190.

43. That Wilde was familiar with the specialized vocabulary of the Urning is beyond dispute: "A patriot put in prison for loving his country loves his country, and a poet put in prison for loving boys loves boys. To have altered my life would have been to have admitted that Uranian love is ignoble. I hold it to be noble—more noble than other forms" [*Letters*, 778].

44. Jacques Derrida, "Otobiographies: The Teaching of Nietzsche and the Politics of the Proper Name," in *The Ear of the Other*, ed. Christie McDonald (Lincoln, Neb., 1988), 4.

45. The pun thus also slyly alludes to our culture's paradigmatic instance of "trivial" meeting: the terminal convergence of father and son at the crossroads called Phokis, where Oedipus meets his father and his fate. "If I understand you," says a darkening Oedipus to his mother Jocasta, "Laios was killed / At a place where three roads meet." Trivial indeed. Against the background of these tragic resonances, we may read Wilde's earnest *and* trivial pun as a gay countersign to the murderous seriousness of Oedipal heterosexuality. Sophocles, *Oedipus Rex*, trans. Dudley Fitts and Robert Fitzgerald (New York, 1969), 37.

46. Roland Barthes, "The Third Meaning," in *The Responsibility of Forms*, trans. Richard Howard (Berkeley, 1991), 41–62; all further quotations from Barthes in this paragraph refer to these pages.

47. Mary McCarthy, "The Unimportance of Being Oscar" in Ellmann, ed., *Oscar Wilde*, 108.

48. No doubt McCarthy would have intensified her antipathy for Wilde's "private joke" had she known, or cared to know, that the Ernest/Earnest/Urning pun did not originate with Wilde; that it made its literary debut two years before Wilde began work on *Earnest*; and that Wilde stole—or, as literary critics like to say, "appropriated"—the pun for the transvaluing purposes of his own genius. A little less "private" than McCarthy would like to believe, the wordplay first appeared in a volume of poetry called *Love in Earnest* (London, 1892) by the Uranian writer John Gambril Nicholson. A collection of sonnets, ballads, and lyrics, *Love in Earnest* included a poem of pederastic devotion entitled "Of Boys' Names":

> Old memories of the Table Round
>   In Percival and Lancelot dwell,
> Clement and Bernard bring the sound
>   Of anthems in the cloister-cell,

And Leonard vies with Lionel
In stately step and kingly frame,
  And Kenneth speaks of field and fell,
And Ernest sets my heart a-flame.

One name can make my pulses bound,
  No peer it owns, nor parallel,
By it is Vivian's sweetness drowned,
  And Roland, full as organ-swell;
  Though Frank may ring like silver bell,
And Cecil softer music claim,
  They cannot work the miracle,—
'Tis Ernest sets my heart a-flame.

Cyril is lordly, Stephen crowned
  With deathless wreaths of asphodel,
Oliver whispers peace profound,
  Herbert takes arms his foes to quell,
  Eustace with sheaves is laden well,
Christopher has a nobler fame,
  And Michael storms the gates of Hell,
But Ernest sets my heart a-flame.

ENVOY.
  My little Prince, Love's mystic spell
Lights all the letters of your name,
  And you, if no one else, can tell
Why Ernest sets my heart a-flame.

Nicholson's book did not go unnoticed among gay readers and interlocutors. I think it self-evident that Wilde knew of it; the joke quoted above about "those chaps, the minor poets [who] are never even quoted" is likely Wilde's oblique acknowledgment of Nicholson's priority, although no doubt Wilde would have happily expatiated upon the (merely belated) originality of his own deployment of the pun. And certainly John Addington Symonds, who died a year before Wilde began composing his farce, caught the pun's gay valence. In a letter of 2 July 1892, Symonds wrote to a friend: "Have you read a volume of sonnets called 'Love in Earnest'? It is written by a Schoolmaster in love with a boy called Ernest." That "Wilde's" pun predates his own use of it would thus seem incontrovertible. "Of Boys' Names" is quoted from Timothy d'Arch Smith, *Love in Earnest* (London, 1970), xviii; Smith's book, a study of the Uranian poets, derives its title from Nicholson's.

49. Dickson, 1:111.

50. Hyde, *Oscar Wilde*, 333.

CHAPTER 5

1. D. H. Lawrence, *Women in Love* (1920; Cambridge, 1987). All further citations to *Women in Love* are to the Cambridge edition and appear parenthetically
in the body of the chapter.

2. Miller, *The Novel and the Police*, 193.

3. Mark Schorer, *"Women in Love"* in *The World We Imagine: Selected Essays*
(New York, 1968), 121. Anyone familiar with Schorer's writing on Lawrence will
recognize my indebtedness to his notion that Lawrence's novel represents a
"psychic drama" in which "the two possible allegiances" wrestle for the fate of
character.

4. A compelling meditation on the somatic implications of reading can be
found in Miller's *"Cage aux folles,"* especially pages 146–56 in *The Novel and
the Police*.

5. *The Letters of D. H. Lawrence*, ed. James T. Boulton, 7 vols. projected
(Cambridge, 1980), 1:544. Hereafter cited parenthetically in the text as *Letters*.

6. D. H. Lawrence, "The Crown" in *Reflections on the Death of a Porcupine
and Other Essays*, ed. Michael Herbert (Cambridge, 1988), 263, 476; hereafter this
text will be cited parenthetically as *DP*. Written originally in 1915 and then substantially revised in 1925, "The Crown" is one of those intractable "philosophicalish" tracts that Lawrence generated in the turbulent wake of his fiction writing, part diatribe and part paean: in any event, indisputable evidence (should any
more be necessary) of an overwrought erotic imagination. I have uniformly cited
the 1915 version, since it bears immediately upon *Women in Love*; the excellent
textual apparatus in the Cambridge edition of *DP* makes it easy to follow the
changes between versions.

7. John Middleton Murry, *Son of Woman: The Story of D. H. Lawrence* (New
York, 1931), 116; hereafter cited parenthetically in the text as *SW*. I will be quoting as well from Murry's 1921 *Nation and Athenaeum* review of *Women in Love*,
reprinted in *Reminiscences of D. H. Lawrence* (London, 1933), hereafter cited parenthetically in the text as *R*.

8. This "highly motivated vacillation" has a fascinating biographical correlative, well known among those conversant with the competing mythologies surrounding Lawrence and his writing. That correlative is appropriately double-
edged, marked, if you will, by a "fundamental equivocation" not unlike the one
against which Murry rails: *Murry himself* was one of the two "real-life" proto-
types for Gerald Crich, a transparent fact that Murry chose not to recognize (con-
sciously at least) at the time of his 1921 review of *Women in Love*. Putting himself under erasure as erotic object, Murry enabled himself to "forget" the

implications of the fact that it was he to whom Lawrence proposed the presumably irrevocable bond of blood brotherhood. As if to say: *Not I Brother.*

9. G. Wilson Knight, "Lawrence, Joyce, and Powys," *Essays in Criticism* 11, no. 4 (1961): 403–17. An understated but monumental piece of Lawrence criticism.

10. Samuel Taylor Coleridge, *The Statesman's Manual*; quoted in *English Romantic Writers*, ed. David Perkins (New York, 1967), 503.

11. D. H. Lawrence, *The Symbolic Meaning*, ed. Armin Arnold (Fontwell, 1962), 18–19; italics original. This text collects early versions of the much-revised critical essays that Lawrence published in 1923 as *Studies in Classic American Literature.*

12. Anyone wishing to resist the sheer arbitrariness of Lawrence's obscene subconscious pun should consider the following passage from another Lawrence letter, this one written to S. S. Koteliansky (or "Kot") on 20 April 1915, the day after he wrote the letter to David Garnett quoted above: "We have had another influx of visitors: David Garnett and Francis Birrell turned up the other day—Saturday. I like David, but Birrell I have come to detest. These horrible little frowsty people, men lovers of men, they give me such a sense of corruption, almost putrescence, that I dream of beetles. It is abominable" (*Letters*, 2:323).

13. The political fate of homosexual desire and misogyny in Lawrence's fiction has been studied with impressive finesse by Cornelia Nixon, *Lawrence's Leadership Politics and the Turn Against Women* (Berkeley, 1986). Although I have learned from Nixon's work, I remain uncomfortable with her complacent deployment of the Oedipal model.

14. It turns out, a little surprisingly, that the fungibility of blood and semen has a literally ancient heritage; see Thomas Laqueur, *Making Sex: Body and Gender from the Greeks to Freud* (Cambridge, Mass., 1990), especially pages 35–51. In an impressively researched argument, Laqueur demonstrates that, until the late eighteenth century (more or less), Western medical and popular thinking on sex and gender presupposed a single-sex model of the human body: a model, that is, in which sexual dimorphism was subordinated to the idea of a single, variable anatomy in which "men and women were arrayed according to their degree of metaphysical perfection, their vital heat, along an axis whose telos was male" (5). Within this androcentric "one-sex body," as Laqueur calls it, "blood, semen, milk, and other fluids" participate in a "physiology of fungible fluids and corporeal flux. . . . A Hippocratic account makes these physiological observations more vivid by specifying the anatomical pathways of interconversion; sperm, a foam much like the froth of the sea, was refined out of the blood; it passed to the brain; from the brain it made its way back through the spinal marrow, the kidneys, the testicles, and into the penis" (35).

15. Laqueur's "physiology of fungible fluids and corporeal flux" displays itself strikingly in Lawrence's phantasmagorical anecdote about the typewriter, Freida,

and the sea: we move from ink to blood to sea to semen. Laqueur's research more than sufficiently demonstrates that this sequence is anything but idiosyncratic; it is, rather, culturally received and transmitted, that is, conventional. The following passage from Roland Barthes, *Michelet*, trans. Richard Howard (Berkeley, 1987) suggests the wide extension of this image repertoire: "*the superlative form of blood is finally the sea. The sea, which is the primordial genetic element, constitutes the archetype of blood and milk. . . . It produces both milk and blood by a kind of progressive organization, of tumescence analogous to all the phenomena of spontaneous generation (in which Michelet firmly believed)*" (128; italics original).

16. Leo Bersani, *A Future for Astyanax: Character and Desire in Literature* (Boston, 1969), 164–65; cited hereafter parenthetically in the body of the chapter as *A*.

17. The *Oxford English Dictionary*'s entry for *allotropy* reads in part: "The variation of physical properties without change of substance to which certain elementary bodies are liable, first noticed by Berzelius in the case of charcoal and the diamond."

18. Obvious question: what versions of it? Most probably (though not necessarily solely) those of Edward Carpenter, the Midlands radical whose writings on nonconforming sexualities were being published in Manchester and circulated in Derbyshire, Nottinghamshire, and beyond as early as 1894; in that year, for instance, The Labour Press Society, Manchester, issued two Carpenter pamphlets on sexuality: *Sex Love, and its Place in a Free Society*; and, "for private circulation," *Homogenic Love, and its Place in a Free Society* (German translation in 1895). Emile Delavenay has plausibly suggested that Carpenter's writing became available to Lawrence through the private library of Eastwood feminist Alice Dax, the young Lawrence's sometime lover and prototype of *Sons and Lovers'* Clara Dawes, whom we know to have owned many Carpenter texts; Delavenay reports that Jessie Chambers, Lawrentian soul mate and prototype of Miriam in *Sons and Lovers,* "was sure that Lawrence had read *all the books* on Mrs. Dax's shelves, being a frequent visitor to her house at Eastwood." Emile Delavenay, *D. H. Lawrence and Edward Carpenter: A Study in Edwardian Transition* (London, 1971), 21; italics original. Like Delavenay, I am persuaded by "internal" textual evidence that Carpenter's *Love's Coming of Age: A Series of Papers on the Relations of the Sexes* was of decisive importance to Lawrence's original, but also highly appropriative literary imagination. Published originally by the Labour Press Society in 1896, this text was variously enlarged, republished, and reprinted in England between 1906 and 1948. The pivotal enlargement occurred with the addition in 1906 of the chapter entitled "The Intermediate Sex," in which Carpenter again advanced a positive valuation of homosexual desire (which he preferred to term *homogenic,* thereby binding a Greek prefix to a Greek suffix); in this chapter Carpenter engages various theories of homosexuality, including the inversion model (which he adopts and modifies), and cites Ulrich's Latin for-

mula, *anima muliebris virili corpore inclusa*. Delavenay reports that "Alice Dax lent Jessie Chambers Carpenter's book *Love's Coming of Age*, possibly in its 1906 enlarged edition" and that this loan is likely to "have taken place around 1909–1910" (22).

19. Jonathan Dollimore, *Sexual Dissidence: Augustine to Wilde, Freud to Foucault* (Oxford, 1991), 275.

20. The relationship between rabbits and frenetic sexuality is of course proverbial; on the connection between rabbits and homosexual desire in Lawrence's fiction, see the prologue in appendix 2 in the Cambridge edition of *Women in Love*: "There would come into a restaurant a strange Cornish type of man, with dark eyes like holes in his head or like the eyes of a rat, and with dark, fine rather stiff hair, and full, heavy, softly-strong limbs. Then again Birkin would feel the desire spring up in him, the desire to know this man, to have him, as it were to eat him, to take the very substance of him. And watching the strange, rather furtive, rabbit-like way in which the strong, softly-built man ate, Birkin would feel the rousedness burning in his own breast, as if this were what he wanted, as if the satisfaction of his desire lay in the body of the young, strong man opposite" (505).

21. D. A. Miller, "Anal *Rope*," *Representations* 32 (Fall 1990): 118.

Index

Compositor: BookMasters, Inc.
Text: Adobe Garamond
Display: Adobe Garamond
Printer and Binder: Thomson-Shore, Inc.